"This new edition of *Solution Focused Team* bring the whole stance and approach of Sol with expansions into narrative and agile m practical tools illustrate everything superbly book you'll need to buy, read and practise."

Dr Mark McKergow, *author of* The Next Generation of Solution Focused Practice

"As both a novice in Solution Focused coaching, and as an experienced team coaching practitioner, this book has been full of fresh thinking, fun analogies and new team coaching 'moves' for me to absorb into my own practice. The writing style is lively, insightful, practical and passionate – the same ingredients needed for a great team coaching session."

Dr Colm Murphy, *Managing Director of Dynamic Leadership Development and senior faculty Global Team Coaching Institute*

"This is a must-read guide for anyone who wants to engage in Solution Focused team coaching. The set of practical team coaching tools and case studies really helped me to become a better leader and transformed the way I coach my team. Read this book – and learn from the best."

Lydia Benton, *Principal Director at Accenture*

"I consider myself very fortunate to have been introduced to coaching by Kirsten. During my studies and all our interactions, I have always been impressed by her honesty and generosity. That is what this book is all about: knowledge and experience shared without reservation. Near or far, the SolutionsAcademy team is my safety net and Kirsten, Carlo, Raf and Cristina are people I can count on. This book demonstrates their ability to apply coaching principles to the team with pragmatism and elegance. The solutions, suggestions and reflections contained in it are the fruit of SolutionsAcademy's experience in this field and will be extremely useful not only to those in consultancy but also to those who manage teams within organizations."

Francesca Caroleo, *Deputy Head of People and Culture and Head of Centre of Expertise – Global Human Resources, Banque Internationale à Luxembourg (BIL)*

"*Solution Focused Team Coaching* presents a positive, hopeful and practical approach to team coaching and is an important addition to the growing discipline of team coaching."

Lucy Widdowson, *Performance Edge*

Solution Focused Team Coaching

Solution Focused Team Coaching offers readers a simple, practical and effective way to coach teams. Its evidence-based approach, which has been applied successfully to many fields, is presented in an engaging, pragmatic and approachable way, making this book a must read for anyone who wants to broaden their horizon within the team coaching space.

This book presents the background and philosophy of Solution Focused team coaching and then moves on to explore its practical application in various formats of team coaching, with different audience dimensions. The reader will find a useful structure for team coaching processes as well as detailed descriptions for facilitating team coaching "moves" (conventionally called "techniques" or "tools") for both online and live settings. With this book, it is easy to plan a Solution Focused team coaching process from contract negotiation through workshop design to follow-up and evaluation. It covers difficult team situations such as conflicts, and different forms of teams from shop-floor to executive teams, Agile teams and special formats of team coaching, as well as how to facilitate larger teams. Additionally, readers who want to achieve certification and/or accreditation will find it extremely useful to read about ICF, EMCC and AC team coaching competencies and how Solution Focused team coaching is an easy way of embedding those competencies.

Solution Focused Team Coaching is a must for any coach, from those who would like to learn a pragmatic, impactful and easy way to move into team coaching to experienced team coaches who would like to learn a new approach and expand their skills, and anybody interested in exploring the fascinating world of team coaching.

Kirsten Dierolf has been coaching teams since 1996 and has been training team coaches since 2008. She is the owner and founder of SolutionsAcademy, an ICF and EMCC accredited coach training school. Kirsten started her journey with the Solution Focused approach when she studied directly with its founders, Insoo Kim Berg and Steve de Shazer, and since then has been passionate about the Solution Focused and other social-constructionist approaches.

Cristina Mühl is an accredited coach and team coach both with ICF and EMCC and also an accredited supervisor, working also with team coaches to develop their own practice. She started supporting teams back in 2010 and her passion for growing teams is transparent in all her team coaching processes and training interactions.

Carlo Perfetto began his career in coaching in 2013, studying and applying the Solution Focused approach in training and in team coaching. He works as a coach trainer, mentor and supervisor for SolutionsAcademy, to which he brings his vast experience and expertise in team coaching and developing people.

Rafal Szaniawski has been coaching using the Solution Focused approach since 2019. Raf also brings his natural enthusiasm and charisma to the training and team coaching space, making it easy to address serious matters in a relaxed manner, creating a safe environment for teams to work on their objectives.

Solution Focused Team Coaching

Second Edition

Kirsten Dierolf, Cristina Mühl,
Carlo Perfetto and Rafal Szaniawski

Routledge
Taylor & Francis Group

LONDON AND NEW YORK

Designed cover image: © Getty Images

Second edition published 2024
by Routledge
4 Park Square, Milton Park, Abingdon, Oxon, OX14 4RN

and by Routledge
605 Third Avenue, New York, NY 10158

Routledge is an imprint of the Taylor & Francis Group, an informa business

© 2024 Kirsten Dierolf, Cristina Mühl, Carlo Perfetto and Rafal Szaniawski

First edition published by SolutionsAcademy Verlag, 2014

British Library Cataloguing-in-Publication Data
A catalogue record for this book is available from the British Library

ISBN: 978-1-032-44075-0 (hbk)
ISBN: 978-1-032-44074-3 (pbk)
ISBN: 978-1-003-37031-4 (ebk)

DOI: 10.4324/9781003370314

Typeset in Times New Roman
by Newgen Publishing UK

This book is dedicated to all our students at
SolutionsAcademy – thank you for teaching us so much!

Contents

Illustrations

Figures

Tables

Cases

Exercises

About the authors

Kirsten Dierolf, ICF MCC, ACTC, EMCC MP, ITCA MP, ESIA
Kirsten Dierolf has been coaching teams since 1996 and has been training team coaches since 2008. She is accredited as Master Practitioner Team Coaching by EMCC and holds the advanced certificate team coaching from ICF. Kirsten is the owner and founder of SolutionsAcademy, an ICF and EMCC accredited coach training school. She is an assessor for ICF MCC and PCC performance evaluation. Kirsten loves team coaching and is passionate about the Solution Focused approach and other social-constructionist approaches. She started her journey with the Solutions Focused approach when she studied directly with its founders, Insoo Kim Berg and Steve de Shazer.

Cristina Mühl, ICF PCC, EMCC SP, ESIA, ITCA SP
Cristina Mühl is an accredited coach and team coach with both ICF and EMCC (ICF PCC, EMCC SP, EMCC ITCA SP) and also an accredited supervisor, working with team coaches to develop their own practice (EMCC ESIA). She started coaching using the Solution Focused approach in 2019 and has since moved into delivering training based on this approach. Cristina studied with Kirsten and is now humbled to be part of the further development of SolutionsAcademy internationally and locally in Romania.

Carlo Perfetto, ICF PCC, ICF ACTC, EMCC SP, ESIA
Carlo Perfetto began his career in coaching in 2013, studying and applying the Solution Focused approach in training and in team coaching. Now he is accredited as an ICF PCC coach and an EMCC SP and ESIA and is closing his path towards the ICF Advanced Certification in Team Coaching ICF. He works for SolutionsAcademy as a coach trainer, mentor and supervisor, and is developing the company in Italy as country director.

Rafal Szaniawski, ICF PCC, EMCC SP

Rafal Szaniawski has been coaching using Solution Focused approach since 2019. He holds PCC accreditation with the ICF and Senior Practitioner accreditation with the EMCC. He works for SolutionsAcademy as a coach, mentor and trainer, and recently took up the project of establishing SolutionsAcademy in Spain and other Spanish-speaking countries.

Why a new edition?

The first edition of *Solution Focused Team Coaching* was published in 2013 (originally in German) with Kirsten Dierolf as the author. Much has changed since then. The world has gone through a pandemic, which expedited online teamwork and online team coaching. The large coaching associations, the International Coaching Federation (ICF), the European Mentoring and Coaching Council (EMCC) and the Association for Coaching (AC), have all published team coaching core competencies. The practitioner and academic literature has seen a flurry of publications on team coaching. In the Solution Focused world, practitioners from narrative, Solution Focused and collaborative approaches have started looking at what unites these techniques as social-constructionist approaches. The last ten years has also seen a lot of Solution Focused theory being developed and applied to coaching. This more than warrants a new edition.

The second edition responds to all those developments: we integrate online "team coaching moves" (traditionally called "techniques") and explore the contributions of the team coaching competences of the large associations and how Solution Focused practice might fulfil them. The new edition integrates what we have learned from the latest literature and describe the specifics of Solution Focused team coaching in terms of social-constructionism and commonalities with the other social-constructionist approaches.

The book is also written by a team: Kirsten Dierolf, Cristina Mühl, Carlo Perfetto and Rafal Szaniawski, who all work with SolutionsAcademy, training, mentoring and supervising coaches, team coaches, mentors and supervisors.

Foreword

When, many years ago, I first heard of the Solution Focused approach, I jumped to several inaccurate conclusions, based on the name. From both personal experience and clinical observation, I was aware that, much of the time, a coaching or mentoring client doesn't want or need a solution within the session. They want an advance in their thinking that enables them to work out a solution in their own time and in their own way. It is the coach who often brings the need for a resolution. And some issues are not solvable – the most beneficial outcome may in fact be acceptance of what is.

Of course, when done well, the Solution Focused approach does not just recognize but works with these realities of the client's world. It creates a safe thinking space, where a client reaches a heightened awareness of who they are, what they want and the resources they can exploit to get there. Unlike simplistic approaches, such as GROW, it does not seek to constrain the client within the coach's model, but rather creates conditions where the client defines their own model and narrative, releasing the creativity that permits them to identify and embrace new possibilities.

The Solution Focused approach draws significantly on the traditions of family and group therapy and the immense research base that underpins both these disciplines. It is not surprising that teams often like to think of themselves as a kind of family – a close-knit, mutually supportive unit. Like families, they are subject to conflicts of process and relationship. They create "voids" (topics it is too painful to acknowledge or discuss), get locked into roles, create shared narratives that reinforce their shared identity and have explicit or implicit power structures.

Our understanding of teams and the role of coaching in helping teams grow and achieve greater collaborative outcomes has increased rapidly over the past 30 years and more. We now have a lot more understanding of team dynamics. For me, one of the biggest advances has been the ability to see the team as a complex, adaptive system nested within other complex, adaptive systems. So many of the widely used models and approaches applied to teams are linear in concept and often badly evidenced. As a result, they can tie the team into time- and energy-wasting activities – for example, by trying to work through the linear stages of the Tuckman model or reducing their attention to a small group of internal interactions, ignoring other potentially more significant and external factors, as in the Lencioni model.

Mechanistic diagnostic approaches that have the well-intentioned goal of building appreciation of team members' cognitive and other differences often have the unintended result of "fixing" the shared narrative when what is needed is to liberate the team from a single narrative.

For teams, the Solution Focused approach is a collaborative process that enables greater collaboration within the team. It is a mutual exploration, stimulating curiosity to release the collective imagination. It allows the people in a system to see the system – a bit like enabling a fish to become aware of the water in which it swims – and to choose energizing paths into a shared future state.

In the following pages, the authors explain how the core concepts of Solutions Focus can be adapted to the complexity of working with teams. They demonstrate differences between the Solution Focused approach and other ways of supporting teams, offer tools and techniques, and challenge the reader to incorporate these powerful approaches into their team coaching practice. I recommend this book to any coach or leader who values an evidence-based approach to good practice.

David Clutterbuck

Preface

Solution Focused Team Coaching aims to enable coaches to move into team coaching using a respectful, resource and progress-oriented approach: Solution Focus. Chapter 1 will provide you with a firm foundation for the approach. You can learn about the history and development of Solution Focus in general and also find out about the philosophical foundation in social-constructionism. A paragraph on the cousins of the Solution Focused approach, Agile coaching, appreciative inquiry and so on, is also included.

In Chapter 2, you will learn about the practical foundations: how a Solution Focused coaching process can be structured, what questions we ask and what search spaces we open. Solution Focus is mainly interested in asking about what is wanted and what is working rather than what is not working and why something is wrong. In the paragraph on the double diamond metaphor, you will find a simple structure on how to partner with your clients in both individual and team coaching. We also present many different ways to facilitate a team coaching workshop.

The differences between team coaching, individual coaching and other modalities of team development are the focus of Chapter 3, which is followed by the Chapter 4, in which "team" is defined.

Chapter 5 provides an overview of the team coaching competencies of the major associations, the International Coaching Federation (ICF), the European Mentoring and Coaching Council (EMCC) and the Association for Coaching (AC). Ethics, coach presence and mindset, trust and safety, coaching agreements, competencies for working with the team in the moment and working with a co-coach are all explored.

In Chapter 6, we walk you through the structure of a team coaching process, from contracting to follow-up. Special team coaching formats, such as Agile coaching, Agile retrospectives, shadowing, team supervision, a decision-making tool and a format for team building, are presented.

In Chapter 7, we talk about different teams: executive teams, shop-floor teams, teams of teams, teams in the education sector and in hospitals. In Chapter 8, you will learn about how to facilitate larger groups in various team coaching formats.

Chapter 9 walks you through difficult situations that can arise in team coaching: negative participants, mandated teams, attacks on the coach, endless chatter vs.

nobody saying anything. Read this to be prepared in the unlikely event of encountering difficulties. The chapter also gives you structures for handling conflict in the team and situations in which diversity and inclusion play a part in team coaching.

Finally, Chapter 10 invites you to think about your continuous development as a team coach. We talk about initial training, reflective and deliberate practice, supervision and accreditation possibilities.

Acknowledgements

This book would not have been possible without the support of my husband, Arnoulf Keil, who managed renovation projects, holidays, food and beverages, as well as my emotional state during and after the COVID-19 pandemic. And of course, the book would not ever have happened without the teams I had the honour to coach and the team coaching students who have continued to ask interesting questions in our training programs: THANK YOU!

Kirsten Dierolf

At the foundation of the ideas shared in this book reside thousands of interactions with colleagues (Thank you Alina and Vlad!), clients and peers. I'm thankful for all those thoughts. Thank you, Kirsten, for welcoming me into the SolutionsAcademy family! It is an honour! Raf and Carlo – it is a true pleasure to work with you! And certainly, big appreciation is due to my family (Chris, Alex, Thomas, Vicky, my parents and Sorin) for constantly believing that I can do whatever I set my mind to. THANK YOU!

Cristina Mühl

My big thanks go to Kirsten for giving me the opportunity to make what I love my daily work. A very special thank you to Chris Bekker, who is a colleague and an incredible mentor but above all a true friend. I also thank Cristina, Raf and the SolutionsAcademy team for all I continue to learn from being a part of it. I thank my wife Angela and my kids for their support, encouragement and the thousand attentions they have reserved for me during these last years of great change. THANK YOU ALL!

Carlo Perfetto

My gratitude goes to all people who have ever invited me to coach, mentor and teach them. I want to thank Kirsten for teaching me what coaching and partnership truly are and giving me an opportunity to do the work I love. Carlo and Cristina, thank you for being such a nurturing team to be part of. I also want to thank my sister Justyna for supporting me throughout our life and finally to my one and only husband, Daniel, for his patience, support, healthy challenge and sense of humour. THANK YOU!

Raf Szaniawski

How to read this book

This book is a workbook. It does not give you one "correct" way to do team coaching, but rather offers a smorgasbord. You can pick and choose and create your own "menu". If you are interested in the foundations of the approach and some philosophy, start with the first chapter. If you are interested in the practical applications, go to the chapter on "moves". If you want to know about difficult situations, go to Chapter 9.

The first edition of this book was often presented to Kirsten in a well-worn, dog-eared state for her to sign. Coaches use the book as they are engaging in team coaching and come back to it whenever they need an idea or an inspiration. It is our sincere hope that this will also be true for this second edition.

Have fun!

Chapter 1

Foundations

Abstract

Solution Focused team coaching is aimed at enabling coaches to move into team coaching using a respectful, resource and progress-oriented approach: Solution Focus. This chapter provides a firm foundation for the approach. You will learn about the history and development of Solution Focus in general and also find out about the philosophical foundation of social-constructionism. A paragraph on the cousins of the Solution Focused approach, Agile coaching, appreciative inquiry and so on, has also been included.

Short history of Solution Focused practice

Solution Focus, along with many other coaching approaches, is based on a psychotherapeutic approach. However, like many other strengths-based and non-pathologizing approaches, Solution Focused therapy is much closer to a coaching approach then to a traditional approach in psychotherapy. Like coaches, Solution Focused practitioners believe that their clients are resourceful and whole. They strive to develop the potential of their clients rather than digging "deep" to "uncover" the root causes of present problems in the past. As Solution Focused therapists already meet their clients with a coaching approach, it has been easy for coaching practitioners to adapt the approach to coaching and consequently team coaching. In this chapter, we provide an overview of the history and development of the Solution Focused approach on which this book is based.

Unfortunately, for many years, the history of Solution Focused practice was mainly handed down orally. There were some articles about its beginnings (Cade, 2007, pp. 25–63; Kiser & Piercy, 2001, pp. 1–29; Lipchick & Derks et al., 2012, pp. 3–19), a few essays and books published shortly after the beginning about the early period (Kiser, 1995; Miller, 1997) and an early article from that time, "A study of Change" by Elam Nunnally, Steve de Shazer, Eve Lipchick and Insoo Kim Berg (Nunnally & De Shazer et al., 1986). However, most of what was taught in educational settings and training programmes for Solution Focused practice was based on stories by Insoo Kim Berg and Steve de Shazer, the founders of the approach.

DOI: 10.4324/9781003370314-1

It is only more recently that members of the Solution Focused community have started writing about the history and the development of Solution Focused practice over time. The European Brief Therapy Association (EBTA) formed a group that published *Theory of Solution Focused Practice* (EBTA, 2020), Harry Korman, Peter de Yong and Sara Smock Jordan (2020) published an article titled "Steve de Shazer's Theory Development" and Mark McKergow (2021) published *The Next Generation of Solution Focused Practice*.

The history of Solution Focused practice can start anywhere from Gregory Bateson's work via Milton Erickson and the Mental Research institute (McKergow, 2021). For the purposes of this book, we will start with the founders. In an article written by Steve de Shazer for the Brief Family Therapy Center website in 1999 (de Shazer, 1999), he describes how he began to study psychotherapy, reading Jay Haley's (1990) book *Strategies of Psychotherapy*:

> Until I read this book, as far as I can remember, I had never even heard the term "psychotherapy". Certainly, this was the first book on the topic that I read. I enjoyed it perhaps more than any other "professional" book I'd read in philosophy, art, history, architecture, or sociology. So, I went to the library and looked at its neighbours – which made so much sense to me – everything else was (poorly written) nonsense.
>
> (de Shazer, 1999, p. 6)

Jay Haley's (1990) *Strategies of Psychotherapy* describes Milton Erickson's hypnotherapeutic psychotherapy. Erickson's work thus became a major influence in the development of Solution Focused therapy. De Shazer continues: "It is not going too far to say that these two books changed my life and shaped my future" (de Shazer, 1999, p. 7). The Solution Focused approach's rejection of the psychodynamic, past-related problem analysis, and the Solution Focused resource emphasis can be traced back to the psychotherapy of Erickson. Erickson (1954) writes:

> The purpose of psychotherapy should be to help the patient in the most appropriate, available and acceptable way. With this assistance, the therapist should give full respect to what the patient is presenting, and it should be fully utilized. What the patient is doing in the present and what he will do in the future should be emphasized more than understanding why a long past event happened. The sine qua non of psychotherapy should lie in the patient's present and future adaptation.
>
> (Erickson, 1954, p. 127)

In Steve de Shazer's first book, *Patterns of Brief Family Therapy: An Ecosystemic Approach* (de Shazer, 1982, pp. 150–152), we encounter both the systemic roots of Solution Focused counselling and the beginnings of the separation from these roots. In the bibliography, you can find the authors to whom systemic family therapy and counselling still refer today: Bateson, Weakland, Minuchin, Selvini-Palazzli, Boscolo, Watzlawick. The representatives of systemic family therapy (if they called themselves that at the time) assumed that psychological abnormalities of a family member were due to the system of the family or to the system of interactions in the family. It is not the family member who "is ill", but the family system or its interactions that make the member a "carrier of the symptom". In this form of therapy, a therapist looks for an intervention that fits the family or the system of their interactions and disrupts this system to such an extent that other patterns become possible. Originally, de Shazer agreed (de Shazer, 1999, p. 10) – his mentor had been John Weakland of MRI and he had collaborated with MRI before their move to Milwaukee. When Kirsten Dierolf asked him whether he had ever considered joining MRI as a member, he replied: "Never join anything as a junior member." In 1978, de Shazer, Insoo Kim Berg and others started the Brief Family Therapy Center (BFTC) in Milwaukee (Korman et al, 2020, p. 50).

At that time, as in other family therapy centres, the BFTC worked with a one-way mirror, behind which a team of therapists observed a therapist's sessions with a family. Contact between the team behind the mirror and the therapist was mainly over the phone. One day, the therapist disagreed with the team and went out to talk to them (de Shazer, 1982, p. xi) and the so-called "practice break" developed. After the interview with the family, the therapist took time to talk to the team and then gave feedback to the family. The team did not see itself as part of the system, but rather as external observers (De Shazer, 1982, p. xii). This understanding changed only once a family expressly asked for the observer feedback and the observers returned compliments, to which the family reacted very positively (de Shazer 1982, pp. xii–xiii). From now on, the therapist, client and team behind the mirror had to be understood as part of a system. This new understanding had far-reaching consequences, which are described in de Shazer's 1984 essay, "The Death of Resistance" (de Shazer, 1984). If the family or the system of interactions in the family is regarded as a relevant system, and the therapist, as it were from the outside, views this system in order to construct a suitable intervention that perturbs this system, the therapist or the team can interpret the behaviour of the clients as "resistance" if the intervention does not work. This understanding is also applied in the systemic theory of that time: a system searches for a state of rest – homeostasis – and wants to return to it; of course it "resists" disturbances and pattern interruptions. De Shazer writes: "Thus, family systems theory, and therapy derived from it, are based on a mechanical notion of how things remain the same" (de Shazer, 1984, p. 1). He adds: "When homeostasis is used as the organizing concept on this more complex level, the 'resistance' is seen as located in the family and is described as something the family is doing" (de Shazer, 1984, p. 2). If the relevant system includes the therapist and the team, the outlook is different. In this case, "resistance" must be described as something that happens between the therapist, the team behind the mirror and the client. So, if resistance arises, the therapist and the team should see this as an attempt by the clients to cooperate: the clients are telling us what they need differently to help the process. Thus, resistance had "died" as a usable concept for family therapy and allegedly was buried ceremoniously in the garden of the house of Steve de Shazer and Insoo Kim Berg.

In the early 1980s, the BFCT team researched effective short-term therapy and experimented with different methods in therapy, each of which was observed by a team behind the mirror. The focus was still on constructing an effective task that clients could perform after the session. The team assumed that the better adapted to the clients this task was, the sooner it would be carried out. De Shazer called the concept "isomorphism" (de Shazer, 1982, p. 7). Therapists at the BFTC subsequently began experimenting with the creation of the task. In the course of these experiments, Alex Molar and Steve de Shazer (Nunnally & de Shazer et al., 1986, p. 83) devised a research project around the "formula first session task". Every team member should – if nothing serious spoke against it – give every client the same task: "Notice what you want to continue happening" (Nunnally & de Shazer et al., 1986, p. 83). Surprisingly, the clients' responses in the next session were very positive: 82 percent reported that something positive had happened in the time following the session, which was new. But if the same task has positive effects on so many clients, the concept of isomorphism, which requires the therapist to search for a "fitting intervention", is obsolete (Nunnally & de Shazer et al., 1986, p. 94). We began to see that the therapeutic task had shifted from *promoting* change to: (1) eliciting news of difference; (2) amplifying the difference; and (3) helping the changes to continue (Nunnally & de Shazer et al., 1986, p. 83).

In 1982, the development towards Solution Focused practice as we know it today began:

> Our epistemological shift in 1982 significantly influenced and changed the interviewing process at BFTC. The questions that we had to ask in order to assess the results of our experiment with the "formula first session task" forced us to increase our push for information about minute differences between past and present behaviours indicative of favourable change. This took us more and more away from details about problems and how they are maintained and more and more toward a focus on solutions and how to help the family construct them. Solutions were seen as a reality different from the one in which complaints lead to unsolvable problems.
>
> (Nunnally & de Shazer et al., 1986, p. 86)

After this discovery, the observation focus of the team at the BFTC was on the interactions between clients and therapists within the session, which led to descriptions of positive changes. The BFTC team experimented with different question forms, which helped to bring about "change talk" or "solution talk" and developed the "tools" of Solution Focused practice as they can still be seen today.

In summary, we can identify the following key points from the history of the development of Solution Focused practice:

• Solution Focused practice is not about a (psychodynamic) explanation related to problem generation, but rather about what clients want for their lives now.
• Solution Focused practice assumes that clients always have resources that they can use.
• Every behaviour of the client is regarded as cooperation.
• The practitioner and the client are the relevant system: the "client system" is not analysed from the outside.
• Solution Focused practice works when clients talk about positive changes – either positive changes they want to achieve or those they have already achieved.

Several meta-analyses show that Solution Focused Brief Therapy is just as effective as other therapeutic methods, but takes less time (and resources) (Stams et al., 2006; Kim, 2008). Solution Focused individual coaching is also recognized as evidence-based (Greif et al., 2022, p. 24).

Initially, Solution Focused practice was itself "practice-based evidence" – there was a lot of experimentation. However, Steve de Shazer had always been interested in the philosophical foundations. After several experiments to link Solution Focused practice with, among others, cooperation theory (de Shazer, 1985) and poststructuralism (De Shazer & Berg, 1992), he "landed" with Ludwig Wittgenstein's philosophy (Shazer, Dolan & Korman, 2007). After Steve de Shazer's death, these philosophical connections were extended by Mark McKergow and Harry Korman (2009) and Kirsten Dierolf (2011), among others, to the related disciplines of discursive psychology, social-constructionism and reflections on the philosophy of "enactive and embodied cognition".

Solution Focused team coaching rests on the same foundations as Solution Focused Brief Therapy. It is a social-constructionist practice that is progress and resource oriented rather than explanation or deficit oriented. As much as Solution Focused team coaching is based on the ideas developed in Solution Focused Brief Therapy, it is still a newer development. Insoo Kim Berg and Steve de Shazer worked primarily in psychotherapy; the only "teams" they encountered in the beginning were families or couples. Some of that work is transferable; however, context matters in the Solution Focused approach, and the approach needed to be adapted.

In the last two years before her death, Insoo Kim Berg also gave workshops on coaching and team coaching, which Kirsten Dierolf had the pleasure to attend as a simultaneous translator for Insoo Kim Berg. Insoo published a book on coaching with Peter Szabo, Brief Coaching for Lasting Solutions (Berg & Szabo, 2005). However, to our knowledge, Insoo Kim Berg did not publish anything on team coaching. After Steve de Shazer and Insoo Kim Berg and others had initiated the Solution Focused approach in therapy, Mark McKergow and Paul Z. Jackson (2002), Ben Furman and Tapani Ahola (2004), Daniel Meier (2005), Louis Cauffman and Kirsten Dierolf (2007), Fredrike Bannink (2010) and many others further developed the ideas of Solution Focused therapy and made them accessible to organizations by adapting the language and processes within the organizational context.

Solution Focused practice as a social-constructionist approach

As Solution Focused practice grew both in the therapeutic and in the organizational world, it became apparent that Solution Focused practitioners were not the only ones operating in a social-constructionist framework. Solution Focused practitioners started to reach out to related approaches. In May 2016, Narrative, Solution Focused and Collaborative practitioners convened a conference on Galveston Island in Texas with the purpose of revitalizing collaborative practices (Gosnell et al., 2017, p. 21). The meeting resulted in a joint "manifesto", similar in structure to Agile's "Manifesto for Agile Software Development" (Agile n.d.). We would like to use this manifesto to describe an expanded view of the foundations of social-constructionist approaches to team coaching, one of which is Solution Focused practice.

Our description aims to create clarity for the reader. It is in no way intended to evaluate or deny the effectiveness of other approaches. We assume that many different consulting and coaching approaches work. It would not be very Solution Focused to recommend changing their practice to people who have been doing something successfully with positive feedback from their clients for years.

On the other hand, this does not mean everything that works is Solution Focused – a mistake often made by beginning Solution Focused coaches. Solution Focus is a distinct approach and clarity is required regarding what it is important. For clients and people who would like to learn the Solution Focused approach, there are many advantages to clarity: you know what you are learning or buying and what you are not. This is our motivation for differentiating the Solution Focused approach from other approaches. This dimension of coaching is often overlooked. We seldom speak about our foundations, philosophies, ontologies, epistemologies and axiologies – and in our opinion, we should do so (Hurlow, 2022).

The Galveston Declaration

Table 1.1 Declaration of values

We *value this:*	More *than this:*
Pluralism – differences of view	**Singularity** – of view
1. Acknowledging multiple "truths"	1. Holding to a singular firm belief
2. Responsiveness to particularities in context	2. Applying generalities (including diagnosis)
3. Exploring multiple social realities	3. Searching for a single reality
4. Exploring multiple cultures, contexts, and interactions, and influences	4. Privileging specific cultures over others
Flux – differences of state	**Static** – fixed states
1. Facilitating the emergence of new identities	1. Stabilizing fixed or rigid identity/identities
2. Regarding "every interaction as mutual influence" with potential for unidirectional influence	2. Assuming "neutrality and objectivity"
3. Recognizing people as persons embedded in relationships	3. Treating people as separate individuals
4. Experimenting with transformational restorative justice practices	4. Implementing traditional retributive justice practices
Opening space – expanding choice	**Closing space** – removing choice
1. Living with curiosity	1. Living with certainty
2. Opening space for enlivened possibilities	2. Closing space for problems to persist
3. Inviting others to entertain change	3. Imposing change interventions upon others
4. Proactively including others (while respecting their possible choice to remain apart)	4. Passively and/or actively excluding others from participating
Responsibility – generativity	**Deficit focus** – constraint
1. Noticing resources, competencies, and possibilities	1. Identifying and diagnosing deficits, possibilities dysfunctions, and limitations for correction
2. Anticipating potential effects of resource use and developing sustainable ecologies	2. Utilizing profitable resources without consideration of the consequences
3. Assuming collective responsibility	3. Projecting responsibility and specifying and accountability to whom it belongs; judging others
4. Enacting an ethics of caring and privileging restorative justice	4. Applying moral judgements and retributive justice

Source: Gosnell et al. (2007, p. 25).

Foundations of social-constructionist and Solution Focused team coaching

Pluralism: Differences of view

We value acknowledging multiple "truths" more than holding a singular firm belief

As team coaches, we are always dealing with multiple perspectives and "truths": each team member has their own "truth" – the manager will have theirs, and so will other stakeholders. If you privilege a singular firm belief, you will not get very far as a team coach as you will be stuck in the middle of differing perspectives, and discussions will be based around who is right and not how to move forward. This might seem obvious; however, there are team coaching approaches in which the team coach will try to figure out "what is really going on", which sounds more like a "singular firm belief".

For Solution Focused team coaches, there is never something that "is really going on"; rather, there are always multiple perspectives that the team coach values and acknowledges. The Solution Focused team coach will also encourage the team to acknowledge and value multiple "truths" and perspectives to generate value out of the diversity of viewpoints. This is in line with the ICF team coaching competency framework, which states that the team coach "fosters expression of individual team members and the collective team's feelings, perceptions, concerns, beliefs, hopes, and suggestions" (International Coaching Federation, 2023).

We value responsiveness to particularity in context more than applying generalities (including diagnosis)

In some team coaching approaches, the qualities of "a good" or "a high performing" (Clutterbuck, 2019; Hawkins, 2021; Wageman et al. 2008) team or the dysfunctions of a team (Lencioni, 2002) are defined in general, as if these qualities were valid for each and every team. Team role models (e.g. Belbin, 1981) assume that a team works best if there is a good balance of preferred roles taken up by each team member. Personality profiles such as MBTI (Briggs Myers & McCaulley, 1992), DiSC (DiSC Profile, 2023) and Insights (2023) propose that the mix of personalities in the team should be a good fit for the main task of the team. It is assumed to be helpful if the team members know about the advantages of other personality types than the one to which they belong. Phase models of team development (e.g. Tuckman, 1965) postulate the existence of a typical development of a team and recommend that the leader of the team and the team members respond differently depending on the phase the team has reached. For example, if the team is in the so-called "storming" phase, it is recommended that people sit down and agree on standard processes and rules of engagement.

These approaches seem to be more in line with applying generalities rather than responsiveness to particularities in context. In Solution Focused team coaching, the practitioner will hold the assumption that every case is different, every team is different and there are no predefined qualities of a high-performing or dysfunctional team. The goals of the team coaching are not defined by a diagnostic instrument, but by the team itself.

One tenet mentioned in a standard tome on Solution Focused Brief Therapy, *More than Miracles* (de Shazer, Dolan & Korman, 2007, p. 1), is "If it isn't broken, don't fix it". If you relate this to team coaching, it sounds simplistic at first. No coach in their right mind would argue with it. In Solution Focused therapy, the goal of the client is the main focus: as soon as the client has found that the situation is sufficiently better for them, therapy ends. The therapist does not enter any of their own goals for the client (for example, "the holistic development of the client" or "maturity") into the process. The same approach is used in Solution Focused team coaching: it revolves around the goals of the team members, the team leader and the team as an entity, and the coaching ends when these goals have been met to the satisfaction of all team members (including the manager) or when the team has run out of goals to pursue. It is the team members who decide which topics are relevant – not the coach and not a diagnostic instrument.

Diagnostic instruments and phase models are therefore not used in Solution Focused coaching. If the client wants to engage in a team coaching process after using such an "instrument", the Solution Focused team coach would acknowledge the results and try to find out exactly, in concrete terms, which results the team wants to achieve. This way you end up working with the goals of the team members rather than working on a postulated ideal that is presumed valid for any team in any situation. One advantage of this is that teams find it easier to buy into team coaching. If it is clear that the team and the team coach are doing everything to collaborate on reaching the goals that the team would like to achieve rather than using a metric or prescribed outside goal, then "resistance" is unnecessary.

We value exploring multiple social realities more than searching for a single reality and *We value exploring multiple cultures, contexts, and interactions, and influences more than privileging specific cultures over others.*

A team in an organization may have the tendency to create one social reality: a team culture or an organizational culture with local norms and distribution of rights and duties. Solution Focused team coaches will not take this for granted but will view "how things are done here" as malleable and renegotiable. Every team member brings in multiple social realities – their cultures of origin, their family cultures, the culture in which they live now, subcultures to which they belong. These multiple social realities are a treasure trove for every team. Solution Focused coaches will value and privilege the creation of safety for each team member to bring in ideas of "how things can be done" from all contexts in which they find themselves, and will encourage the team to do the same.

In a way, this preference is a contradiction in terms. By valuing multiple social realities and exploring multiple cultures, Solution Focused team coaching may clash with organizational cultures where "how things are done" is predefined, and rights and duties are distributed in such a way that a few powerful people get to define the single reality. This ties in with the old misunderstanding of postmodernism or social-constructionism as "anything goes" or relativism. By stating that we value exploring multiple social realities and cultures, and that we value different perspectives, we are positioning ourselves. The basis of postmodernism and social-constructionism is that all human beings should be listened to and valued, and there should be an equitable distribution of rights and duties – otherwise the above preferences do not make any sense at all. Case 1.1 illustrates this dilemma.

Case 1.1: Hierarchies and team coaching

Kirsten was hired for a team coaching session in the Middle East. The focus was to enable the highly qualified team members to generate more value through increased participation in the planning process. Previously, the team leader had generated all the plans and they were not always very realistic. When deadlines ended up not being met, he got angry and started shouting at the team members. Obviously, they did not appreciate this, so morale and productivity were affected negatively.

Kirsten started by interviewing all the team members and the team leader on what was going well and what could be improved. She then fed the results back to the team leader and the team. The team leader got extremely angry. As he had no appreciation of the competence of his team, he felt that they were making excuses for not meeting his deadlines. Kirsten's perception had been that the team was very motivated – they wanted the same thing as the team leader: realistic timelines and deadlines kept. However, Kirsten could not convince the team leader to appreciate any other view of the situation than his own, and he was not willing to accept the help nor the feedback of his team members.

Kirsten learned to ask a bit about the organizational, leadership and team culture before engaging in a team coaching exercise: Solution Focused team coaching may clash with very hierarchical settings. If she had to do this again, she would first ask whether the organization wanted to move toward a more participatory culture. If it did, she would suggest some leadership coaching or training first, or taking a look at the entire organization to identify where pockets of participatory leadership already existed to learn from them what worked in the given culture.

A suitable team coaching process will look different for every culture. We have a preference for diversity, equity and inclusion as guiding principles. Every coach will have to decide themselves what kind of culture they would like to support and where they draw the line. We strive to be respectful of the cultural environment of the team be it national, religious, organizational or other. We won't assume that "everyone is like us" and always strive to ensure that differences are respected in a way that furthers trust and safety for all participants.

Another consequence of our preference for exploring multiple social realities and cultures is that the team coach will encourage everyone to contribute their perspective during the coaching. Even when there are conflicting views, the team coach will let them stand as equally valid and support the negotiation of either a shared perspective or the acceptance of different views.

Flux: Differences of state

We value facilitating the emergence of new identities more that stabilizing fixed or rigid identity/identities

In our view, individual and team identities are connected to the stories that are being told about the individual or the team by the individual themselves or by others. We strive to invite our clients to "tell their stories in ways that make them stronger" (Wingard & Lester, 2001).

During the contracting phase, a team coach often hears stories about what is not working. This can help to "stabilize" the identity of the team as "problematic". The more stories about the horrible past and the dreaded future are generated, the more the team is identified with the problematic state. As social-constructionist team coaches, we strive to separate the team from the problem. To paraphrase Michael White, "The team is not the problem, the problem is the problem" (Morgan, 2022). No team is unproductive and miserable all the time: there are always times when it is slightly better and slightly worse. The problem-saturated narrative hides these occurrences and make it harder for new and more favourable identities to emerge.

Explanations can also be part of the problem narrative. There seems to be a human need to understand exactly why the undesirable situation exists: "The team is dysfunctional because there are incompatible personalities" or "The leadership is non-existent" or, even worse, a specific team member is isolated as the source of all the problems or is even described as "the problem". These descriptions usually stand in the way of finding a way to a better situation as they also solidify the story or identity of the team as problematic. To avoid this, Solution Focused coaches would rather invite the team to describe what is wanted instead in great detail. The Miracle Question (see below for a detailed description) is one way of inviting the team to do this: "Suppose all issues were solved, which differences would you be noticing?"

We value regarding "every interaction as mutual influence"
with potential for unidirectional influence more that assuming
"neutrality and objectivity"

As mentioned above in the paragraph on the history of the Solution Focused approach, we believe that a coaching process always changes both the coach and the client(s). The relevant system consists of all stakeholders, including the coach.

This is different from some other approaches in which the coach's position is described as one of "neutrality". Sometimes there are even warnings that the coach should not get "sucked into" the team dynamic as if there was a possibility to not be part of the process. Of course, the coach has a different role than the team, but that does not mean the coach's view of the situation should be privileged in any way. The team coach is part of the relevant system and needs to maintain a different perspective only to the degree that they can invite the team to ponder meaningful differences.

We value recognizing people as persons embedded in relationships
more than treating people as separate individuals

Team coaching processes that start by analysing the personalities of the team members miss an important point: the team is not just a mix of personalities. How the team members can shine (or not) very much depends on the interactions in the team. We have often seen highly intelligent and motivated team members become completely ineffective in a team that did not value their contributions. The International Coaching Federation's (2023) team coaching competencies also mention this in Competency 1: Demonstrates ethical practice, where one of the performance markers is "Coaches the client team as a single entity" and in Competency 4: Cultivates trust and safety: "Promotes the team viewing itself as a single entity with a common identity". The EMCC core standards for team coaching state under "Systems thinking and group dynamics":

> Understands models and thinking on group dynamics and the impact of systems on behaviour and appropriately intervenes to highlight and raise curiosity within the team about such dynamics and behaviours and their impact on the team's performance.

Solution Focused practitioners are a bit weird here. On the one hand, we firmly agree that "taking the team apart" does not make sense. We know that people are embedded in relationships and that context and environment of other people matters a lot. On the other hand, "We value regarding 'every interaction as mutual influence' with potential for unidirectional influence more that assuming 'neutrality and objectivity'." We therefore do not make any attempt to "analyse the client system" or to map them in any way. We know that human systems are complex and that you cannot influence them strategically from the outside. You can only collaborate to make things better.

The way team relationships can be used fruitfully in coaching is by asking perspective change questions, such as:

- Suppose you got better at collaboration, who would notice it?
- What would they be noticing?
- How would they respond?
- How would you respond?

The descriptions elicited through the above questions make it easier for the team to notice when things are going in the right direction, and this in turn motivates change.

We value experimenting with transformational restorative justice practices more than implementing traditional retributive justice practices

The questions "How do we make it right?" or "What can we learn?" are much more important than "Who is at fault?" or "Who is responsible?" We try to help teams to stay away from "blamestorming" and instead enter into a future-oriented "brainstorming".

Of course, personal conflicts do not simply go away by ignoring the hurt feelings. The "What can we learn?" and "How do we make it right?" responses include the interpretations that conflict parties might have of each other. We ask ourselves the question of how "viewing" the other person needs to be different and what the "doing" is that needs to be different so that the conflict turns into collaboration.

Case 1.2:   Job-sharing conflict

Martha and Sabine worked part time, sharing the position of marketing manager. Sabine often found that Martha changed decisions she had made. For example, Sabine had decided that one of the team members, John, could not take Friday afternoon off, as he had already accumulated quite a deficit in his hours. Sabine thought it would be unfair to the team. Martha overruled Sabine's decision when John approached her, not knowing that Sabine had already decided. Sabine thought Martha wanted to endear herself to the staff in order to get a promotion. When she confronted Martha, Martha got the impression that Sabine was being unnecessarily strict – after all, it was John's grandmother's funeral on the Friday (a fact that John had not shared with Sabine).

Does this sound familiar? Simple misunderstandings can lead to very unfortunate interpretations of the character of another person. If we only invite Sabine and Martha to talk about how they want to handle such situations in the future and ignore the hurt feelings and interpretation, lasting collaboration can probably not be achieved. So a bit of helping Sabine listen to Martha and her motivations and helping Martha listen to Sabine and her motivations beyond discussions of "whose fault it is" will go a long way towards helping the situation.

Whenever there is a conflict, misunderstanding or perceived/actual wrongdoing, we try to figure out how to make it right rather than opting for retributive justice by punishing someone – that rarely makes things better.

Opening space: Expanding choice

We value living with curiosity more than living with certainty

"In the mind of the beginner, there are many possibilities. In the mind of the expert there are few." This quote is attributed to the Zen master Shunryu Suzuki. Solution Focused team coaches will try to be curious and aware that their own assumptions are just that: assumptions and not truths. Of course, we are human and there is no way to be human and not have assumptions – for example, you can't live if you are constantly questioning your assumptions that the floor will hold and a new day will be there tomorrow. The difference is that we try not to turn our assumptions into truths.

In team coaching, this "not knowing" attitude of the coach can be seen in how the coach partners with the team. The coach will invite and suggest rather than determine and direct. The coach will give the team choices about what will be discussed and how it will be discussed, what will be decided and how it will be decided. When the coach sees something happening in the team that they think is not so useful, they will not "confront" or "point out", but rather mention their observation without attachment to it being right as a potential interesting space at which to look.

Case 1.3:   Everything has been said, but not by everybody

In a team coaching session with a preschool, the team members often rehashed each other's points, making the discussions very long. Kirsten noticed this and was feeling herself getting impatient. Thinking that if she was becoming impatient, maybe others were feeling this too, she commented, "I see that many of you seem to show agreement with the others by restating what was just said – or am I off here?" The teachers nodded. Kirsten continued: "I am wondering, would you like to continue doing this or might we look at a more effective way?" Two ladies started laughing and said: "Ahhh, this is why we are running around in circles a lot!" Kirsten asked what their ideas were regarding how to change it. One of the team members suggested that if you want to agree with someone, you could just say: "Plus 1" instead of reiterating what was just said. The team experimented with this and everyone was very happy.

The team coach's "knowledge" is always provisional, tentative and curious. Our preference for curiosity also calls into question the team's assumptions, thereby opening up possibilities of doing and viewing things differently and potentially better.

We value opening space for enlivened possibilities more than closing space for problems to persist

Of course, no team coach (or any coach) in their right mind wants to "close space for problems to persist". However, this sometimes happens inadvertently when coaches assign labels to clients. If a coach labels a team "dysfunctional" or an individual coach assigns a "diagnosis" like "impostor syndrome", the problem solidifies. Instead of a team that is working to improve collaboration, we have a team that is dysfunctional. Instead of a person working on feeling comfortable, we have someone who "has" impostor syndrome. These descriptions can start to define the team or the individual. In the medical field, you can sometimes hear a doctor speak about "the depression in room number 4". Everything about this person has disappeared apart from the problem that defines them.

Solution Focused team coaches invite clients to talk about what they are wanting rather than what they are not wanting. They focus on what is already going in the right direction, thereby opening space for more possibility: the team coaching is more about describing the preferred future than about analysing and classifying the past. Traditional ways of inviting clients to do that are mentioned in the sections on "moves": the Miracle Question, the "best hopes" or "best team" question.

We value inviting others to entertain change more than imposing change interventions upon others

As coaches, we are sometimes asked to submit proposals with "deliverables" or prove that our "intervention" created a return on investment for the organization we serve. The idea behind this is that the coach creates a targeted intervention that, if followed, will create the desired change and, as already mentioned, Solution Focused coaches don't believe this will work. Human beings simply are not "trivial machines" where a given input guarantees a certain output (von Foerster, 2011).

Thinking in terms of interventions opens the room to the concept of resistance. If the team coach carefully analyses the situation, takes exactly the right intervention and the team then does not think this intervention is a good idea, the team coach will interpret the team's behaviour as resistance. This interpretation, in turn, is not very useful for the further collaboration between team coach and team. At SolutionsAcademy, we prefer the term "dance moves" rather than "interventions" or "tools". The team coach always responds to the situation and the team, and it is a co-creation rather than the targeted use of the fitting tool by the team coach.

When the Solution Focused team coach invites the team to entertain change, the team coach will usually invite the team to think about smaller experiments rather than revolutionizing everything at once. Our world is so complex that we think it is impossible to know exactly what the consequences of our experiments are going to be. In alignment with Agile project management, we think it is safer to experiment with small steps and then evaluate whether it was a step in the right direction or not.

We value proactively including others (while respecting their possible choice to remain apart) more than passively and/or actively excluding others from participating

We always strive to include all members of the team and maybe even other stakeholders in the team coaching process. Sometimes there is a view that the team will not be open if, for example, the team's manager takes part in the team coaching. However, the team's manager is a crucial part of the team. We think it is strange to separate the team into manager and team. This will actually cement the difference and perceived hierarchy rather than facilitating collaboration and conversation. If the members of the team feel they cannot talk to the manager, this might be a good topic to raise respectfully in the team coaching. It definitely does not get better by excluding the manager.

Another important principle is the principle of voluntary participation. A team coaching process that some members have to be forced to join does not start off on the most promising basis. If in an initial interview it transpires that some team members do not want to join the team coaching process, the question should be what could make the team coaching process attractive to them. We assume that everybody has good reasons for their actions and attitudes. Maybe they have experienced team coaching that was uncomfortable or useless. In any case, it makes a lot of sense to surface these issues before the team coaching process begins, and to make sure we design something in which everybody actually wants to participate.

Responsibility: Generativity

*We value noticing resources, competencies, and possibilities more
than identifying and diagnosing deficits, possibilities dysfunctions,
and limitations for correction*

As mentioned previously, the Solution Focused approach is resource and progress oriented rather than deficits and explanation oriented. It is not that we ignore
problems, lack of resources and competencies – Solution Focused does not mean
problem phobic. It is simply that we assume that whenever the team is able to
develop a goal, they will have had experiences which gives them hope that this goal
can be achieved. Surfacing these positive experiences and paying attention to them
generates hope and can point to skills, knowledge and resources of which the team
had previously been unaware.

The title of a classic Solution Focused book is *It's Never Too Late to Have a
Happy Childhood* (Furman, 1998). Of course, this title is playful, but there is a
philosophical background to it. Social-constructionist philosophers use the metaphor of Wikipedia rather than that of a hard drive for human memory. Yes, the team
has a past but how the team members come to view this past depends strongly
on the stories they continue to tell about it. If we invite the team to tell stories of
their resilience in the face of difficult situations, the team members will experience
themselves as strong and resilient. If we invite stories about helplessness and vic-
timization, the team members will tend to experience themselves as victims. The
facts of this story might be the same. Again, this is not about viewing the world
through rose-coloured glasses. It is about our preference of paying attention to
resources, competencies and possibilities. If the team wants to talk about problems
and hardships, we obviously acknowledge them. But we will listen with our atten-
tive ears to the stories that will make the team stronger (Wingard & Lester, 2001).

*We value anticipating potential effects of resource use and
developing sustainable ecologies more than utilizing profitable
resources without consideration of the consequences*

"Suppose you achieve everything you want to achieve, what difference would that
make?" and "Who will notice this difference and what will they be noticing?"
are standard questions in the Solution Focused approach. These questions help to
elicit descriptions of differences that might make a difference. They also take into
account the environment of the team and the consequences that their actions might
have on others. No team lives in a vacuum and by taking as many stakeholders'
perspectives into account as necessary and useful, more sustainable solutions can
be developed than with a plan that was developed in isolation. Moreover, our preference for incremental experiments rather than white-knuckle revolutions makes
the approach safer. When after the second experiment you find out that what was
thought as beneficial for everyone has negative consequences for some, it is easier
to back-track and find a different solution.

We value assuming collective responsibility more than projecting responsibility and specifying accountability to where it belongs – judging others

Kirsten does not have a green thumb. In her care, even the hardiest of plants don't survive long. But even she would never blame the individual plant for her lack of gardening success. When a plant does not grow as anticipated, we fix the environment, not the plant. So why does this suddenly become so different when we are talking about human beings? As mentioned above, blamestorming is rarely useful. I think we all know someone who was a star in one team and after transfer to another didn't thrive as anticipated.

Even if the team has identified one person who is seen as "the problem", a Solution Focused team coach would not start by assuming that focusing on this person will help. We try to treat team problems at the team level. If someone is behaving "originally", it often makes more sense to try to create an environment in which this behaviour no longer needs to occur rather than to try and "fix" this person.

Case 1.4:   Why are you not like us?

Kirsten was coaching a team of software developers. The team consisted of five developers under 30 years of age whose greatest joy in life was programming. It was very hard to keep them from working in their free time. Another member of the team was in his mid-forties with a family and other interests that he wanted to spend his time focusing on. The manager had a very hard time helping the team to develop some cohesion and acceptance for the different phases of life of his team members. During the team coaching, Kirsten and the team had a discussion on "what can reasonably be expected". The team members were able to recognize the differences and develop more acceptance for each other. If the "problem person" had been singled out and identified as the cause of the difficulties, the team would not have had that chance.

We value enacting an ethics of caring and privileging restorative justice more than applying moral judgements and retributive justice

The team coach is the advocate for team collaboration, not the advocate for any individual team member. This is even the case when there are serious accusations or difficulties that have happened in the team. As you will see in our chapter on conflicts, the question is always about how things can be right again rather than analysing what happened exactly and who was at fault. This doesn't mean that wrongdoing is not acknowledged. The focus is different: we acknowledge what happened and invite the team members to listen to one another. In most cases when someone is accused of doing something wrong, that person has a story about a need or a positive motivation. Eliciting the stories can be helpful to create peace. At the same time, acknowledging the hurt on the other side, perhaps an apology or other ways of trying to make things right again can open the space for future collaboration.

Exercise 1.1: Your personal statement

Now that we have shared where we are coming from, we would like to invite you to respond. EMCC asks practitioners to fill in a personal statement of their understanding of team coaching. If you were to summarize in 300-500 words, what your basis for team coaching is, what would it be?

Other approaches: The cousins

Agile

Agile is an iterative approach to facilitating project management in software development. It is based on the assumption that a team can deliver value to the customer (internal or external) by delivering works in small increments rather than using big "jumps" with great effort. In this way, the results are evaluated continuously by customers so the team can receive immediate feedback and can adjust quickly.

The Agile approach originated in 2001, when 17 people met together to reflect upon the future of software development in Snowbird, Utah. The group all perceived difficulties with the way software was being developed, yet they disagreed on how to address these difficulties. The biggest frustration arose from the fact that the companies involved in software development were so engaged in planning and documenting their activities that they often lost sight of the value they were engaged to deliver to the client. Software development took a long time. First, the customer was asked to describe their requirements in detail, then a project plan was designed with sub-projects, deliverables, timelines and so on. When the software was finally delivered, it sometimes did not meet the requirements of the business, which had changed during the time of the development. The group of people who met in Snowbird decided to invest their time to solve this dilemma and explore how they could deliver value to the client quickly, adapting the work to the change needed rather than following a "waterfall" project-management approach.

Their reflections were documented in the "Manifesto for Agile Software Development" (Agile, n.d.), a set of values that defined a new culture. These are the values of the Manifesto:

We are uncovering better ways of developing software by doing it and helping others do it.
Through this work we have come to value:

- Individuals and interactions over processes and tools
- Working software over comprehensive documentation
- Customer collaboration over contract negotiation
- Responding to change over following a plan

That is, while there is value in the items on the right, we value the items on the left more.
We follow these principles:

1　Our highest priority is to satisfy the customer through early and continuous delivery of valuable software.
2　Welcome changing requirements, even late in development. Agile processes harness change for the customer's competitive advantage.
3　Deliver working software frequently, from a couple of weeks to a couple of months, with a preference to the shorter timescale.
4　Business people and developers must work together daily throughout the project.
5　Build projects around motivated individuals. Give them the environment and support they need, and trust them to get the job done.
6　The most efficient and effective method of conveying information to and within a development team is face-to-face conversation.
7　Working software is the primary measure of progress.
8　Agile processes promote sustainable development. The sponsors, developers, and users should be able to maintain a constant pace indefinitely.
9　Continuous attention to technical excellence and good design enhances agility.
10　Simplicity – the art of maximizing the amount of work not done – is essential.
11　The best architectures, requirements, and designs emerge from self-organizing teams.
12　At regular intervals, the team reflects on how to become more effective, then tunes and adjusts its behaviour accordingly.

The similarities between the Agile approach and the basic tenets of the Solution Focus are impressive: delivering value in brief cycles, receiving feedback from an external point of view, measuring the steps done, empowering people, trusting their abilities to do a good job, simplicity and adjusting the path using the feedback are all elements that align this approach with the Solution Focused approach. Many agile coaches therefore find it easy to improve their coaching skills by learning the Solution Focused approach.

You can also see how the "Agile Manifesto" inspired the "Galveston Declaration" referenced earlier: valuing one thing over another without claiming that we hold "the truth".

Appreciative Inquiry

Appreciative Inquiry is an approach to organizational development that also shares a lot of the assumptions of Solution Focused team coaching: it is a strengths and future focused approach and is more concerned with what is right with an organization than what is wrong. It was developed by David Cooperrider (2008).

The foundational idea is very similar to Solution Focus. Appreciative Inquiry also assumes that it is not possible to observe without influencing. What a team pays attention to has implications for what it deems possible or not, and what it will move towards. Appreciative Inquiry starts by eliciting detailed descriptions of what is going well rather than describing the preferred future, like the Solution Focused approach. What makes sense to us about this is that when a team has described highlights, resources and past successes, the description of the preferred future may change as the team now sees more things being possible than before. As stated above, Solution Focused team coaching does not set any structures in stone: whether you want to start with the preferred future or the successful past really depends on where the team is at. If there is little hope, a description of the successful past might be the best way to start.

Appreciative Inquiry also works with rich and detailed descriptions rather than with generalizations. The way Appreciative Inquiry generates these is by "appreciative interviews". The team divides into pairs and one partner interviews the other about concrete highlights in their experience of the team with the help of a questionnaire. They then switch roles. This is called the "discovery" phase of Appreciative Inquiry. The other phases are "dream", in which a vision of the future is generated (much like Solution Focused's preferred future), "design", in which decisions for concrete actions are made and "destiny", the implementation of the new ideas.

Systemic team coaching

"Systemic" is a term that is used for a wide array of approaches (Dierolf, 2012). Some are closer to Solution Focused work; some are quite different. The systemic approaches to team coaching that are most similar to Solution Focused team coaching also include the team coach as part of the relevant system, rather than assuming that a completely neutral outside view of the team is possible or desirable. All approaches to systemic team coaching consider the stakeholders outside of the team that might be impacting the team's performance and work with "circular questions", which are very similar to Solution Focused perspective change questions ("How would your customers notice if you ...?").

In some forms of systemic team coaching that are not so close to the Solution Focused approach, the team coach will assume that insights from systems theory or cybernetics can be brought in helpfully for the team (von Bertalanffy, 1968). It is sometimes assumed that the team as part of the entire organization will mirror what is going on in the organization, as in fractals in natural systems. The team coach can notice these "parallel" processes and offer them to the team as an observation. The Solution Focused approach would not start with these assumptions.

Systemic constellations

"Systemic constellations" are a very specific approach within systemic team coaching. They involve a practical activity that can allow all those involved (team members, the leader and all stakeholders) to "visualise" the interactions and unspoken dynamics of the team, particularly during difficult moments or throughout difficult situations. The constellation creates a spatial and 3D visible model (a "living map") that can enlighten sources, patterns, relationships and dynamics between team members and/or the team and its environment so they can face difficulties and to provide clarity and possible resolutions. In a constellation, the team members are positioned in a room and the spatial dynamics, the distances and the directions team members face form a representation of the team's interaction. This technique can also be used to let the 'inner map' that every team member is carrying inside emerge so everybody else can see it and confront their own personal map, with the purpose of restoring the system coherence so all members are given a place and can be free to operate at their best. Constellation work also comes in many different forms, some closer to Solution Focus, some quite far away. Insa Sparrer and Matthias Varga von Kibéd founded an approach called "Systemic Constellation" (Sparrer, 2007; Varga von Kibéd & Sparrer, 2005). They assume that constellations are a transverbal language in which humans also communicate.

The first use of constellations workshops was to elicit individual personal complex patterns. The client invites up to 20 people who they think are relevant for solving the situation in their mind. The client then positions these people in the room to build a "map", spatially describing the relationship between themselves and every person, and between every person. The construction of the map in itself is already able to give the individual some fresh insights and more clarity about the "structures" behind this representation. By changing this map, the shape and the distances between the people can support the individual to change their perspective and the way the client relates to the system in a more useful way. Constellations don't always have to involve people – the map can also be built using stones or other placeholders that represent the people involved.

This methodology can also be used for teams: after having introduced the methodology to the team and defining the goal of the intervention, the team and the relationship between members and stakeholders are mapped through placeholders and the coach/facilitator starts to facilitate the discussion about it by inquiring about the meaning of the positions and the possible future changes.

What is similar to Solution Focus is the form of the questions (especially in systemic constellations founded by Insa Sparrer and Matthias Varga von Kibéd) and the idea that in a complex environment, small changes can create big differences. Everything is always connected to everything else.

Solution Focused coaching structures and moves

There are two structures that we mainly use for Solution Focused team coaching: the metaphor of an art gallery with four different rooms and the structure of a double diamond.

The art gallery metaphor

The metaphor of the art gallery was invented by BRIEF in London. However, BRIEF's founders, Chris Iveson, Harvey Ratner and Evan George, did not publish anything about the metaphor to our knowledge. Only later did a detailed description become available in *The Next Generation of Solution Focused Practice* (McKergow, 2021, pp. 109–114) (Figure 1.1).

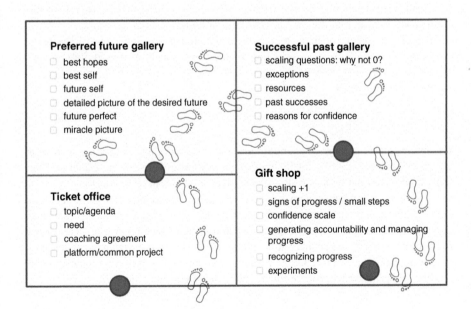

Figure 1.1 The Solution Focused art gallery.

The idea is to liken a Solution Focused conversation to visit to an art gallery or museum. Before you may enter the museum, you must buy a ticket. You can then wander through the rooms of the museum and look at the pictures on the walls. At the end of your visit, you will probably leave the museum through the gift shop with an umbrella featuring a nice Monet print or a cup with a Klimt.

The metaphor of the art gallery also includes one of the specific characteristics of Solution Focused team coaching. While we are walking through the museum, we see the pictures on the wall. We are describing in observable behaviour what we see rather than interpreting what is going on or engaging in other explanations. Solution Focused team coaching invites all stakeholders to describe signs of progress and past successes rather than explaining why something is not like the team and why other stakeholders would like it, or identifying the deficits of the team.

Here is a description of the rooms in the museum and the opportunities this metaphor offers for Solution Focused team coaching.

Ticket office

Just as you need to buy a ticket when you are entering a museum, you also need permission to enter a team coaching session. Both the EMCC and the ICF codes of ethics state that clients have the right to terminate their coaching at any point in time: nobody can or should be coached against their will. This may be a little tricky in team coaching, given that organizations have ways of mandating team members to be in a team coaching session whether they want it or not. It is crucial for the team coach to state that this will always be a voluntary process.

To make it easier for team members to develop a positive view of the team coaching process, a good introduction of the team coach, a nice invitation, and clarification on what team coaching is and what it isn't may help (more details below under "moves").

Good working relationship

As already stated, it is important not to lose the good working relationship with your clients. This is mainly true for the working relationship between the coach and the individual team members as well as the team as a whole. In team coaching, it is not only the relationship between coach and client that is important, but also the relationships of the team members with each other. It can be very useful to take care of this good working relationship at the beginning of the team coaching process. The aim is to evoke a confident and positive atmosphere. The more hope the team has that something can improve, the more likely the improvement will be to occur. Suggestions to facilitate this atmosphere can be found under "team coaching moves".

Listening

Listening is another very important tool for Solution Focused team coaching. Solution Focused listening is different from "active listening". Active listening is about enabling the coach to understand the client as exactly as possible. The techniques for achieving this are a coach's repetition of what the clients say in the coach's own words. The technical term here is "paraphrasing". Behind this lies the metaphor of communication as information transmission.

Solution Focused listening is not about exact understanding. We assume that in each interaction meanings are created and negotiated between the conversation partners and that understanding 100 percent correctly is neither possible nor necessary. Listening is more about not disturbing the relationship between coach and team, and the team having the impression that a coach understands what they are trying to say and is working on a solution with them. The Solution Focused team coach listens most intently when the team members are talking about what they want, such as resources or other things that give the team confidence that improvement is possible.

Exercise 1.2: Listening

Watch a debate on television (e.g. in a talk show) and listen in a goal and resource-oriented fashion. Take a piece of paper for each participant in the discussion. Jot down: "What does this person want?" (stated as the presence of something, not the absence – for example, not "What does this person want to avoid?" and "Which resources can I perceive in this person – what makes me confident that he or she can reach this goal?").

Using the language of your clients

Nothing creates the feeling of being understood better than when the coach is using the language of the team. This can be quite difficult, especially when the team is working in a field that is completely foreign to the coach. Therefore, we have always found it very valuable to know a little bit about what the team does, which words are being used and which context the team is working in before engaging in team coaching. We are not engaging in a diagnosis or analysis (even though it might look that way from the outside), but we are trying to learn the language of the team to be able to connect.

When we are talking about language, we are not only talking about the vocabulary; we are speaking more generally about the culture, the "grammar" of the team. If everybody shows up every day in jeans, we will not wear our pinstriped suit. If it is a team of down-to-earth high school graduates, we will not boast about our university degrees. If we are working for an international consultancy in which intelligence and qualification play a large role, it might happen that we mention our credentials quickly. We believe that, just as in individual coaching, the trust and confidence of the team concerning the coach and their belief that their ability will help them move forward is one of the main success factors of coaching.

In Solution Focused team coaching, we are looking for a common project to which all team members, superiors and we ourselves can subscribe. Since we can't enter into the whole process without the ticket, this step is crucial: the team coach needs to help the team to find something that they all want to work on. The criteria for a promising common project are:

- Everyone agrees that the desired outcome is something on which they want to work.
- The desired outcome is described in positive, observable terms as the presence and not the absence of something.
- The desired outcome is something that is under the influence of the team.
- The desired outcome is beneficial for the whole organization.

EVERYONE AGREES THAT THE DESIRED OUTCOME IS SOMETHING ON WHICH THEY WANT TO WORK

The team coach might ask, "Suppose this team coaching process is really useful, what difference will this make to you and the team?" If team members answer with conflicting goals, the team coach might ask again, "What difference will that make?" For example:

Team member A:	I want us to start planning in a lot of detail.
Team member B:	No, I hate the micromanagement – I need the big picture!
Coach:	What difference will it make if you have the right level of planning?
Team member A:	I will be clear on what to do and where this will lead to.
Team member B:	I will know which direction we are taking and what I need to do as next steps.
Coach:	Ok, so clarity on the direction, desired outcome and next steps?
Team members A and B:	Yup.

The team coach really needs to be tenacious – don't start without establishing a desired outcome that everyone wants to achieve. The Solution Focused approach is very useful here. Most often people have difficulties agreeing on what the real problem is, but if you ask what they want instead, team members usually can agree much more easily. The minimal compromise is, "We want to come to work every morning looking forward to our day and willing to do our best." If somebody does not want to be part of the team or doesn't want to be productive, they probably have no business being in that team. There is always this minimal goal that a team can work towards, irrespective of what their vision of the "real problem" is.

The details of the solution or forward movement to which the team is aspiring can then be additive rather than controversial. Maybe person A wants more quiet in the room and person B would like a better meeting structure. If this is formulated in terms of "all of the things we want", there usually isn't much contention. You can have more quiet in the room and a better meeting structure at the same time.

THE DESIRED OUTCOME IS DESCRIBED IN POSITIVE, OBSERVABLE TERMS AS THE PRESENCE AND NOT THE ABSENCE OF SOMETHING

Often the initial request of the team or other stakeholders is framed in negative terms: "There is a lack of accountability in the team" or "There is no psychological safety in the team." There are two issues with these kinds of descriptions. One is that the goals are formulated negatively. The other is that the description is very general. Of course, most clients will mention what their problem is before they can be invited into a description of what they want instead. Sometimes they even don't know what they want instead. It is the task of the team coach to elicit positive descriptions about what is wanted. The team coach might use Solution Focused questions like:

- Suppose there was accountability, what would be different?
- What would be some signs of psychological safety appearing?

With these kinds of questions, you not only get a positive description of what is wanted but you also invite the team to give more details on big words such as "accountability" and "psychological safety". Many of these words are popular as triggers for team coaching. Leoncioni (2002) has even categorized them as five dysfunctions of a team: "Absence of trust, fear of conflict, lack of commitment, avoidance of accountability, inattention to results". However, even when you "know" what the team "dysfunction" is, you still don't know what the team wants to work towards. And as mentioned above, many things can be hidden behind a word like "accountability". The Solution Focused team coach therefore takes great care not to start a team coaching process before they know in positive, concrete and observable terms what it is that the team wants.

THE DESIRED OUTCOME IS SOMETHING THAT IS IN THE INFLUENCE OF THE TEAM

No team lives in a vacuum. There are always other teams, customers or other stake-holders around the team, which may cause problems for the team and might lead them to ask for a team coaching session.

Case 1.5:   When the team cannot change the environment

Kirsten once worked with the team of social workers confronted with a sudden change and legislation. They would have a lot less resources available to help the underprivileged children they were serving. Of course, the team coaching started with many of the team members being very concerned about the feasibility of their work, given the new regulations. While acknowledgement of the difficulty is important, it really doesn't help to spend a lot of time talking about things that cannot be changed. The team was invited to describe their goal as within their influence and framed the goal of the team coaching as "How do we continue to serve our clientele well under the changed circumstances?"

Of course, it is the decision of the team members whether they would like to use their team coaching time to think about how they might advocate for a change in policy or whether they would prefer to use the time to find ways to respond to the change. In any case, the team coaching needs to be something that within the influence of the team: how to respond to the change or how to advocate for a policy change.

If a team is very stuck on descriptions of what other people need to be doing differently, the team coach has a few options but to invite the team to focus on what they can change:

Coach: Suppose the policy did change, what would be possible for you that is important?
Team: We would be able to serve our clients well.
Coach: So is this your main concern for our session: How to serve your clients well given the changed circumstances?

Another option is to invite the clients to draw a circle of concern and a circle of influence (Covey, 2020) and ask them to position their team coaching goals into either the circle of concern or the circle of influence. Sometimes you can start by collecting all concerns on Post-It notes and then invite the team to select those they can influence. The main point is that it does not make any sense to start working on a limitation, which the team cannot influence.

In individual coaching, coping questions are used in situations in which the client has little confidence that something can be done in order to improve the situation. It is also used when the client seems very burdened by the problem, and no alternatives or resources are accessible to the client. In individual coaching, you can acknowledge how difficult the problem is and validate the client's perspective of feeling stuck or hopeless. Of course, this is only the beginning. Questions that can help the client regain access to existing exceptions can be coping questions like, "I can see that this is very difficult; how have you been able to cope?" or "Under these circumstances, how do you manage to still go to work every morning and do your job well?" How you phrase the question obviously depends on the language the clients use and the general disposition of the clients.

When the team is in a similarly difficult situation, it also helps to think about asking a coping question. There are sometimes difficulties in team coaching that are determined by the environment. For example, they might have to adhere to a certain process, use certain software or collaborate with a specific department. As much as you might understand the team's anger about unfortunate and unchangeable structures and processes, it is not useful to spend a lot of time talking about things that cannot be changed. Coping questions can help.

We first ask whether the topic at hand is something that can be solved or improved today. It is important not to assume anything at this point and try to judge yourself what can and cannot be changed. I have experienced situations in which the team was suddenly able to talk about things and change things that I thought could not be changed. For example, when Kirsten was meeting with a team of executives for a strategy meeting, they decided to throw out a performance management system that was not doing what it was supposed to, on the spot.

However, if the team states that something is set and cannot be changed, it is most helpful to discuss with the team how they can best deal with the situation. It also helps to "normalize" the situation, agree that situations like these happen in other companies and perhaps share your experiences with other teams in similar situations (obviously without mentioning any names). No organization is perfect. You will always find processes and structures that are difficult for some parts of the organization. This is simply the nature of organizations, and it is helpful for teams to be content with the situation if they know this is not merely the fault of their own less-than-perfect organization. As a Solution Focused team coach, I take the dissatisfaction of the team with structures and processes that they are perceiving as unhelpful as engagement and enthusiasm for the success of the organization. Team members want to give their best and be useful for the organization. They are committed to the organization and want to create improvement, even in situations in which improvement is impossible. Acknowledging and respecting their wish for the efficiency and success of the organization is usually greatly appreciated by the team members.

As a team coach, it is very important not to fall into the trap of describing the team as "resistant to change" or in any other negative way. We have heard colleagues describe teams they are working with as "resistant" or as "having a complaining culture". In coaching, one of our main jobs is to hold the client in unconditional positive regard, so we are not helping if we describe the team negatively. When you feel tempted to do that, you might explore your good reasons for your negative description. Are you afraid that the team coaching process might fail and need a cop-out? Would you like some acknowledgement of the difficult situation yourself and paint the situation as dire so you can shine as the rescuer? No team coach I know is free from these thoughts, and pushing them away doesn't usually help – but examining them does. What helps Kirsten to deal with these impulses is to remember that her own descriptions of the team are also stories that make the collaboration either stronger or weaker.

In Solution Focused coaching, we try to invite clients to describe preferred futures more than problems. However, sometimes clients would really like us to acknowledge the hardship that they are experiencing. It is as if clients need us to understand how difficult life is before they can start moving on towards finding ways to make things better.

Narrative practice has found a really creative and useful way of talking about the problem without solidifying the description of the situation into one that is only dominated by the problem story. When people are telling us about their problems, they often identify with this problem, or – worse – they are being identified as the problem. In these cases, the team, the sponsor or the team leader may talk in language such as, "Our lack of commitment, our lack of alignment, our lack of motivation, etc."

As coaches, we can invite a useful difference between describing the team as the problem and the problem as the problem. If the team is the problem, then team members are identified with it and their story revolves around the problem description. Many other experiences and stories are left undescribed and therefore are not noticed.

Narrative practice uses the externalizing technique to separate the person from the problem. The problem is given a name and clients are invited to describe their responses to the problem, how they live with the problem or their preferred relationship to the problem. The problem is metaphorically taken from inside the person or the team to outside the person or the team. This is also where the term "externalizing" comes from.

The atmosphere becomes much more hopeful and open to new descriptions if a team rallies against an externalized demotivation rather than seeing itself as the cause of the trouble, or as "the demotivated team". Questions that the team coach may ask to facilitate the externalization might be:

- What is the name you have for the issue that you're experiencing? Does it have a shape or a form? (Creative teams might even draw the "monster".)
- What does *this name* invite you to do as a team that you would rather not be doing?
- How does it get the better of you?
- What are its sneaky ways of tricking you into doing what you don't want to be doing?
- What is *this name* keeping you from doing that you would rather be doing?
- What kind of relationship would you like with *this name*?
- Have there ever been times where you were close to having this relationship with *this name*?
- What did you do at that moment that you are currently doing less of?
- What is this response to *this name* tell you about you as a team?
- Instead of *this name*, what would you like to invite into your team *instead*?
- If the *instead* was present more than *this name*, how would you notice? If the *instead* was a close companion over the next weeks, what would you and others be noticing?

THE DESIRED OUTCOME IS BENEFICIAL FOR THE WHOLE ORGANIZATION

It doesn't happen very often that a team develops a goal that would not be beneficial to the whole organization. When it does, it is almost always about something that is wrong in the whole organization. It might happen, for example, that the targets that two teams have been given are contradictory or mutually exclusive. Usually this happens only in large organizations where the complexity makes it difficult to see when these kinds of issues arise.

In this case, it doesn't make sense to continue coaching the team to reach a goal that would not benefit the entire organization or would be detrimental to another team in the organization. Here, the team coach might ask the team whether they would like to escalate the issue after it has become transparent that they are pursuing a goal that is in conflict with other important goals of the organization. Often it is then possible to continue the team coaching at a higher level – for example, coaching the team of team leaders to align targets and goals in such a way that no team is in conflict with another team.

THE DESIRED OUTCOME CAN BE REACHED BY A SERIES OF SMALL STEPS OR EXPERIMENTS – EVOLUTION BEATS REVOLUTION

It is always so much safer if the goal that the team wants can be reached by a series of small steps or experiments. This gives the team coach and the team the opportunity to check whether they are going in the right direction along the way. Most organizations these days are very complex, so it is hard to anticipate what the consequences of the changes a team might make will be.

Exercise 1.3: Team coaching goals

Take the following goals (which come from our real work with clients) and determine what is "wrong" with them – why they would not be taken at face value as goals in a Solution Focused process. You will find the solution below.

1 The legal department should stop being so overworked and incompetent.
2 We need better communication.
3 We should stop constantly blaming each other.

Solution:

1 This goal is not in the influence of our clients and is stated negatively. It also sounds like a negative value statement. Basically, you do not know what should be there instead of overwork and incompetence. A better way to put

it could be, for example, "Our collaboration with the legal department has improved so that we get answers quickly when we have an important request for information."

2   This goal is in the influence of our clients; however, "improved communication" can mean a lot. Ludwig Wittgenstein and Steve de Shazer would call it a term that is defined by "family resemblances". As coach, you would have to ask how people would notice "improved communication". If you clarify the goal in this way, you usually receive the first ideas for a solution: "Every morning when everybody is there, we will have a 10 minutes stand up meeting, and we will tell each other what is on our plate for today and discuss the priorities."

3   In this case, the topic is also what *should not* be there instead of what *should* happen. Clarifying the goal again gets you closer to the solution: "When we have a problem, we will talk about how we can solve it. It's not about who's to blame."

Preferred future

Rich description of the preferred future

After we have established what the team and the relevant stakeholders want as an outcome of the team coaching process, we can invite the team to describe a rich picture of their preferred future. As mentioned above, this description of the preferred future can be additive. Whatever people want is fine unless it is the exact opposite of what another person wants. If this is the case, the team coach might go for the goal behind the goal and inquire what difference this description may make.

The description of the preferred future is the space in the team coaching process where teams can be creative and brainstorm, draw or otherwise describe their preferred future stories. In the section of this book on team coaching moves, you will find many ideas on how to facilitate this. Here, we would like to explain the general format of the questions and what a team coach needs to take care of when inviting a team to a rich description of the desired future.

The Miracle Question

There are many stories on how the "Miracle Question", a signature move of Solution Focused practice, came about. A predecessor might have been Milton Erickson's crystal ball technique (De Shazer, 1978). In Kirsten and Guy Shannon's conversations with different members of the original team at the Brief Family Therapy Center (personal communication), different stories emerged. Maybe there wasn't an exact "origin", but instead a collaboration of people who came up with the idea that it made sense to describe in rich detail what clients wanted rather than trying to explain the problem.

Steve de Shazer describes the development of the miracle question in an interview from 1997 (Norman, McKergow, & Clarke, 1997):

The Miracle Question evolved out of one day Insoo asked a question and the answer was, "Oh it would take a miracle!" and Insoo said, "Well, yes, suppose ... a miracle did happen" ... and that started the whole thing. The answer was pretty nice, whatever it was. The answer was nice, so almost all our stuff like that is invented by clients first.

The miracle question was subsequently developed further at the Brief Therapy Center. In 1988, it was first published by Steve de Shazer (1988, pp. 5–6). It invites clients to imagine a world in which the problem or challenge no longer exists. Clients explore observable differences in that situation and possible approaches for initial changes for the better.

You might think this is the same as the above "ticket office" questions for goal setting. However, there is a difference between the Miracle Question and goal-setting questions. In the Miracle Question, you do not assume a linear connection between problem and solution. You invite your clients to focus on what the world would look like if the problem or challenge had disappeared. This draws the attention of the clients to what happens outside the problem. The question is often completely against our first impulse to want to understand the problem in as much detail as possible in order to be able to find a solution.

There are many ways of usefully posing the miracle question. Here is a standard variant:

I would like to ask you question. It is a little bit strange and requires some imagination.

Suppose our workshop/conversation is over and you go home. At home you do all the things you usually do in the evening. Maybe you'll have some dinner, watch television, brush your teeth ... and then some time that evening you get tired and go to sleep. And while you are fast asleep, in the middle of the night, a miracle happens – just like that. And the miracle is that everything that we have been talking about and maybe even what we haven't talked about, has been solved – just like that. Now you are fast asleep, and that is why you cannot realize that a miracle happened. The next morning, nobody is telling you about the miracle either. How are you going to start noticing in the morning that a miracle happened?

Often teams do not know what to answer right away. The coach can make it easier by asking a few follow-up questions:

What would be a first small sign?
What else?

People then usually start to smile and find answers that range from the trivial to the important. The team coach takes care to get a rich description of the differences after the miracle that can serve to identify small observable differences and possible steps afterwards. How are the team members going to notice? What is everybody doing differently after the miracle? What are observable, interactional signs that the miracle has happened? Perspective change questions (e.g. "How are other people going to notice?") can be useful to help the team generate answers that draw it forward:

How will your customers notice that the miracle happened for you?
What would others say was your contribution to the miracle picture?
How will your family notice?

Asking about an outside perspective serves to identify observable differences, just like when you are working on goals. We only imagine the outside perspectives – what the others will actually notice is unknown, and stays that way. There is a similarity to the "circular questions" in systemic practice. The difference in Solution Focused coaching is the fact that integrating an imagined outside perspective only serves to identify observable differences. In systemic practice, these questions are sometimes used to uncover circular processes and patterns of relationships in order to gain greater clarity on the interwoven patterns of interactions or collect other information.

Peter de Jong and Insoo Kim Berg (1998) suggest the following structure for posing the Miracle Question:

- Start slowly and tentatively.
- Mark the question as unusual or strange.
- Start in future tense or conditional: "How would you notice?"
- When you are asking about observable signs in follow-up questions after the Miracle Question, change to the indicative: "When the miracle happens, you ..."
- Gently and persistently confirm the team's change of attention to what will be different when the team is starting to revert to describing the problem (which also has its place, but not here).

Some people think it is difficult to pose the traditional Miracle Question in the context of companies and corporations. They presume clients think the question is frivolous or silly. In our experience, the Miracle Question works well in an organizational context. In 15 years, it has only happened once that a participant refused to answer it because "it is too New Agey". Even in this situation, we think the reason was probably more that the participant was not particularly interested in developing solutions. We should probably have realized this earlier and refrained from asking him the Miracle Question – but hindsight is always 20/20.

Steve de Shazer once said (personal communication in workshops) that if you want to pose the Miracle Question, you should take care to prepare the ground, just as the frying pan needs to be hot when you want to sear a steak (or tofu). Signs that the frying pan is hot include:

- *The team has developed a goal that is in their influence.* If the team coaching goal is outside the team's influence, inviting the team to a description of the preferred future often results in the team describing what other people would be doing differently. This is not very helpful. However, in this situation, the team coach might "save" the situation by going back to "And if these other people did … differently, what difference would it make to you as a team?" or "How would you respond to their action?".
- *The team has some hope that the team coaching can be successful.* If there is no hope, an invitation to a description of the preferred future might be an exercise in cynicism: the team describes what it might want, but it is a "pie in the sky" description. If this happens, the team coach might go back to questions like: "What gives you hope that something can change?"

If you don't feel comfortable asking the Miracle Question in its traditional form in an organizational context, you can also experiment with other formats. The crucial element is that the linear connection between problem and solution is dissolved – independent of the question that you use. The world after the miracle makes things possible which would not be possible without a miracle. So instead of speaking about miracle you can also ask about "an unforeseeable development".

Reauthoring (from Narrative)

Narrative practice also has a way of inviting clients to a description of the preferred future. The starting point here is the team mentioning something that is really important to them. It might be that the team mentioned that they would like to trust each other more. Another example could be that they discover in the goal-setting phase that they would like to show each other appreciation – any word that holds a positive meaning or intention will work. A rich description of the desired future might then be invited by asking the team:

- If trust were a close companion over the next weeks, how would you notice in your team?
- Who else would notice?
- What would they be noticing?
- How would they respond?

It might also be that inviting the team to describe their preferred future is triggered by an externalizing sequence. Maybe the team described that they do not want "distrust" to influence their teamwork. The team coach can then ask what they would like to invite into their teamwork instead and then work with whatever word the team comes up with in order to gather a rich description of the preferred future.

A positive self-description of the team could also serve as a springboard for a rich description of their preferred future. Let's say the team wishes to be a high performing team, or they want to be a team of superheroes. The team coach here might invite the team to describe themselves as this high performing team or this team of superheroes. As you will learn from the section on concrete moves, this description can be very creative and joyful and be accompanied by drawing pictures or finding symbols or whichever way taps into the creativity of the team to invite them to describe the state that they would really like to be in.

Successful past

We believe no one can imagine a preferred future without having seen signs of it in their life. If a team would like to be high performing, its members probably have had instances of high performance in their past. If a team's members wish to be appreciative of one another, they have had experiences with teams that were appreciative. Therefore, whichever goal the team can describe usually has precursors in their experience. Asking the team to describe what tells them they can get to where they want to be is very helpful because it enables the team to perceive the small signs that tell them they are already on the way. The perception of not starting from zero but building on something that already exists creates more hope and confidence and thereby makes it more likely for the team to achieve what they want. Below you will find some questions that a team coach may ask in order to facilitate this discussion.

Scaling

Scaling questions serve to identify useful differences in individual as well as team coaching. They are different from objectively measurable key performance indicators or benchmarking data. Solution Focused scaling is not about measuring something objectively. The questions are about helping clients to identify relevant differences that can point to more options for solving or improving a situation.

This is how scaling questions work:

1 The scale usually runs from 1 (or 0) to 10. 10 means that the situation has been solved satisfactorily. You can also define 10 as "a time when the problem has vanished", "the day after the miracle", "when you are this high-performing team" or in another way that is appropriate for the situation. This all depends on the situation and the client. In any case, 10 should be a realistic possibility that can be achieved by the team. A 10 that is not in the sphere of influence of the client – for example, "the outsourcing program has been taken back, and we return to doing the accounting in Germany" – would not serve to identify small possible differences in the behaviour of the client. The first step is therefore the definition of an attractive goal, a 10 (which you should already have done in the two first "rooms" of the gallery).

Insoo Kim Berg always used a scale of 1–10 because she thought 0 seemed too hopeless. Steve de Shazer self-identified as a scientist and preferred to use 0 because the scale does start at 0. There are no studies into what is more effective – why don't you try it out to determine your own preferences? Another possibility is to work with the negative scale. Minus 10 means the worst situation and numbers toward 0 or into the positive section of the scale mean a positive difference. The minus scale has the advantage of being able to talk about differences in situations that seem rather hopeless to the client.

2 The next step in asking a scaling question consists of asking the team members to assess the current situation on the scale. It is important to mention that everybody's assessment is completely individual, and the team does not have to agree on a common assessment of the situation. Every team member has their own idea of what a 10 is. Some people are more ambitious, while others are more realistic. This is why there is no need to agree on a common number or to create an average. Again, scaling is not about measuring; it is about noticing small differences.

   For many teams, this may sound a bit strange, and it is therefore important to mention that it is okay for team members to have different numbers before engaging in this step. Otherwise, team members may feel offended by the differing assessment of other team members: "What – you think our collaboration is only at a 3? How terrible! How can you?" It is best if the coach mentions beforehand that nobody can know what the numbers mean exactly for every team member. Finding out what is already working well and what could be the next step are important, not the discussion about differing assessments of the current situation.

3 After learning the number of the current situation on the scale, the team coach turns the attention of the team towards what is still working and on the actions of the team that led to the fact that the team is now at an overall point on the scale that is higher than 0. If most team members are at 0, the team coach can go on with a coping question.

4 The question about a next possible step in the direction of 10 is only asked after what is still working has been explored sufficiently. Questions for the next step are:

- Which next step in the direction of 10 would you notice? How would you notice this step?
- What will tell you that you are at an X +1?
- Who else would notice this step? (This can be the customers, other teams, the boss of the boss etc. If the team forgets to mention an important stakeholder – often the customers are not mentioned – the team coach can ask the question directly: "How would the customers notice?"
- What would relevant stakeholders notice about you that would tell them that you are at an X+1?
- What else would you be doing differently after the step you are doing now?

Exceptions (Solution Focused) and unique outcomes (from Narrative)

There are many possibilities for asking the team about exceptions, unique outcomes and resources. The wording that the team coach uses probably works best when it is adapted to the team. If the team is working on "a problem", "exceptions" may be a good word to describe a successful past. If the team is working towards something, "resources" or "unique outcomes" might be more suitable.

Steve de Shazer and Michael White once had a discussion at a conference on the difference between "unique outcomes" and "exceptions" (the recording is available at Vancouver Narrative Therapy Center; however, it is behind a paywall and not publicly accessible. Steve de Shazer liked "exceptions from the problem" as it calls into question the assumption that the entire situation is dominated by the problem. Michael White preferred "unique outcome", as it is more future oriented and about something that was wanted and is already happening. We prefer "unique outcomes" for team coaching because usually a team wants to work towards something and not away from something. However, as stated above, when the team is experiencing a "problem" – for example, a conflict – we might choose to work with "exceptions".

The team coach may help the team to identify exceptions and resources by talking about times when the problem did not occur as intensively or when something went better than was expected. This way, the team can gain confidence that the situation can improve. By analysing the exceptions to the problem or the instances in which the situation was a little bit like the way the team would like it to be, the team often comes up with strategies that have been successful and promise to be successful in the future.

The team coach can invite the team to describe unique outcomes once they are clear on their preferred future: "Were there times in which you already saw this preferred future, or even a glimpse of it, appear?"

A good time to ask about exceptions, unique outcomes and resources is after a scaling question – or during a scaling process. You can use questions like, "When did you have a time where it was a little bit better?" or "What kind of situations did you have that were higher on the scale than you are now?" Afterwards, you can ask, "What was your contribution? What did you do to make that happen?" to identify possible alternatives for the team.

If there are several exceptions, you can ask the team to split into small groups and determine what made the exception possible and what their contribution was. In our experience, it makes sense to write down the question, "What was your contribution?" or "What did the exception enable you to do differently?" on the flipchart or into the chatroom of the virtual space, or invite the participants to record their findings on a handout with the questions. Without written instructions, the discussion might revert to talking about why the exception is not the norm (and that would not be very helpful at this point).

You can also connect appreciative feedback with the search for exceptions and resources. You ask the group to identify a "highlight" or "sparkling moment" and invite them to talk about who in the group contributed to it. Nobody is allowed to talk about themselves. Everybody shares their positive observations of what other people have contributed. If this seems too artificial or embarrassing, you can also ask the group to note the observations on Post-It notes and stick them to a flipchart or wall. This way, however, you run the risk that you have somebody whose contributions are forgotten, and this might be hurtful to that person. To avoid this, you can ask everybody to write one Post-It note for each of the other participants. To ease the logistics, you can also prepare Post-It notes with the names of the participants on them. In our experience, simply talking about each other's contribution is the easiest (at least in Central Europe).

You have probably realized by now that there are many different starting points for the "gallery":

- You can start by asking the team what they are doing well, even before asking for goals. Appreciative inquiry works this way.
- You can start by inviting the team to describe a preferred future and then narrow it down to what needs to happen as a next step.
- You can start with a scaling question, describe 10 and go from there.

What you end up doing, depends on the clients and the situation. The golden rule of team coaching is: "It all depends."

Gift shop

In every museum, there is a "gift shop" where you buy an umbrella with a print of a Monet or a cup with the logo of the museum, or other things that collect dust in your home. The gifts the team takes away in this room aren't there to collect dust but rather to enable the team to take the learnings and insights from every individual team coaching session forward.

As in all the other rooms of the gallery, the gift shop also focuses on description. This description is already built into the scaling process: "If you move up one step on the scale what would you and others be noticing?" We invite the team to describe what they will be noticing when they move up on the scale rather than coming to action planning for concrete steps right away. It is often easier to describe what you will see as sign of progress than to start going into to-do lists, responsibilities, roles and accountability structures. Once the signs of progress have been described, it is often very clear what the team would like to do to make this progress happen.

In any case, we would invite the team to be tentative and frame their ensuing actions in terms of experiments rather than appearing sure that what they are planning now will definitely lead to the result they are aiming to achieve. If an action plan doesn't work out, it is a failure. If an experiment doesn't work, you have gained more information and are still on track.

Observation

Sometimes it is not yet clear what needs to be done. Maybe the team is still a little bit stuck, there aren't a lot of useful experiences that they can draw on or the situation is completely new and nobody has ever experienced something like it before. In these cases, it might be useful to ask the team to observe what is going in the right direction before coming to experiments that involve doing something. The team coach may ask the team to pay attention to what is going right, to write it down somewhere or even to take pictures of moments that are like the preferred future. More ways of inviting the team to observe what is going right can be found in the section on moves.

Confidence

At the end of a team coaching session, it can be useful to ask the team for another scale: "How confident are they that the result of the team coaching process is going to lead to an improvement?" The team coach can then invite a discussion about what makes the team confident and what else still needs to happen so the team can become more confident.

Distribution of tasks

In Solution Focused team coaching, we have a preference for voluntary tasks. If people agree to carry out a task or project, they are usually more motivated and the chances of success are higher. Of course, every organization will have their own ways of dealing with task distribution, so as a team coach, we can also just go with whatever it is that the team is already used to and successful with.

Visualization of results

Having agreed-upon concrete actions and to-do lists in the time after the workshop are a sign of success to many of our customers. There is a difference between Solution Focused team coaching and Solution Focused therapy or Solution Focused individual coaching. In Solution Focused individual coaching, we would usually not write down or visualize the steps the client wants to take. We would probably leave this to the client. Visualizing agreed actions for the team, however, generates more commitment and fits well with the culture of many teams, so as team coach we might take over this task for the clients.

The double diamond metaphor: Partnering with the team

The Solution Focused gallery described above is one metaphor for Solution Focused (team) coaching. It may help a coach to experience the team coaching in a structured way and to know where to invite the team to focus their attention next. As already indicated, this never happens in the orderly fashion that the metaphor of the gallery suggests. There will be walks into the different rooms, three steps back, one step forward, depending on the situation and depending on what may be a useful next step for the team. It is important is that the team coach is able to partner with the team around where the attention should go. Of course, as stated, as Solution Focused team coaches, we have a strong preference for focusing on what is wanted and what is already working. However, it is not us as team coaches who decide where the attention goes; we always coach in collaboration and partnership with the team.

If you are just beginning to coach or act as a team coach, it may be difficult to let go of the idea of controlling or facilitating the discussion in ways that the team coach finds useful. As individual coaches, we partner with our clients by inviting them to choose what happens in this session. We suggest that team coaches operate in a similar way: We ask the team where they would like to go next, whether a topic has been explored fully or whether there is still something missing.

Partnering with our clients is a little trickier when it comes to coaching a team. As a team coach, you deliberate carefully whether to partner with the team at any given moment. The team coach has to be able to assess whether to hold the discussion more tightly and choose the direction in which the discussion is going and when to let go and let the team determine the pace and direction. We suggest that whenever the team is moving forward, when they have constructive discussions, it is time for the team coach to stay out of the discussion. When the situation is trickier and the team is in danger of getting stuck, this may be the time to hold the reins of the discussion more tightly. Again, only the team can tell you whether you are doing it "right". It is important to collect regular feedback from the teams with which you are working: is your way of coaching teams useful for everyone or is there something that you could change? We suggest getting feedback at least once in the middle of each team coaching process, at a time when you can still do something different (not at the end, when everything is done).

We admit that this sounds a bit daunting when you are just starting out as a team coach. Not only are you asked to find a suitable structure for a potential workshop or series of workshops, but you are also asked to partner with the team and to be flexible. And all this when you are basically just starting out to learn the steps. It sounds like you are being asked to improvise dancing on ice when you've just learned how to put on your skates. Individual coaches experience a similar dilemma. They first learn a structure like the gallery, but the more experience they gain, the more they are able to let go of that structure and partner with their clients as to where the attention should go. In our classes on individual coaching, we are using another metaphor to help beginning coaches find good places at which to partner with their clients. We call it the "Double Diamond of Coaching" (Figure 1.2).

The Double Diamond of Coaching integrates Solution Focused and Narrative ideas to loosely structure a (team) coaching session. The fundamental structure is a

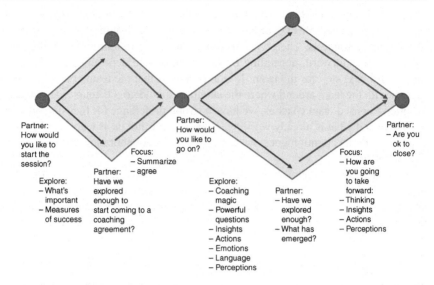

Figure 1.2 The double diamond.

first, smaller diamond that describes the goal-setting process in which coach, team and other stakeholders find a common project to work on. The second, larger diamond is what happens in the "main body" of the (team) coaching.

The top part of the diagram describes discussions around the "landscape of action" and the bottom part describes the "landscape of identity". Landscape of action and landscape of identity are concepts deriving from Jerome Bruner's (1990) book *Acts of Meaning*. The landscape of action is described in conversations when the "doing" is described: the plot, who does what, who did what. The landscape of identity is described when the conversation revolves around what the client intends, believes and values. Both landscapes also happen in team coaching: We can invite the team to talk about what they did and want to do or invite them to talk about what is important to them – what they intend or believe. The conversation may oscillate between both during the process, and you can see possible questions for each landscape in Figure 1.2.

Case 1.6:   A merger of two teams

Two teams of a consulting company were in the process of merging and coming under the same line of service. The director contacted Cristina for an initial conversation around creating the joint team vision. As there were two teams who were not completely separated, they had been outsourcing personnel from one team to another for some time now; it was not about creating everything from scratch. The team members were used to working with each other. Cristina suggested a workshop structure along the lines of "Landscape of action/Landscape of identity.

Cristina invited the team to look at what they were currently doing and what their current projects were. From this "landscape of action", the conversation moved to what they valued about this work and how they were transmitting this in the organization or to their customers based on the work that they were delivering currently – "landscape of identity".

In the next step, Cristina invited them to look at past projects and the work they were most proud of (again "landscape of action" in the successful past) and from there to draw upon what the organization valued and appreciated about the team ("landscape of identity" in the successful past).

Once the picture of what was being valued and intended became clearer, the team was invited to look at what want to be recognized and valued in the future ("landscape of action" in the future).

Of course, from there it was only a natural step towards the actions that they wanted to design to ensure that what that they wanted to be recognized for in the future could materialize ("landscape of action" in the future).

At the follow-up session after a couple of months, the team was energized and well-equipped to work with iterations on what they wanted to be known for and how that should be brought to fruition.

The round dots in the middle of the double diamond diagram in Figure 1.2 depict standard places where the coach may invite the team to partner with them. At the beginning, the team coach might explore how the team would like to start the session. Do they know each other and do not need a round of introductions? Would they like to engage in an icebreaker? When talking about the objectives of the team coaching session, a point will be reached when it seems sufficiently clear what the team wants. This is another place where the team coach may partner with the team and ask whether what they want from the team coaching session has been explored enough or whether they would like to spend more time on it. After the confirmation of common projects of the team coaching, there is yet another place where partnering is quite easy. The team coach may ask the team about their preferred way of working on these goals: plenary, small groups, and so on. The team coach might also the team about how the coach might support them in this process. After the discussion of each project, there might yet be another possibility to partner up when the discussion comes to an end and potential closure is in sight. The team coach may yet again ask whether this topic has been discussed enough and whether the team is ready to close. The last possibility for partnering is at the end, when the team coach can ask whether the team is ready to close or there is something else that needs to be discussed.

Differences from other modalities

Differences from individual coaching

There are a few differences between Solution Focused individual coaching and Solution Focused team coaching. When you are dealing with several people, each of them is likely to have a different goal for the team coaching. It is therefore more difficult to reach a good definition of the goal with the team than it is with an individual. A situation can also arise where team members have conflicting goals. The solution-focused approach offers several possibilities to set goals with groups in such a way that everybody is happy with the process and the resulting goals. You can find out more about these possibilities in the section on moves under "goal setting".

Another important difference is that facilitating the conversation is more difficult when several people are involved. Every team coaching participant wants to be appreciated. It is important to facilitate each contribution in such a way that every team member feels heard. In order to achieve this, the team coach not only needs to have coaching skills, but also needs facilitation skills. To facilitate well (and also in order to coach well), the team coach needs the acceptance and trust of the team. For Steve de Shazer, rapport was something that needed to be protected, but that should come naturally. Generating trust and acceptance, in his mind, was not something that required a lot of extra effort.

Also in our experience, it becomes more difficult if you do too many things to generate rapport that you would usually not do in a normal encounter with a group of people. The whole situation quickly becomes unnatural and awkward, which can lead to a bad start in team coaching. In many other approaches, you can find recommendations for how to generate rapport. The coach is asked to "pace" movements and body postures of individual team members by imitating them. Once they have done this for long enough, they can start "leading" the group and get the team members to follow their movements and body language. The idea is based on the fact that similarities can be observed in the movement patterns between two people in a successful therapeutic conversation (e.g. Ramseyer & Tschacher, 2008, pp. 329–348), but are the patterns of movement similar because people understand each other well, or does a good understanding lead to people's patterns of movement becoming similar? Using Occam's razor and following the old adage that "the simplest explanation is always the best", Solution Focused coaches assume a good relationship exists and try not to lose it.

So maybe it makes sense to think about the opposite. What does somebody have to do to guarantee the destruction of a good working relationship between the coach and their clients? Here are some recommendations (which we definitely hope you won't take seriously).

Most importantly, the coach should avoid listening to their clients. The coach should insist on their own interpretations and take any reply from the clients as a sign of resistance. The agenda of the team coaching should primarily consist of points that are important to the coach. There should never be room for any agenda items with which the team wants to deal. A good idea for the destruction of the working relationship is also taking the side of one of two groups. It is especially useful for the destruction of the working relationship if you consistently agree with the boss and fight on the side of the boss against the team. It is probably also useful when the coach uses a completely different language than the team. If the team consists of elegant bankers, the coach should take care to use soft pedagogical language. Distinguishing yourself by adopting a completely different outward appearance than that of your clients can also prevent a good working relationship. For example, if the team dresses in suits and ties, the coach could wear a miniskirt or torn jeans and a t-shirt. If the team is used to elegant PowerPoint presentations, the coach should insist on using badly written flipcharts in their facilitation.

When the Solution Focused coach adheres to Steve de Shazer's advice and simply takes care not to disturb the good working relationship, it is helpful to turn the above advice around. We don't think that you can produce a list of things that a coach needs to do in order not to endanger a good working relationship. There are coaches who always wear jeans and t-shirts and work effectively with a wide range of clients. There are other coaches who wear a suit and tie even when they are working in the public sector. When you look at photos of Steve de Shazer, you may not see someone who conveys the image of timeless elegance or therapeutic authority. What disturbs the respective working relationship is always decided in the interaction between coach and client. It is very difficult to give general advice. In Solution Focused coaching, we try to speak the language of our clients. Experience shows that this tends to lead to a good collaboration between coach and clients; therefore, the only advice we give is to listen really well to the words of our clients. If you concentrate too hard on all the other things that you have to get right in order not to endanger the relationship, you will have less time and attention to spend on the important things: listening and exploring the client's goals, resources, exceptions and first steps.

When you are working with teams, there is also the question of who belongs to the team, who needs to be asked and who needs to participate in which event. In Solution Focused family therapy, you work with everybody who is interested in coming and working on a solution. It is important that everybody feels welcomed and invited. This is also a good strategy for team coaching. In an organizational context it makes sense to understand who belongs to the team, who has which competence to decide what, who has a stake in the solution and so on. In organizations, there are more formal rules for that than in families, and in our experience you can avoid misunderstandings if you know beforehand who decides what and what the relevant framework for decisions is.

One advantage in working with teams is that you have many involved people in the room with you. In individual coaching you would have to ask, "What do you think your boss would say?" In the team coaching situation, the boss is probably in the room and you can ask directly. Many conversations that happen after the coaching sessions in individual coaching can happen immediately and are facilitated by the team coach.

Multipartiality

In the team coaching process, there are usually several people with differing interests. We deal with this point in a similar fashion to Solution Focused couples or family therapy. These ideas go back to Ivan Boszormenyi-Nagy and Geraldine Spark (1973), who were the first to speak about "multi-directional partiality". This concept of multidirectional partiality was then taken up by Solution Focused therapists. Phillip Ziegler and Tobey Hiller (2001) explore this helpful standpoint for therapists. It is a standpoint of "active neutrality" or of "multi-partiality" (Ziegler & Hiller, 2001, pp. 39–41) The benefit for clients is that the therapist seems to be standing on both sides. They aren't "neutral", but rather involved and engaged for the benefit of both parties. We also recommend this attitude for team coaches. The only difficulty here is that there are more than two people involved. It is therefore a little more difficult yet very rewarding to strive for a "multi-partial" standpoint. The coach is engaged, is not drawn into the accusations or complaints of any one party, and is collaborating with everyone to find a solution.

Nothing is easier than this, right? So how does it work? How do you maintain a standpoint of multi-partiality? Ziegler and Hiller (2001) discuss two very important points:

1 The coach should accept the assumption and demonstrate that reality can always be seen from various perspectives. The meaning isn't fixed, but changeable, and differing perspectives are normal (as discussed above when we were talking about the Galveston Declaration).
2 The coach should also try and subscribe to an attitude of curious "not-knowing".

The first point is especially important in team coaching. Participants notice when the team coach doesn't try to level differences. The team coach listens to each participant's opinion and contribution, and is interested in it. They don't try to question anybody's perception. For example, if an employee claims that they are constantly working overtime because a colleague fails to enter data into the system correctly, the team coach will accept this perception at face value. If the colleague then contradicts it, their perception is taken as equally "true". The team coach will then try to achieve a constructive conversation that acknowledges both perspectives. After acknowledging the problem, they might ask: "Suppose this problem was solved for both of you, how would you notice?" or "What kind of exceptions have you already noticed?" For the Solution Focused team coach, each participant's perspective is equally "true" in that moment.

Curious "not-knowing" is also important for the team coach. Instead of engaging in elaborate analyses of which structures and processes brought forth the current situation or otherwise indulging in their own theories, Solution Focused team coaches try to listen intensively. Of course, Solution Focused team coaches also have their own frame of reference and cannot "not use their own frame of reference". Our frame of reference, however, stands back in favour of the exploration of the frame of reference of our clients. If this proves too difficult, we just pretend.

When you look at it pragmatically, there are a few behaviours that are useful to support the multiparty of the coach. If there are interviews before a possible workshop, it is important to be transparent about who is being called, who isn't being called and why. If possible, it is best to be able to talk to everybody beforehand. It is equally important to take care to talk to the team leader. During a workshop, it makes sense to give everybody similar speaking time (if they wish to speak). If somebody conveys confidential information to the team coach, it is important to deal with it sensitively.

Each contribution during the workshop should be accepted with appreciation. In contrast to other coaches, Solution Focused team coaches do sometimes interrupt. If a participant has a difficult time getting out of the complaining mode, we try to turn the conversation around and ask, "What needs to be different?" Such a process makes it easy to stay curious, and to acknowledge and validate the perspectives and goals of each team member.

Exercise 1.4: Multipartiality

Think about how you would notice that somebody is on your side in a controversial conversation or a meeting. How does this person act and what does it look like exactly? Write "guidelines for being on my side". Then think about which of these behaviours would also be good for multipartial facilitation and experiment with these behaviours in your next team facilitation.

Exercise 1.5: "Together in the middle of the bed"

The video *Together in the Middle of the Bed* by Steve de Shazer and Insoo Kim Berg provides a good opportunity to observe multipartial behaviour. It is a first session in couples therapy with a married couple. The first minutes of this session provide many clues. Steve de Shazer is the therapist. It is very noticeable that he does not evaluate or interpret the statements by the husband or by the wife, but simply lets them stand. He takes care to allocate equal speaking time to each partner. He asks the husband about the possible perspective of his wife and vice versa. When one of them starts entering into a longer phase of complaining, he interrupts softly and says, "We'll get back to that." Steve de Shazer works on small, observable signs of improvement. These are all means that you can use in team coaching, especially in conflict situations. Watch the video (you can order it at www.sfbta.org and find excerpts on YouTube) and maybe you will notice other techniques that you can transfer and use in your team coaching.

Other team development modalities

The International Coaching Federation (2023) mentions several "modalities" under the heading of "team development". Team coaching is only one of them. In the following, we would like to mention some of the other most important modalities and describe the differences and how you might approach them in a Solution Focused way.

Team-building

The ICF defines team-building as a modality with a short duration. The team gets together for a day and does exercises to create awareness around what it takes to be a well-functioning team. These exercises may be "build a bridge out of flip-chart paper" or exercises in joint problem-solving or any other team exercises. You will find instructions on how to use such exercises in the section of the book where we talk about how to turn any exercise into a Solution Focused exercise. When we are using such exercises as Solution Focused team coaches, we take care to focus on the existing strengths of the team and on what the team is learning from the exercise. We do not point out what the team is doing wrong or take a deficit focus in any way.

As Solution Focused coaches, we believe context matters (see our section on the Galveston Declaration), so we don't necessarily assume that the team behaves in similar ways when they are solving a physical puzzle and when they are working in their daily life as a team. Our preference is to work with reality rather than simulations. However, if a team would like to engage in "team-building" and also have some fun together, we would use the "exercises" as possibilities for learning without assuming the team's behaviour in the exercises is indicative of anything they are doing in real life. Instead, we invite the team to make connections (or reject them) in a partnering way.

Team training

Team training aims at strengthening generic team skills in a group of people. Participants in team training may or may not be part of the same team. The trainer walks the participants through a structured, generic, curriculum. As Solution Focused practitioners, we are not so interested in generic approaches. Every team is different, and the skills needed are also different. If invited to do a "team training", we would need to get a common project first. What would be different for the participants after the training? What would they like to be better at? Who would notice if they got better at this? What would these people be noticing? Once we know that, we can build a curriculum for the team training. If it is communication, we could train them in Solution Focused communication skills. If it is conflict management, we could teach about Solution Focused conflict management.

One of the issues with which Solution Focused practitioners contend is that the training and coaching world has dominant narratives and concepts that don't fit our social-constructionist understanding of the world. HR will contact us to do a generic team training, figuring we will simply pull something off the shelf. They are then surprised when we start asking a lot of questions about the desired outcome. Sometimes this leads to an impasse. HR wants to do something, but they don't have a lot of time for our questions. In this case, the Solution Focused team coach can either step back or get permission from HR to ask the potential participants for a common project. As we learned in the metaphor of the gallery earlier in this chapter: no ticket, no museum!

Team consulting

Team consulting is defined by an expert sharing their expertise. A team might want to learn best practices of project management or ideas on how to create great retrospectives. There is quite a lot of material that a Solution Focused expert might be able to share if asked as an expert. In this book, for example, you will find a lot of expertise and "how to" instructions. The Solution Focused team consultant may share the gallery, the double diamond, future focus vs problem focus and so on. However, the most important thing is that context matters! Nothing works all the time, even Solution Focus. We are sorry if we are disappointing you, but a Solution Focused expert shares expertise with the idea that it may or may not be helpful for the team. The next step will always be that the team evaluates what they want to try and starts to experiment to design its own solutions.

Team mentoring

Team mentoring happens when a team would like to learn an approach from a seasoned professional. Agile coaching has elements of team mentoring. The Agile coach knows how other teams have implemented Agile principles and helps a team to adopt the approach by engaging with them for a few hours every few weeks. Of course, the same Solution Focused caveat applies to team consulting.

Team facilitation

The team facilitator helps the team to have productive discussion. They are there to help provide clarity and manage the team discussion in a meeting or workshop. As they facilitate the dialogue, the focus is less on enabling the team to manage their own dialogues and grow as a team, and more about helping them to do it this one time.

Solution Focused facilitation will use similar principles to Solution Focused (team) coaching. The facilitator will invite the team to define outcomes, talk about preferred futures and successful past and signs of progress. When there are conflicts in the discussion, they will assume good intentions on every side and will attempt to ask for the "goal behind the goal", for interests rather than positions. A Solution Focused team coach will also be able to facilitate a team discussion; in our opinion, the skills are a subset of the skills of the team coach.

What is a team?

Definition of a team

There are about 1,217 definitions (rough estimate) of a team in the literature and every author seems to have their own spin on it. As we believe the meaning of a word becomes apparent in how it is used, let us attempt a pragmatic definition rather than going for "what a team really is".

Here are some "differences that make a difference" in coaching teams.

Common goal

A team will have a common goal – something they want to achieve together. A football team wants to win; a team of investment bankers wants to enable customers to make money to fulfil their dreams and also make money for the bank; a management team wants to see employees happy and the company successful. It makes sense for a team coach to inquire about the common goal before engaging in a team coaching. If there isn't one, contracting will be extremely hard and the whole endeavour may be futile. Kirsten once supervised two team coaches who were struggling with this issue. A manager had invited them to coach their direct reports. When the coaches interviewed the direct reports, it became apparent that they did not have the same goals. Two of the direct reports were acting as internal consultants, the other six were a development team responsible for a piece of software. It made no sense to coach them as a team, even though at first glance they might have appeared to be a team because they reported to the same manager.

Interdependence

Another difference that is important for team coaching is whether the team works interdependently. Does the work of one person in the team depend on the work of another person? For example, you might have sales "teams" consisting of individual sales representatives. Each of them might be responsible for a different region of a country – they have very little overlap in what they do. The work of the sales representative in the Eastern Region does not influence the work of the sales representative in the Western Region. This group of people can still be coached by a team coach, but not really as a "team" – they don't have enough interdependence and overlapping goals. A "group-coaching" around "best practice sharing" or learning from each other might still be very useful, however.

Duration

There is also a difference between coaching project teams and teams that work together over a longer period. If team members know that they will be "stuck" with one another for the next several years, relationships become more important. You may be able to ignore the quirks of someone more easily if you know that the collaboration will end in a few months. Moreover, the definition of success is different in a project team and a longer-term team. A project has a (hopefully successful) end, a team has to self-define milestones and KPIs.

Leadership

We don't think teams are defined by the leadership; however, it makes sense to inquire about what kind of leadership the team you are being invited to coach has: is it a self-organized team, does it have a manager, two managers, matrix structures? Knowing how decisions are being made makes the life of a team coach much easier.

Size

Teams come in many different shapes and sizes. The largest team that Kirsten was invited to coach consisted of 28 people, which was a problem. They all reported to one manager who was hopelessly overwhelmed. Of course, you can coach larger structures such as departments or even whole organizations (find some tips on our section on larger teams), but they would no longer be "manageable" without substructures. Most teams consist of no more than around 12 people – it is simply very hard to organize the collaboration otherwise. When asked to coach a large number of people, the team coach might inquire what the decision and meeting structures are: probably there are substructures, however informal. The team coach can then partner with the organization to determine the best approach: coach the whole "team", the team of managers, sub-teams?

Competencies and core standards

All the major coaching associations, the International Coaching Federation, the European Mentoring and Coaching Council and the Association for Coaching, have published team coaching competencies (ICF) and team coaching core standards. They are available on the respective websites (www.coachingfederation.org, www.emccglobal.org and www.associationforcoaching.com). As they are subject to change and as we don't want to prepare our readers only for one certification, we will not quote the competency models here, but rather give you a collated summary of the points mentioned by all associations with some pointers as to how Solution Focused Team Coaching demonstrates these competencies.

Ethics

All the above-mentioned team coaching competency models start by stressing the importance of ethical practice. EMCC and AC mention adherence to the global code of ethics and ICF the ICF code of ethics. If you are not aware of these documents, please go to the respective organizations' websites and read (and maybe sign) these codes. They are foundational documents for any individual or team coach. As detailing the content of these documents would lead us too far from the purpose of this book, we will concentrate on the specific ethical considerations raised by team coaching in the following.

Coaches the team as a single entity

ICF mentions that a team coach should have the competence to coach the team as a single entity. They are multipartial (as mentioned above) and are the advocate for collaboration and progress for the entire team. Coaches will need to be aware of differing interests and positions and know how to invite the team to define a goal that is beneficial for all stakeholders. Solution Focused practice already includes this stance. Of course, you will not learn how to do that by reading a book. We learned by practising, reflecting, getting feedback from teams, and partnering with the team and practising again.

Communicates different modalities

Customers deserve transparency about what they are buying. A team coach therefore needs to communicate what their services entail and what they do not. There is a lot of confusion about team development modalities on the market and most customers are not team coaching specialists. When a client asks for a "team coaching", it is possible that they want team-building, facilitation, training or something else entirely. As you will see in our section on contracting, it is very important for the team coach to ask exactly what the client wants and then decide whether this is something they would like to provide. This capability is built into the Solution Focused process: we always start by asking what will be different after our work together. Once we know that, we can agree with our clients about the best modality for getting there.

Takes care of own wellbeing and ability to perform professionally

It is part of any professionalism that the provider of a service takes care that they are in a position to provide the service. Especially in the helping professions, it is crucial for the provider to be aware of any impediments that may hinder a professional performance: after all, we are working with people and their lives. It might be that the team coach is experiencing personal issues, which draw on their attention so that they might not be able to be present to their clients, or health issues that prevent full attention being given to the clients. In this case, the ethical response would be to take care of one's own wellbeing first before entering into a (team) coaching process.

An advantage of Solution Focused coaching is the orientation toward what is wanted and what is already going well. Solution Focused (team) coaches assume that everybody would like to create a better situation and interpret experiences of "resistance" as a lack of communication between clients and coach rather than as a personal attack on the coach (see our section on difficult situations). Therefore, Solution Focused coaches are much less prone to professional fatigue. Viewing clients as competent and willing helps coaches to experience the team coaching work as joyful rather than as a burden, which positively impacts coach wellness. A study by Coert Visser (2012) found that solution-focused coaches suffer less emotional exhaustion, and experience more personal accomplishment and less depersonalization.

Conflicts of interest

As described above, multipartiality is an important skill in Solution Focused team coaching. The ethical corollary is that if a team coach notices they are not able to be multipartial, they should recuse themselves from the process and hand over to someone else. It sounds a bit far-fetched, but it happens more often than you might think. The most common example is an executive coach being asked by their executive client if they could also coach their management team or facilitate an offsite coaching session. In most cases, the team will not perceive the coach as multipartial in such circumstances. Other cases may be that the coach is too invested in the success of the team (for example if they just bought shares to the startup where they are going to coach) or if they are working for a competitor simultaneously. The answer is simple: if you cannot be 100 per cent committed to the entire team's growth and happiness, fingers off and make a phone call to a colleague.

Adheres to any applicable laws (local and/or international)

We don't think we have to say a lot about this – of course, as an ethical coach, you stick to all legal requirements and don't do anything that is outside the law! Most common issues that arise are data protection and privacy, and clear agreements on sharing of results within or outside the organization.

Data protection needs to be taken seriously. The team coach should have a specialist look over their information technology structure and check it for safety. Please do not solely rely on this book, as every coach has a different set-up and different challenges. Some hints (not all-encompassing): using a VPN when in public networks; two-factor authentication on data storage; automatic deletion policies of soft and hard copies of client results; disposal of flipchart paper and results; privacy regulation-compliant storage of customers' personal data; automatic assistants (Google, Siri, Alexa) switched off during team coaching sessions; double encryption for any collaboration sites; hosting on European or other data privacy safe servers ... There is a lot to take care of and it depends on your special situation. Check with a specialist in your jurisdiction and any other jurisdictions you may work with.

It is also very important to clarify with the sponsors, clients and stakeholders of the team coaching process who will get access to the results, progress reports and so on of the team coaching process. Once agreed, the coach needs to stick closely to these agreements and always err on the side of team privacy.

Coach presence and mindset

A team coach stays a coach and partners with clients to maximize their potential. They hold the clients in unconditional positive regard and see the clients as experts for their growth and progress. This aligns very well with the Solution Focused stance toward clients. We venture to say that Solution Focus might even take this mindset a bit more seriously and radically than many other approaches.

The coach's presence includes self-awareness of their own position and what they believe and value. As we don't think "neutrality" is really possible, what remains is the awareness of our biases and attempt at reminding ourselves of the resources of the clients. We interact with the team to invite them toward positive interactions among themselves. We invite them to pay attention to certain things (what is wanted and what is working) more than others – but everything in partnership with the client. A coaching never just changes the clients; it always influences both parties.

As the coaching influences both parties, the coach may also notice what is going on personally during the team coaching and offer the observation to the clients as potentially helpful. One time, Kirsten was getting really bored during a team coaching. The clients were discussing detail after detail, and she was feeling rather useless. She offered her observation: "I am feeling a bit useless at the moment, the discussion is mainly around details, and I am wondering if I am needed here – is this relevant in any way?" The team looked a bit perturbed, then one team member spoke up: "Okay, actually, we can take care of these details alone. Should we take this discussion out of today and put it on our next meeting agenda?"

Maybe the competences around presence and mindset become clearer if you think about the opposite. A team coach who is not present and does not have a coaching mindset might design a workshop for the team, run the team through the previously planned facilitation, stick to the predesigned questions at all costs, interpret any request for adaptation of the process as "resistance" and so on. Turn this around, and you might find a descriptions of a present coach with a coaching mindset: flexible, secure, partnering and aware of the limitations of their own perspective. Does this remind you of the Galveston Declaration, discussed earlier? Good.

Trust and safety

A trusting and safe relationship between team coach and team (and manager, other stakeholders and sponsor), and between the team members, is very important for the success of a team coaching. The coach needs skills to invite such a relationship without overcomplicating things (see above). Partnering with the team is also key in this area: the coach will ask permission to ask sensitive questions and accept the team's response. They respect the team and their way of being without judgement. The team coach is able to manage the discussions in ways that further acceptance and appreciation and is able to help the team discuss conflicts constructively (see our section on conflict).

One sign of a trusting and safe relationship between team member is that team members feel free to speak about sensitive issues, raise concerns or disagree with one another. One skill of a team coach is also to help the team feel safe to do that. A Solution Focused attitude that assumes positive intentions is very helpful here, even if there are strong emotions and judgements coming from team members. The team coach can demonstrate ways of responding to such incidents, which the team can then apply themselves.

Case 1.7:   Always me

We were almost at the end of a team coaching session in a school and Kirsten was about to wrap it up by inviting the team to create a plan. Tasks were distributed and the teachers all seemed happy with the result. As Kirsten was almost ready to pack up her flipcharts and markers, a teacher stood up and said, "Yeah, we know that none of this is going to happen, right? It'll be on a few people's shoulders, and we'll all be frustrated as hell. What a waste of time!" Kirsten was quite shocked as she could not understand the timing of this contribution and what the (positive) intention behind it might be. So she said, "Wow, I am really surprised. I thought we were on a good path, yet your experience seems very different. Is there anything you would like us to change at this point so you feel more hopeful?" The teacher seemed a bit shocked too, and replied, "No, I just wanted to say what I have to say." Kirsten insisted: "Can I explore what was your intention behind it – I don't quite understand." "Well, I just wanted to make sure that we don't get our hopes up." Kirsten started to get a glimpse of what was important to the teacher and asked, "So are you happy for us to try this plan without great expectations and we'll see how it goes?" "Sure, but can we talk about where we are in our next conference?" Kirsten asked the group, "Would it be helpful to set yourselves a reminder for the next meeting to follow up?" Everybody, even those who had been rolling their eyes throughout the whole interchange, agreed. We think this interaction, while it began as a nuisance, might have helped the team to voice their concerns more safely in the future.

In addition, the team coach takes care of confidentiality. They mention the level of confidentiality of the team coaching at the beginning. A Solution Focused twist here may be that we would aim at a richer description of the confidentiality than just stating "We will treat everything that happens here confidentially." Instead, negotiating what may or may not be shared and with whom may help to create even greater clarity and safety:

Can we have a discussion on what may be shared with whom? Are you happy for the results of this team coaching to be shared with the manager's manager? Should we discuss which results can be shared at the end of the team coaching? How would you like to deal with personal information of the team members? Is it ok if we can share the learnings from this team coaching with others without mentioning names or other identifying information?

What happens in Vegas never stays in Vegas: people talk to their significant others or their family and friends. If we describe more closely what the team is comfortable having shared, the commitment to "confidentiality" is clearer and more realistic.

Of course, establishing a trust-based relationship also includes treating team members equitably and valuing diversity. The Solution Focused approach has a built-in appreciation for differences and multiple viewpoints (see the section on the Galveston Declaration). Social-constructionist approaches are also aware of the unequal distribution of rights and duties in our contexts and take systemic privileges seriously. While Solution Focus has traditionally neglected societal issues,

Narrative Practice includes a keen understanding of power relations and dominant discourses that strengthen them. We believe that this is one of the great advantages of combining both approaches. A good team coach will be able to help a team raise and discuss issues of discrimination, or positively put increasing inclusion in ways that strengthen the team (more see our section on diversity and inclusion).

Self-management and self-development of the coach

The team coaching competency models of all associations mention the ability of the team coach to self-manage. As in individual coaching, the team coach needs the ability to centre the clients and at the same time be present as a human being. Narrative practice calls this stance "de-centred and influential".

One of the competences of a team coach, therefore, is the ability to notice what is currently going on with oneself, what may be a response to what the team is currently doing or experiencing, and what may be a totally unrelated response. It is useful to know for a team coach if there are topics to which the coach is sensitive and to which they may respond more strongly due to the sensitivity. Being able to notice when the team coach's attention starts centring the coach rather than the team is key to being able to recentre the team. Some team coaches use mindfulness exercises such as meditation, while others engage in self-reflection and journalling, and still others go for a run or swim. Some coaches have this ability without having to engage in any additional practice. The Solution Focused approach traditionally has not mentioned a lot about the coach's self-management. The stance is the same, though: the conversation is about the client and not about the coach. Taking care that the team coach is in a position to be able to centre the team is part of the responsibility of a team coach.

Sometimes team coaching sessions can get heated and strong emotions can surface. A good team coach will have the ability to self-manage, and not be swept away by what is happening. We love the mindfulness metaphor of the raging river: the emotions that may surface are like a raging river, the team coach should aim at staying on the riverbed rather than being sucked under. Team coaches are part of the interaction, but should retain the ability to respond constructively. Being able to keep the assumption of positive intentions (as described above) goes a long way here. We think emotions are not something "special" and more important than actions or thoughts. We don't even assume that it is very meaningful to separate out our experience into these categories. It is best to simply accept the team's and our own experience as it is, without interpretation or any initial desire to change it. We can move on from there.

This is also very important when the team coach feels pressured. At the beginning, team coaches might feel responsible for ensuring a positive outcome for the team. There may be a need to "prove themselves" or "make sure the team gets value for the money spent". Of course, we want to deliver good service and show ourselves as valuable professionals. However, this thought can also lead team coaches beginning to centre their own "performance" rather than that of the team with which they are working. A team coach might notice themselves taking over tasks the team might do themselves, or talking too much, or feeling insecure and not able to interact freely with the team. When this happens, take a step back and remember it is about them, not you.

All associations mention the duty of the team coach to continue their professional development and growth. This can initially be achieved by learning about team coaching through books such as this one, or workshops and training programs. However, for continuous development, we recommend deliberate and reflective practice. It is important to separate "practice" from "performance". No violinist in their right mind would practise on stage! While you are engaged in the team coaching with the team, it doesn't make much sense to focus on whether you are doing a good job or on what you are currently learning. As mentioned above, this would centre your experience rather than that of the team. The point where learning can happen is before and after a team coaching session. Before, you might plan and engage in supervision to be best prepared for the situation at hand. After, you might sit down and think about the feedback you received and what you might have done differently, and reflect on what went well. This might also be done with the help of a supervisor. EMCC requires practitioners to keep both a practice log, where the practitioner notes the engagements, and a reflective log, where the practitioner keeps track of their learnings throughout their career. We highly recommend a Solution Focused reflective log that focuses on what the team coach would like to develop over the next period and what already went well in the last engagement together with a plan for incremental improvements for the next time.

Sometimes, team coaches are invited to work with teams that have aims they do not agree with. As mentioned in the section around the Galveston Declaration, Solution Focused team coaches tend to prefer equality and progress rather than exclusion, judgement and explanation. It is part of good self-management to know when a team's culture and aims are too far from what the team coach wants to bring into the world before entering an engagement.

Self-care is also part of self-management. Team coaches are human beings too, so noticing when your batteries are starting to go empty before they are on low and recharging in any way that helps is another important skill of a good team coach.

Coaching agreement

Coaching agreements are trickier in team coaching processes than in individual coaching. The same Solution Focused questions apply: "What are your best hopes from our working together?", "How would you know this that these best hopes have been fulfilled?", "Who else might notice?" The difference is that you need to invite more than one person to co-create a goal. Solution Focused team coaching already has a systemic perspective built in. All stakeholders are asked about their best hopes and the team coach is constantly in search of an objective that is meaningful and can serve as a common project.

The competency frameworks of the associations mention a "systemic perspective". The Solution Focused preference for inclusion (see the earlier section on the Galveston Declaration) and perspective change questions guarantee that the "system" is taken care of. One important difference is that the Solution Focused team coach will not assume that they can take on an outsider perspective and analyse or diagnose the "system". This would be privileging one perspective over another.

A detailed description of how Solution Focused team coaching takes care of the inclusion and alignment of the various perspectives of the team, the manager, the organization and other stakeholders can be found in the section on contracting, as well as the other important aspects of creating a coaching agreement such as clarity of roles, logistics and definition of team coaching.

Case 1.8:   What difference would it make?

Cristina was approached by another team coach to work together on a project. The co-team coach had already initial conversations with HR to clarify the scope, but they were more in the line of pricing. As a Solution Focused practitioner, Cristina was interested in the benefit for the team of going through this process beyond the perception of HR that they need someone.

A contracting meeting was arranged with HR, the general manager and both team coaches to further explore the request. It became clear that HR was simply aiming at ticking the box of contracting someone. The general manager was actually interested in finding someone to facilitate a day for the team, as he believed that, for a change, he should not do it.

Using Solution Focused questions such as "What would be different if we facilitate the day?" and "What would the team see as benefit from having two team coaches facilitating the day?", it became clearer that the intent of the general manager was to have someone who would simply facilitate through the agenda. Based on that, the decision was made not to engage further with the project. At the end of the day, the general manager decided to facilitate the day as usual.

Competencies for working with the team in the moment

Another group of competences mentioned by all three associations consists of skills for working with the team in the moment: effective communication, inviting awareness and insights, facilitating progress, "group dynamics" and "knowledge of models and interventions". Some of these are very easily to demonstrate for a Solution Focused team coach, while others are a little trickier as they imply an outside perspective and are based on a seemingly incommensurable philosophical framework. In the doing of team coaching, these differences are rarely important, however.

Effective communication

A good team coach knows how to communicate effectively. As stated multiple times, Solution Focused communication skills are highly effective. Having as few assumptions as possible makes it easy for the coach to listen for what is important to the team. Listening for what is wanted and what is already working, replaying this to the team and checking whether the team coach has picked up the important bits fulfils the competency requirements for active listening. Inviting the clients to walk through the "gallery" generates powerful questions that evoke awareness. In the "gift shop", the team is invited to generate their own progress and measures of accountability.

In addition to the Solution Focused questions and summaries, a Solution Focused team coach also has an easier time facilitating the discussion in a constructive way. The Solution Focused assumptions of positive intention (as mentioned above) make it much easier than if you were working on the assumption that change is difficult and will be resisted.

Just as the Solution Focused team coach will not take an "outside" perspective and will not analyse, diagnose or categorize a team, they will also not deal with "group dynamics". This term implies someone looking at "the dynamics" from the outside and analysing them. This is alien to a social-constructionist mindset. We think that what the associations' competency frameworks mean here is the ability of the team coach to engage effectively with the team and facilitate constructive discussions to which everyone can contribute. This can be done without a prior "analysis" or outside perspective, as described above.

Another set of team coaching competences revolves around the "knowledge of team development models". As mentioned in the section on the Galveston Declaration, Solution Focused team coaches would not revert to any diagnosis of the team. So why do the associations demand a "knowledge of team coaching models"? One the one hand, it is about tradition – rightfully or not, these models have been part of team coaching or leadership training for years. On the other hand, beginning team coaches do sometimes view these models as helpful. They can be a helpful "crutch" for the team coach to figure out what to do next. If we assume that one of the main practical purposes of the models is to find out a suitable "intervention" ("what to do next"), we can provide the benefit these models have without reverting to privileging an outside "expert" view on the team. Solution Focused team coaches might simply be braver by throwing away or never picking up the "crutch" and admitting they don't know what may be "the best" next step. Rather than adopting the expert stance, they are collaborative in knowing that the next step can only be determined in collaboration with the client.

Working with a co-coach

Working with a co-coach is mentioned by all three competency models as an important skill of a team coach. Some frameworks mention that it might be better for the team coach to have someone as a partner who can observe the team while the other person is doing the coaching. Again, this presumes that an outside perspective is necessary or in any way valid. Personally, we would not appreciate being "observed" and not interacted with as a team. Still, having two people as team coaches brings a lot of benefits: they can take turns, one can facilitate while the other visualize, the team coaches can facilitate two small groups, they can interact positively and act as role models, they can have conversations about the team's strengths and have the team listen in and much more. Our favourite stance toward a co-coach comes from improvisational theatre and states: "Make your partner look good!" Holding this saying in mind when interacting with a co-coach, a team, a team leader, a sponsor and other stakeholders makes the whole endeavour much easier.

References

Agile (n.d.) *Manifesto for Agile Software Development.* https://agilemanifesto.org

Bannink, F. (2010). *Handbook of solution focused conflict management.* Toronto: Hogrefe.

Belbin, R. M. (1981). *Management teams. Why they succeed or fail.* New York: Wiley.

Berg, I. K., & Szabó, P. (2005). *Brief coaching for lasting solutions.* New York: W.W. Norton.

Boszormenyi-Nagy, I., & Spark, G. (1973). Invisible loyalties: Reciprocity in intergenerational family therapy. New York: Lippincott, Williams and Wilkins.

Briggs Myers, I. & McCaulley, M. H. (1992). *Manual: A guide to the development and use of the Myers-Briggs type indicator.* Palo Alto, CA: Consulting Psychologists Press.

Bruner, J. S. (1990). *Acts of meaning.* Cambridge, MA: Harvard University Press.

Cade, B. (2007). A history of the Brief Solution Focused approach. In T. S. Nelson (Ed.), *Handbook of Solution Focused Brief Therapy: Clinical applications.* New York (pp. 25–63). New York: Haworth Press.

Cauffman, L., & Dierolf, K. (2006). *The solution tango: Seven simple steps to solutions in management.* London: Marshall Cavendish.

Clutterbuck, D. (2019). Towards a pragmatic model of team function and dysfunction. In D. Clutterbuck, J. Gannon, S. Hayes, I. Iordanou, K. Lowe, & D. MacKie (Eds.), *The practitioner's handbook of team coaching* (pp. 150–160). New York: Routledge.

Clutterbuck, D., Gannon, J., Hayes, S., Iordanou, I., Lowe, K., & MacKie, D. (Eds.). (2019). *The practitioner's handbook of team coaching.* New York: Routledge.

Cooperrider, D. L., Whitney, D. Kaplin, & Stavros, J. M. (2008). *Appreciative inquiry handbook: For leaders of change* (2nd ed.). Brunswick, NJ: Crown.

Covey, S. R., & Covey, S. (2020). *The 7 habits of highly effective people. Powerful lessons in personal change* (rev. ed.). New York: Simon & Schuster.

De Jong, P., &. Berg, I. (1998). *Interviewing for solutions*. Pacific Grove, CA: Thomson Brooks/Cole

de Shazer, S. (1978). Brief hypnotherapy of two sexual dysfunctions: The crystal ball technique. *American Journal of Clinical Hypnosis*, 20(3), 203–208.

de Shazer, S. (1982). *Patterns of brief family therapy: An ecosystemic approach*. New York: Guilford Press.

de Shazer, S. (1984). The death of resistance. *Family Process*, 23, 1–17.

de Shazer, S. (1985). *Keys to solution in Brief Therapy*. New York: W.W. Norton.

de Shazer, S. (1988). *Clues: Investigating solutions in Brief Therapy*. New York: W.W. Norton.

de Shazer, S. (1999). Beginnings. Unpublished manuscript from the website of the Brief Family Therapy Centers.

de Shazer, S., & Berg, I. K. (1992). Doing therapy: A post-structural revision. *Journal of Marital and Family Therapy*, 18, 71–81.

de Shazer, S. , Dolan, Y. M., & Korman, H. (2007). *More than miracles: The state of the art of Solution Focused Brief Therapy*. New York: Haworth Press.

Dierolf, K. (2011). SF practice as an application of discursive psychology: Discursive psychology as a theoretical backdrop of SF practice. *InterAction*, 3(1), 21–34.

Dierolf, K. (2012). Is SF a systemic approach? *InterAction*, 4(2), 10–26.

DiSC Profile (2023). What is DiSC? www.discprofile.com/what-is-disc

Erickson, M. H. (1954). Special techniques of brief hypnotherapy. *Journal of Clinical and Experimental Hypnosis*, 2(2), 109–129.

European Brief Therapy Association (EBTA) (2020). Theory of Solution Focused practice. www.ebta.eu/definition

Furman, B. (1998). *It's never too late to have a happy childhood: From adversity to resilience*. New York: BT Press.

Furman, B. & Ahola, T. (2004). *Twin star: Lösungen vom andern Stern*. Heidelberg: Carl Auer.

Gosnell, F., McKergow, M., Moore, B., Mudry, T., & Tomm, K. (2017). A Galveston Declaration. *Journal of Systemic Therapies*, 36(3), 20–26.

Greif, S., Möller, H., Scholl, W., Passmore, J., & Müller, F. (2022). Coaching definitions and concepts. In S. Greif, H. Möller, W. Scholl, J. Passmore, & F. Müller (Eds.), *International handbook of evidence-based coaching: Theory, research and practice* (pp. 16–34). Cham: Springer.

Haley, J. (1990). *Strategies of psychotherapy* (2nd ed.). Norwalk, CT: Crown House.

Hawkins, P. (2021). *Leadership team coaching: Developing collective transformational leadership* (4th ed.). London: Kogan Page.

Hurlow, S. (2022). Revisiting the relationship between coaching and learning: The problems and possibilities. *Academy of Management Learning & Education*, 21(1), 121–138.

Insights (2023). A new era in the world of work has begun: Hybridization. www.insights.com/de

International Coaching Federation (2023). ICF Team Coaching Competencies. https://coachingfederation.org/team-coaching-competencies

Jackson, P. Z. & McKergow, M. (2002). *The solutions focus. The simple way to positive change*. London: Nicholas Brealey.

Kiser, D. (1995). The process and politics of Solution Focused therapy theory development: A qualitative analysis. Dissertation, Purdue Universität.

Kiser, D., & Piercy, F. P. (2001). Creativity and family therapy theory development: Lessons from the founders of Solution Focused therapy. *Journal of Family Psychotherapy*, 12(3), 1–29.

Korman, H., de Jong, P., & Smock Jordan, S. (2020). Steve de Shazer's theory development. *Journal of Solution Focused Practices*, 4(2), 46–70.

Lencioni, P. M. (2002). *The five dysfunctions of a team: A leadership fable.* San Francisco: Jossey-Bass.

Lipchick, E. &. Derks, J. et al. (2012). The evolution of Solution Focused Brief Therapy. In C. Franklin (Ed.), *Solution Focused Brief Therapy: A handbook of evidence-based practice* (pp. 3–19). New York: Oxford University Press.

McKergow, M. (2021). *The next generation of solution focused practice: Stretching the world for new opportunities and progress.* London: Routledge.

McKergow, M., &. Korman, H. (2009). Inbetween: Neither inside nor outside: The radical simplicity of Solution Focused Brief Therapy. *Journal of Systemic Therapies*, 28(2): 34–49.

Meier, D. (2005). *Team coaching with the Solutioncircle: A practical guide to Solutions Focused team development.* Cheltenham: Solutions Books.

Miller, G. (1997). *Becoming miracle workers: Language and meaning in Brief Therapy.* New York: Aldine de Gruyter.

Morgan, A. (2022). *What is narrative therapy? An easy-to-read introduction.* Adelaide: Dulwich Centre Publications.

Norman, H., McKergow, M., & Clarke, J. (1997). Paradox is a muddle: An interview with Steve de Shazer. *Rapport*, 34, 41–49.

Nunnally, E., de Shazer, S., Lipchick, E., &. Berg, I. (1986). A study of change: Therapeutic theory in process. In D. Efron (Ed.*), Journeys: Expansion of the strategic, systemic therapies* (pp. 271–286). New York: Brunner/Mazel.

Ramseyer, F., & Tschacher, W. (2008). Synchrony in dyadic psychotherapy sessions. In S. Vrobel, O.E. Rössler, & T. Marks-Tarlow (Eds.), *Simultaneity* (pp. 329–348). Hackensack, NJ: World Scientific.

Sparrer, I. (2007). *Miracle, solution and system: Solution-focused systemic structural constellations for therapy and organisational change.* Cheltenham: Solutions Books.

Stams, G. J. J., Dekovic, M., Buist, K., & de Vries, L. (2006). Effectiviteit van oplossingsgerichte korte therapie: een meta-analyse. *Gedragstherapie*, 39(2): 81–95.

Tuckman, B. W. (1965). Developmental sequence in small groups. *Psychological Bulletin*, 63(6), 384–399.

Varga von Kibéd, M. & Sparrer, I. (2005). *But on the contrary. Tetralemma work and other basic forms of systemic structural constellations.* Heidelberg: Karl Auer.

Visser, C. (2012). How the Solution-Focusedness of coaches is related to their thriving at work.   http://solutions-centre.org/pdf/How%20the%20solution-focusedness%20of%20 coaches%20is%20related%20to%20their%20thriving%20at%20work.pdf

von Bertalanffy, L. (1968). *General system theory. Foundations, development, applications* (rev. ed.). New York: Braziller.

von Foerster, H. (2011). *Wissen und Gewissen: Versuch einer Brücke (1. Aufl., [Nachdr.]). Suhrkamp-Taschenbuch Wissenschaft: nr. 876.* Frankfurt: Suhrkamp.

Wageman, R., Nunes, D. A., Burruss, J., & Hackman, J. R. (2008). *Senior leadership teams: What it takes to make them great.* Cambridge, MA: Harvard Business Review Press.

Wingard, B., & Lester, J. (2001). *Telling our stories in ways that make us stronger.* Adelaide: Dulwich Centre.

Ziegler, P., & Hiller, T. (2001). *Recreating partnership. A solution-oriented, collaborative approach to couples therapy.* New York: W.W. Norton.

Chapter 2

Structure of a team coaching process

Abstract

This chapter provides the overall structure of the team coaching process. It covers a generic process, including how to contract with the team as a whole, with stakeholders and with the team leads. You will learn about concrete "facilitation moves" for team coaching workshops and gain insights into special team coaching formats such as Agile coaching, Agile retrospectives, shadowing a team, regular supervision of teams, Solution Focused reflecting teams, and a technique to explore decisions, the Tetralemma. A section on team-building provides an introduction to how Solution Focus can be used for this modality.

Introduction

"Every case is different" is an important basic tenet of Solution Focused coaching. Defining standard processes is therefore a little counter-intuitive. Our suggestions for processes are best understood as ideas and inspirations. It is like being in a big outdoor shop trying to gear up for your expedition. You think about where you will be going and check out the wares with that in mind. You know what you will probably need, but you also are inspired by the deals on offer.

The process we use most often is structured like this:

- Contracting with the sponsor(s) and team leader
- Interviews with individual team members
- Mind map or summary of the interviews
- Creation of an agenda / invitation to the team coaching workshop
- Workshop

  - Presenting the results of interviews
  - Working on the topics identified
  - Planning of experiments or actions

- Follow-up.

DOI: 10.4324/9781003370314-2

Contracting

General remarks

To clarify a contract or a proposal for work in team coaching, it is possible to use the same questions as were used for goal negotiation. Here is a short summary of what is relevant before entering into a team coaching process.

At the beginning, it is most important to find out from the sponsors of the team coaching what should be different after the team coaching process compared with the situation before. Often, people and organizations do not have a clear picture of what would be an ideal or better state. Sometimes this ideal or better state can only be elicited by working with the team members. It is important not to fall into the "language trap" and believe you know what the sponsor or team means when they are using a general term. For example, if you are asked to "increase motivation", you do not really know as a coach what should be better afterwards – you have to ask. It is best to get the sponsor or team leader to describe in detail what that change will be and which context it can be measured in or how it will be noticed.

Some team coaching processes last for months, and you cannot assume that you can "clarify" the process and the contract once and for all at the beginning of the process. With longer processes, it makes sense to plan "update conversations" or "fine-tuning meetings" right from the beginning. No plan survives the clash with reality.

The grammar of the team: Language and style

When sponsors choose a team coach, they often ask about relevant experience in the sector or industry of the company. The assumption is that it is useful if the team coach has already worked together with people from similar professions. For Solution Focused coaching, such experience is not so important. For us, knowing about a similar problem or a similar group has two sides: on the one hand, it is useful to know a little bit about the language of the team members and what they might mean. On the other hand, it is always dangerous to assume you know what somebody means and therefore stop asking questions.

Knowing the language and the working style of clients can be useful for the "standing" of the coaches. You can ask yourself why it is necessary for coaches to give a good impression and to demonstrate standing. What is in focus here is the confidence of the team members. The coach who does not fulfil any of the competence markers of the team will not be taken seriously by the team members. They will have a difficult time thinking seriously about the questions of the coach. Knowing about the team's competence markers is therefore interesting: is it a certain presence, a certain language or outfit, or something entirely different? The coach can then choose to fulfil these competence markers within the limits of their own possibilities to feel credible.

Context: What do I need to know?

In contrast to systemic coaching, Solution Focused coaches do not assume it is necessary to collect information about the system before the start of the work. Solution Focused practice aims at useful interactions between the coach with active people and it always happens in "person grammar". The language is about who does what and how, and who would like to change what they do or the way they do things. It is about the concrete actions and thoughts of people. The coach does not assume an observer stance and does not think that information about structures can be separated from the people within these structures. Learning about how the organization functions, the organizational structures and ways of decision-making are only important insofar as it helps the coach to interact with the people in the organization.

Therefore, it is also not important for the Solution Focused coach to become aware of their own "inner picture" or ideas about organization. Reflecting one's previous experiences with systems like family or school is often an important part of systemic coaching training. The goal here is to ensure the coach remains independent from possible unconscious assumptions about how systems function. Since these are irrelevant to Solution Focused coaching, it is not necessary to delve into these issues in training sessions for Solution Focused team coaching. This is why our training sessions are usually shorter. The devil is again in the detail – it sounds simple, but it is not easy. As Solution Focused coaches, we know our own assumptions and ideas are not relevant for the coaching process. But how do you manage to let go of your own assumptions and how do you create an "assumption-free" conversation with clients? For beginners in the Solution Focused approach, it is useful to start by pretending not to have assumptions. Notice your own assumptions as they arise, let them go and return your focus to the client by asking questions about goals, the miracle, resources and exceptions or small steps. But let's get back to the contract negotiation in which working without assumptions is so important.

Steve de Shazer often started Solution Focused interviews by asking, "So what do you do with yourself the whole day?" which is a very relaxed question about the daily life of his clients. The answer to this question provides clues about the resources of the client and an overview of the context in which the client would like an improvement to take place. For the same reason, we want to find out a little about what everybody does the whole day before starting the Solution Focused team coaching. We ask the following questions (which incidentally are not so different from those that would be asked in systemic coaching; the difference is mainly the philosophical background and the kinds of information that is picked up from the answer):

- Who is part of the team?
- What are the people like (age, education, general mood, competence markers)?

- What is going well and what would they like to keep doing?
- Who should participate in the team coaching? (This question can also be asked later.)
- What is the team doing the whole day?
- What is the main task of the team within the organization?
- What is the company strategy, mission and vision? What is important for the company?
- What does the team have to get right next year?
- What are the interfaces of the team? (The answer to this question is very useful for ensuing questions about who would notice a change.)

It is also important to find out a little about the decision-making limits of the team. It can be very frustrating if the team identifies useful steps in the team coaching process, then it turns out that they cannot be carried out. Naturally, the team knows whether things that have been decided on in the team coaching sessions can be implemented by the team members and lie within their responsibilities. We usually confirm this when we are asking about what the next steps are when we are creating action lists. It can be very helpful to talk to the HR department or the team leader about the decision-making limits regarding what can or cannot be changed by the team before entering into a team coaching process.

Contracting with the whole organization

When working with teams, you will most likely expand your contracting to include the team leader/manager, HR stakeholders within team organizations and potentially other stakeholders – such as functional stakeholders. Identifying them and then ensuring you contract properly with everyone are crucial for establishing the framework for your team coaching work.

Let's start with the organization level. You will need to ensure that there is a contract between you and the organization whose employees are members of the team(s) you are going to coach. Your contract with the organization should cover legal and organizational areas of your relationship with the organization.

Legal and organizational elements of your contracting should be mutually agreed terms and conditions of your collaboration with the organization. These include areas such as scope of work (coaching teams), method of delivery (in person/virtual/blended), your remuneration, terms of payment, confidentiality of your work with the organization and the clients who you will coach, and any form of reporting.

The next level of your contracting is less legalistic and administrative, but equally – if not more – important. It is contracting with the people development function. We can call it HR for simplicity, but we know that your stakeholder responsible for people's performance may be a member of variously called organizational functions, such as talent or people, and sometimes you may be contracted/hired directly by the business.

Contracting with this stakeholder is more focused on creating and agreeing the framework of your work and accepting rules and boundaries to ensure ethical and constructive work. You need to remember about few crucial aspects:

- expectations
- communication
- confidentiality
- follow up.

It is important to gain clarity on the expectations that people function has about the work you are about to do as well as challenges that nudged them to ask for your help. It is a time for you to ask questions that will help you ensure you are engaging in the coaching work, not anything else, as well as getting to know their expectations about the process, reporting, communication and outcomes.

When we say "communication", we refer to the agreed flow of information between you, your client(s) and the organization/stakeholders who hired you. It is very important to agree on things such as the content, scope of the communication, frequency, format and key contacts of the communication. All parties to that contract, including the client, need to be clear who communicates what to whom.

Clarifying confidentiality is an ethical demand of all of the coaching associations. You want to make sure all parties of your contracting – particularly stakeholders who will not be coached – are clear about rules of confidentiality in the coaching process. This helps you to create trust with the client(s) and navigate any further conversations with the organization/stakeholders who hired you. It will also help you if any of the stakeholders are not fully aware what coaching is and how it works and/or want to get insights into the content of the coaching sessions when the collaboration starts. Both parties to the process need to be satisfied and clear with the framework you have created before you move forward with the actual work.

Depending on the structure and/or characteristics of the organization with which you are engaging, you may need to contract with the team leader/manager. Your contracting with them may differ, depending on whether or not they are part of the team that you will coach and will be actively participating in your work.

If not, your contracting with them may be similar to your contracting with the people development stakeholder, agreeing the framework of the work, highlighting the expectations, communication and confidentiality. This is extremely important for you as a coach, and getting it right is critical to ensure the constructive nature of the work you will deliver.

In the following paragraphs, we explore the contracting in details, depending on the different origins of the request.

Request by HR

We are most often approached for team coaching by the HR department, which usually has been notified by someone in the company who indicated that there was room for improvement in the team. Perhaps the team has approached the HR department, the team leader is asking for help, or one of the team leader's superiors, who sees that something might be changed for the better, may have initiated the process.

When the coach is approached by HR, you are not speaking directly to the client in the first step. HR usually talks to several coaches about the issue at hand before recommending a team coach. HR has been told about the issues and tasks of the team and usually knows what should be improved.

Therefore, in the clarification phase with HR, you are usually dealing with two issues. On the one hand, it is important to find out as much as possible about the goals of the team coaching and make the request for the proposal as clear as possible in order to be able to decide whether this is a contract the team coach can and would like to enter into. On the other hand, the conversation with HR is also a form of "sales pitch" in which the coach would like to convince the organization that they are the right partner for these kinds of jobs. In our experience it is important to focus on the fit between company and coach. If an organization has clear ideas about what should happen in the team coaching, and these clear ideas do not fit with a Solution Focused approach, it is often better not to put in a proposal.

Case 2.1:   But where is your feedback?

We had been asked by an internationally operating bank to conduct a simple team coaching process for them. The team had been working together for three years. Six months ago, they had a change in the team leadership and were now working with the new team leader. Collaboration was working very well, and the team wanted to take some time out to make sure it could continue this good beginning. We thought that this suited the Solution Focused approach very well. We would scale with the team where they were on the scale of 0 to 10, with 10 being optimal collaboration (whatever this meant for the team) and take it from there.

HR had asked to join in. The woman in question was a young, motivated and very friendly member of the training and development department. We thought she could help with her perspective and observational resources, and generally be very useful to have in the team coaching process since the team also trusted and respected her, so she attended the team coaching days.

The team members had wanted to talk about what was going well and what could even be a little bit better. They had also said that they would like to have some fun together and that they really appreciated interesting team exercises. Such kinds of exercises are easily integrated into Solution Focused team coaching if you follow them up with a conversation about the strengths and resources of the team that appeared in the exercise. You can then talk about where these strengths and resources are visible in the daily life of the team. If the team cannot spot the same strengths in daily life, you can talk about how the exercise made it possible for the team to demonstrate their strengths and how they could show up in daily life too.

In this case, we carried out a rather traditional team exercise: building a bridge. The team got the task to build a bridge which would hold two water bottles using the facilitation materials available. The team was very successful and creative in its solution-finding approach. In the debriefing phase of the exercise, the team members realized that they were able to integrate and build on different ideas very well. They also appreciated the careful team leadership by their boss. They also realized a few other strengths that had become visible. The team was able to plan how they would use these strengths in their daily lives, and everybody left with the feeling that this had been a very useful exercise and a meaningful conversation.

You can imagine our surprise in the debriefing discussion with the training and development specialist when she said she was very disappointed with how this exercise had been conducted. She knew this exercise from other workshops. Her expectation was that we, as team coaches, would observe the team in the solution-finding approach with detailed observation sheets or questionnaires (like in an assessment centre), then give every team member feedback on their team roles, their communication style, and so on. She expected us to give each team member advice on how to improve their collaboration skills. In Solution Focused coaching, we assume that every situation is different; therefore, we cannot really draw conclusions that are valid for daily life in the team from the behaviour of the team in an exercise such as bridge-building. The exercise only shows which kind of positive behaviour is possible for the team. Transferring these positive behaviours into daily life requires deliberation and planning. For us, such an exercise is more an occasion for constructive conversation similar to a question about team resources or exceptions then a diagnostic tool.

Only in the debriefing with the training and development specialist did we notice what we should have clarified beforehand. What were her expectations about the debriefing and use of experiential exercises? Which methodologies in team coaching did she know and what had she experienced as useful?

Apart from questions about the context as they are listed above, the following questions to the HR department would have proven useful:

- Which kind of team coaching processes have you observed in the last few months?
- What was important for you?
- What is important for you about this coaching process?
- What is important for you in the collaboration with external coaches? What were some of the most positive experiences with external coaches?
- Have you been trained as a coach? Which training did you attend? What did you like about it?
- What would you like to know about us?
- What tells you that we could be the right coaches for this project?

Other interesting questions could be:

- What are some of the instruments for HR management that the company uses?
- What are your company "values"? Are there competency frameworks, leadership guidelines or other important instruments that you use?
- Are there regular surveys for example employee opinion surveys?

The answers to these questions can help us to understand a bit about the context in which an improvement for the team needs to fit. For example, it would not be very helpful if the team decided to do something that was in stark contrast to the company guidelines. If you as a coach are interested in the instruments used by HR, you show respect and appreciation for the work of the HR department. If there are regular employee opinion surveys, you might be able to "measure" the effect of the team coaching and how the team rates its collaboration in these surveys. The results of the work of coaches is often very difficult to measure, just like the work of the HR department in general. Often, the HR department is happy to be able to show how measures that it initiated affect employee opinion or, even better, the bottom line. In this way, you can also demonstrate to the top management that your work has represented a good return on their investment.

The HR department naturally also has an idea or an image of the team that you want to coach. The team members or the team leader have talked about their needs with the HR department. It is therefore useful to talk to HR about the exact goals that should be pursued in the team coaching. Of course, this does not replace talking to the team and the team leaders about what should be different after the team coaching.

Questions for the HR department which relate to the goal could be:

- Suppose this team coaching is very useful for the team and the company – who would notice?

- How would these individual stakeholders notice the improvement? What would be different for the team?
- How confident are you that the team can reach their goals? What makes you confident?

- What do you appreciate about this team?
- What do you appreciate about the team leader?

It is always helpful if you can partner with the HR department and ask about their experiences with coaching processes with the team in question to make sure the methodology you are using in the team coaching fits the team. Here you could ask:

- What kind of coaching or training sessions has the team had in the past?
- What did they like? What did the team find less useful?
- What is the general approach of the team to measures such as team coaching? Are they looking forward to it? Are they a little bit more sceptical?
- What is the atmosphere in the team like?

If you are able to partner with the HR department, you create the best conditions for the success of team coaching. In our experience, it is much easier to design any type of coaching if you have a supportive HR department covering your back. In this way, if there are any difficulties you can start looking for a good solution together. Mutual appreciation prevents finger-pointing in difficult situations. Instead, you can think about how you can continue in a way that benefits everybody. Nothing is more frustrating than when the HR department is blaming the coaches, the coaches are blaming the HR department, and so on when something is not working. Partnering in coaching and training makes much more sense for both sides. The good thing is that, as Solution Focused coaches, we have the necessary know-how to build on our good relationship with the HR department.

Contracting: Request by the team leader

Direct requests for team coaching by the team leader are rare. Most often, the conversation with the team leader or team members is the second step after clarifying the contract, following the sales meeting with the HR department. It is mandatory for the success of the team coaching to talk to the team leader before you start. Here you can also ask a few questions about the context. It is most important to find out about the goal of the team leader and the methodology with which the team is comfortable. Questions about the context are the same as those listed above.

Here are a few more possible questions:

- Suppose the team coaching process is very useful for you and your team. Who would notice a change? What would they notice?

- Which of these changes would be especially desirable or important for you?
- On a scale of 1 to 10, where 10 is that you have already reached these individual goals and 1 means you are just starting to think about them, where is the team in your view? (Here you can use one or several scales depending on the goals of the team.)
- What do you notice about the team that tells you that you are already at an X and not at 1?
- Who would notice X+1? What would that tell them? What should stay the same in your team?
- What do you appreciate about your team?
- What makes you confident that these improvements can be achieved?

We often jot down the answers to these questions on a piece of paper. It can be quite practical to conduct such conversations over the telephone – this way you can type away while you are talking, and you have a good overview of the starting point of the process. The results can also be made available to the team before the team coaching session.

Contracting: Other sponsors/stakeholders

On rare occasions, the request for coaching may come from a different source- a functional stakeholder, a business executive or anyone else who is eligible to make such a request. Most often, such conversations are part of clarifying the contract after meeting with HR. Equally important and crucial for the success of the team coaching process, these conversations should help you to understand the expectations and the context of the request. We advise using the same set of questions as we propose for the team leader. The answers will offer you unique insights into the expectations of a diverse and important group of stakeholders in your team coaching project:

- Suppose the team coaching process is very useful for you and your team. Who would notice a change? What would they notice?
- Which of these changes would be especially desirable or important for you?
- On a scale of 1 to 10, where 10 is that you have already reached these individual goals and 1 means you are just starting to think about them, where is the team in your view? (Here you can use one or several scales, depending on the goals of the team.)
- What do you notice about the team that tells you that you are already at an X and not at 1?
- Who would notice X+1? What would that tell them? What should stay the same in your team?
- What do you appreciate about your team?
- What makes you confident that these improvements can be achieved?

Contracting with the co-team coach

Both ICF and EMCC recommend using a co-team coach in certain situations. It might be that you are working with a team that is large (above 15 members, there should be a co-team coach according to ICF competencies) or the complexity of the project would signal the need for one (EMCC core standards).

In any case, there is value from working as a team of team coaches. It also means we should engage in a contracting step to ensure that both (or more) team coaches have clarity on the project, explore the best hopes of the team coaches' team, ways of working together and so on.

Questions that you could use for the contracting stage between team coaches include:

- What are your best hopes from us working together on this?
- How will the team see a difference from having us as a team of team coaches?
- How will we be noticing that we are working as a team?

At the same time, project management-type questions should also be addressed:

- What would be the best way we could schedule our work (regular meetings, planning meeting only, etc.)?
- What do we need to keep making each other look good?
- What issues of confidentiality need to be considered?
- How will contracting be done (only one company signs the contract and the other one is subcontracted, or both are part of the client contract)?
- What are the reporting needs of the organization and what do we want to report upon? KPIs?

It would be especially important to go through the contracting step if the co-team coach with whom you will be working is "speaking a different language", hence coming from a different coaching method/approach. This is even more the case when the organization selects the other team coach internally or externally.

What can we coach and what not?

As you may have noticed, your contract with the organization does not include any outcomes of your coaching work. We would like to reiterate here that your obligation is to deliver the best service you can, not the outcomes the company may want to achieve by hiring you.

Is coaching the best method?

When discussing your work with the stakeholders and/or decision-makers, be sure to ask questions that will allow you to truly understand what they would like to achieve. You need to be sure that what they want is "coachable" and a "well-formed goal" (see Chapter 1) and you can commit to work in full alignment with the nature and ethics of coaching. If not, we always advise stating that clearly as well as helping the stakeholder(s), if possible, to identify the right approach for their challenge – for example, training, mediation and so on. However, please remember that it is not always possible, and it is not really your role to do it. In simple terms, you want to commit to the work of the coach, not anything else.

While you go through the above contracting processes, it is useful to remember and be cautious about certain typical situations we have encountered in our work, discussed below.

Coaching leader and team separately

We always applaud leaders who want to engage in a coaching relationship. If you receive an offer to deliver team coaching, but the team leader is not willing to join the team in the process, we encourage you to be curious and understand their reasons. We always coach the team and its leader. That is our gold standard and an approach that allows the team to gain the benefits and move forward in the best possible way. Therefore, if the team lead is unwilling to join the team, be curious and try to understand their concerns. This will allow you to respond to any questions or ideas they may have about the process and its benefits. We hope you are able to encourage them to join the team. If, however, they still are not willing to join their team in the process, maybe team coaching is not the right modality. There are very rare cases in which it makes sense to separate team and team leader. Potentially, if there is distrust between them, you might interview them separately first; however, even in this case, solutions can only be found together.

The team is not a team

When the team that is in scope of the potential coaching work turns out not to be a team as per the definition we discussed earlier in this book, you may be unable to apply the team coaching framework that we intend to promote and use. A team has a common purpose, common objective and common function, and our coaching work helps it achieve its goals and potentially improve the way it functions and delivers. A team's work is interdependent and every team member relies on every other team member's work. If you are asked to coach a group of individuals who are not a team, then this is no longer a team coaching engagement and it requires a different approach, further investigation and constructive conversation about how to help this group address its challenges. This, however, is not a team coaching work and we encourage you to think carefully about such situations and not undertake a commitment that falls outside the scope of team coaching work. You might still engage in group coaching, action learning, reflective work, best-practice sharing and so on, but it is simply not "team coaching" if it is not a "team".

Conflict of interest

As in several aspects of business and personal relations, a conflict of interest may arise. This can have various forms – for example, your business and/or personal relationship with the organization, with their competitor, with an individual in the team. This short list does not definitively cover all possible options. In our work, such situations happen – it is not unusual. What is important here is to disclose the conflict to the potential client/stakeholder and be transparent. Conflicts of interest can be managed and they don't always close the door to the potential business relationship. However, we strongly encourage you to rethink if the project you are discussing can be delivered in the best interests of the participants – your clients.

One common conflict of interest is when you are coaching the leader as an individual and are asked to coach the team of this leader – we recommend using another coach for that engagement.

The team is not responsible for the solution

While you are discussing the contract and coaching work with the client, we encourage you to be cautious if you realize the team you are asked to coach is not responsible for the solutions that is sought by the stakeholders and or client organization. This is one situation when we would advise you to raise it with the client, and if they don't change the goal, decline to enter this coaching agreement. As you know, coaching is a partnership created to help the client (in this case, the team) to achieve the outcome (in this case, the solution) they seek. In the absence of the link between the team and the possibility of the outcome (solution), we don't see this as a coaching partnership.

This is tricky – sometimes it is not obvious that the solution that is sought is not in the team's hands. If you realize this during the team coaching, go back to square one and re-contract with the organization. You might not be able to coach this team, but maybe you can help someone else in the organization who is responsible for the outcome desired.

Taking over team leadership

Another situation we would like you to be mindful of is when you are asked to take over leadership of the team. Such requests may be a result of lack of understanding of the coaching work, desire to quickly "fix things" or some other "get this sorted" approach. Naturally, this is something that falls outside your scope of work and should not be accepted while contracting with the potential client and/or stakeholder.

When team leaders or HR ask you to "lead" the team as a team coach, it is best to help the people whose function it is to lead by offering to coach them. One example is that the team leader is asking the team coach to manage the performance of the team. It is much better to then coach the team leader to be able to do it themselves.

Being the messenger of "bad news" and coach at the same time

We have encountered some situations when we found ourselves asked to communicate some difficult decisions to the team we coached or even solve the actual problem the team faced. If you sense and/or are asked to deliver a difficult message to the team (e.g. headcount reduction, restructuring) and/or solve the actual problem, you need to identify and communicate the clear boundary here for your work as a coach. A coach never accepts these types of responsibilities within coaching work because they belong in other types of support and intervention.

Interviews

Interviews with the team members and key stakeholders are an important element of Solution Focused team coaching work. After clarifying the contract with the HR department and the team leader, we often ask to carry out short interviews with the team members and other stakeholders in the process. These interviews provide the possibility to get to know each other and offer the opportunity for a more exact goal-setting process. These interviews are Solution Focused interviews – so they often increase the confidence of the team members that something can change for the better as well as provide better understanding of the context in which the process is going to happen.

Case 2.2:   A second chance

A high-tech company had conducted the standardized employee opinion survey: "A great place to work". They had found out there were significant deviations in one German team in contrast to other international teams. They did not seem happy with their leadership at all and there were other topics that popped up in the survey that made it seem useful to conduct a team coaching process.

In the interviews, Kirsten asked the team members about their general assessment of the team situation first: "On a scale of 1 to 10, where ten means that you come to work every morning happy and willing to give your best and one is the opposite, where are you now?" Many were around 7. When she then asked, "What tells you that you are already on a seven and not on a one?", she found that they thought their work was very interesting and provided a great technological challenge. Team cohesion and the atmosphere within the team were very good. However, before Kirsten could get in the next question, many team members told her that everything else – especially their boss – was a catastrophe.

One team member especially had taken on something like an unofficial leadership role and was very upset about his boss: "He is a complete loser! Our meetings are completely chaotic. Whenever he has to defend our interests internationally, he simply gives in, and we end up with only those tasks that are too difficult for everybody else. He also does not ask about the general strategy or takes care that we get the resources we need. I would be much better at this! He never gives us feedback and we feel completely left out in the cold."

Kirsten was surprised by how strongly he felt. She would not have expected this from this rather rational and dry engineer. So she mumbled something along the lines of, "That sounds terrible – I am impressed that you still like your work that much, anyway." When she had recovered from the shock, Kirsten tried a confidence scale: "On a scale of 1 to 10, where 10 means that you are extremely confident that something can change with regard to this topic and 1 is the opposite, where are you now?" The engineer looked at her, very surprised. He started thinking and there was a relatively long, not extremely comfortable silence. He finally said, "So you mean that for this thing to be successful at all, I really need to give my boss a second chance?" Kirsten could see in his eyes that he was also seeing the humorous element of the situation. So she threw her hands up in the air and said: "Meeee? I'm not thinking anything – you just said this!" Both laughed and continued with a very constructive conversation.

This episode shows that the interviews are not mainly for data collection. They prepare the ground for a successful beginning of the team coaching.

The questions for the interviews naturally depend on the task or the request. The main difference is what you take as a 10 on the scale. Here are some sample questions:

- What is your role in the team? What is your task? What would you do the whole day?
- On a scale of 1 to 10, where 10 means

  - that you go to work in the morning happy and in a good mood willing to do your best
  - that your team problem has been solved so you work well together with 1 for the opposite/the beginning/the most difficult moment, where do you see the team now?

- What tells you the team is on X and not on 1? What else? Who contributes what to that? What else?
- Who would notice an improvement to X+1? What would they notice that would tell them?
- What are some of things that we should definitely talk about in the team coaching?
- What do you appreciate about your team?
- What is your experience with team coaching workshops? Which methods have you already used that you found useful?

You can also decide to opt for a different set of questions if you think these will bring you more clarity about the situation and expectations. The following set can be used for interviews with team members as well as key stakeholders:

- What are your best hopes from this team coaching?
- What is some good advice you would give yourself and your team?
- Who will notice what?
- What's the matter and what do you want to happen?
- What have you already tried?
- What is working well and what would you like to change?
- How would you like your collaboration to be instead?
- On a scale of 1 to 10, where 10 is you are going to work every morning, happy and willing to do your best, where are you?
- What do we need to talk about in the coaching?

The team interviews most often happen on the telephone or virtually, so you can type while talking. Please make sure you let them know you will be typing to ensure that they understand that you are listening.

Our experience is that the relative anonymity of the telephone call sometimes makes it easier for people to confide in you and to speak about what they really want to see happening after a team coaching process. You can also successfully build this sense of safety in the virtual meeting, ideally tapping into your coaching abilities.

After every interview, we read our notes to the interview partners to make sure that we did not misunderstand them. The interviews take around 15 minutes, so for a team of eight people, you have an interview time of approximately two hours.

Results as mind map

When you finish conducting the interviews, it is important to summarize the observations and results, and to present them back to the team and the contracting parties. While there are various models for doing so, we recommend that you approach this as a mind map, clearly presenting the information you collected during the interviews, their interdependencies and potentially emerging themes and trends.

Mind maps are a powerful information presentation method. They not only highlight important facts, but also help you present the overall structure of a subject and the relative importance of individual parts of it. They are really useful and can help you to make new connections between ideas. They also help your audience, stakeholders and team to visualize and understand the key messages you want to convey.

As with our approach in general, we encourage you to apply simplicity that will ultimately help to clarify and communicate the outcomes of the interviews. To use mind maps most effectively, remember to apply simple and consistent wording and labelling, use different colours to separate ideas and add visual impact, and use cross-linkages to help you show how one part of the subject affects another part (Figure 2.1).

So what exactly is a mind map and how do you create one? In the simplest terms, we would say a mind map is a diagram that represents tasks, ideas, concepts, words and conclusions connected to or arranged around a central idea/theme that allows a user/reader to understand the framework of a central subject. Some would say it is a tool that allows others to understand the thinking that goes inside your head. In our case, the mind map will allow you to present your findings from the interviews you held in preparation for your team coaching process.

How do you then create the mind map? Let's walk you through the process we recommend. While interviewing all the relevant stakeholders, you collect notes – probably a lot of them. When you start reviewing them, you may start noticing some themes or patterns, so you can note them down on paper or on your virtual mind map. If you cannot see anything at the beginning, do not worry; simply start jotting the information and keywords down as you move through your notes.

As you go through the outcomes of your interviews and add more information to your mind map, you will start noticing connections, patterns and interdependencies. That's when you can start connecting and grouping the information on your map. Remember that it is a living document, so you may want to move things around and shift ideas as you progress through your notes. The key is to map the information in the way that creates a picture, a landscape of reality, which you can present back to your stakeholders.

It might help to put some "targets" on your map, which may help you to start creating your mind map. The first targets can be whatever key ideas/concepts structure the results of your interviews – for example, key targets that made the team invite a coach (e.g. collaboration, communication, change). When you add more information to your mind map, you can decide what branches you can create and how best to connect the information, observations and ideas to crystalize and present the outcomes in the most impactful way. As much as it is aimed at presenting the outcomes to the stakeholders, we often discover that it helps us see the big picture as well as important details of our interviews.

As you progress through mapping the ideas on your mind map, you may experiment with using different colours and/or shapes, as this helps with presentation of ideas, their connection and emerging themes. This may be a bit of a messy process. You will start with a few headings/targets that may fit together and, as you

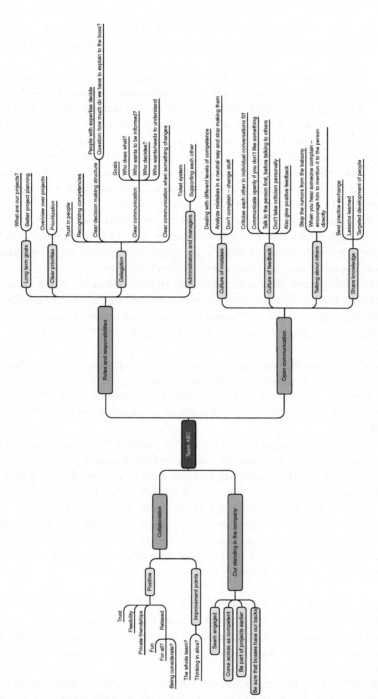

Figure 2.1 A mind map.

are adding interviews or notes from your interviews, a different way of sorting the topics may appear. If you are using an online mind-mapping tool, it is very easy to reallocate topics and to switch around headings and ways to summarize different topics.

Explore deeper the observations/notes, adding sub-topics, facts, observations and any additional information. Then link them to the targets/themes to which they belong – ideally using different colours for clarity. As mentioned above, you can always add more headings and different subheadings, and choose different ways of sorting the contributions from the interviews as you go along. That is an exercise in creativity! As you can see from Figure 2.1, we have added several pieces of information, color-coding them for clarity and thematic grouping. Repeat the process with new sets of acts, observations and data, again connecting them with the relevant targets and color-coding them consistently for clarity.

We advise you to remember that the mind map may have a lot of topic/subject lines radiating from the centre and then branching out. The important thing is to remember to connect the information in the appropriate groups, using consistent colour-coding and shapes to ensure clarity of the presentation.

This is a fairly basic process of mind map creation. However, while we love simplicity, we also want to add few ideas to consider while creating your mind map and presenting the results of your interview in the team coaching process.

Here are some of the most useful ideas we have collected over the years:

1 *Use simple words or phrases.* Single words or simple phrases convey messages best, and they reduce the risk of potentially confusing the reader.
2 *Use symbols or images.* Pictures can help you remember some information and/or help the reader understand and absorb the information presented in the mind map.
3 *Use colour to code separate ideas/level of information.* Colour usually helps to add clarity as long as it is used consistently and intentionally.
4 *Use cross-linkage.* If the information in one part of your mind map relates to another part as well, draw a line to show this interdependency. Always check whether the connection is clearly marked and consistently coded.
5 *If you are running interviews online, then you can share your notes while you are talking to the team member.* This allows them to see what you are capturing. Of course, be mindful of not sharing input from other team members, only the elements that you are capturing from them.

We encourage you to experiment with the mind map before you even propose it in your team coaching work. Maybe use it to present themes in your coaching experience so far? Or maybe try drafting a mind map to present your coach education. Starting small will allow you to become comfortable and confident in using this concept.

Additionally, as we live in a digital age, you will find numerous applications and software that will help you to prepare mind maps. As with other tools, we recommend trying them out and reflecting how they help achieving your objective. Our golden advice is that the format should always help the content to speak and the message to be understood and received by the audience.

Thematic analysis

If you want to be very thorough academically, you might opt to transcribe the interviews and run through a thematic analysis process. Thematic analysis is a method of analysing qualitative data. The researcher reads the texts (in this case, the interviews) in order to identify common themes. There are a number of software products that facilitate such reading: the researcher can mark themes and use the same marker each time the same theme is mentioned, and can also add sub-themes as they go along. If two researchers do this at the same time without knowing of the results of the work of the other, something like "intersubjectivity" (as objectivity does not exist) can be achieved.

We usually don't opt for this step – it is very time-consuming and does not add a lot to simply creating a mind map through "playing it by ear". However, in cases when stakes are high and cost is not an issue, this might be a good way of proceeding: thematic analysis is a valid academic research method. It can create trust in the results and the team coaches. It is very important, however, that these results are also presented as "the themes we saw" and that the team uses this as a springboard for discussion and not as "this is what the themes objectively *are*". As you may have noticed, we are really not fond of an "outside expert" position for the coach.

Workshop(s): Concrete facilitation moves

We use the term "coaching moves" for what are traditionally called "facilitation techniques" or "coaching tools". We believe that coaching and team coaching are always emergent, and you can most often forget your plan as soon as you have written it down. No plan survives first contact with reality. As in a dance, we respond to what the client is doing and partner with the team to create a team coaching process that fits their needs.

Trust and safety

There is no impactful coaching without trust and safety. As we mentioned earlier in the chapter discussing the differences between team and individual coaching, we do not advise creating unnecessary and often unnatural trust building exercises such as walking blindfolded or jumping into the arms of the team from a table (actually, our insurance doesn't cover this, and we really don't like it).

Within the coaching agreement space, you move as a trusted guide by asking about and recognizing needs of the clients with regards to the space and group with which you are working. We use Solution Focused questions to elicit what the team means by "trust and safety", and what that will look like, and by asking what needs to happen for the team members to offer their trust in the coaching processes. This is a great starting point where you can not only embody coaching presence and mindset, but also naturally build rapport and trust without creating artificial exercises or activities.

Trust and safety before the workshop

INVITATIONS

A well-written invitation acts like a catalyst to create interest and curiosity for the team coaching process. It can reduce the level of concern each team member has about what will happen. The team coach should engage with the team leader to construct and coordinate the invitation. Not every team leader has the skills and time to craft a careful, trust-building invitation. The worst Kirsten has seen went something along the lines of: "Ms Dierolf will interview you to see if you are able to be part of a high-performing team." Such a comment may not be very conducive to trust building! The aim should be that the team leader sends the invitation, introducing the team coach and the agenda for the workshops, as the responsibility for the overall process and leadership remains with the team leader.

Invitations may contain a short biography of the team coach, a short description of the process and logistic details. It should also build the "hope" that this is a common project and that the team and all team members will benefit from the exercise.

CLARIFICATION OF ROLES

An important element before the start of the process is to clarify the roles with the team leader and any other relevant team members. You can organize a short kick-off call where the roles and expectations are spoken about openly and expressed in a manner that brings clarity. The same approach should be used in relation to other stakeholders (HR, CEO, etc.).

It is really helpful if the team coach asks for a mandate from the team and also asks how they would like to be coached:

- Are they okay with the team coach facilitating?
- Can the team coach ask difficult questions?
- Is it okay for the team coach to interrupt them when they seem to be veering off topic?
- How would they like to capture the off topic (e.g. in a "parking lot")?

Trust and safety in the beginning of the workshop

INTRODUCTION ROUND

At the start of the workshop, the team coach should aim to create an environment of trust and to set an atmosphere of sharing and constructive interaction. A carefully selected "warm-up exercise" (not icebreaker, as we don't assume there is ice to be broken) is one of the elements that should be on the to-do list of team coaches.

Depending on the desired approach to the entire team coaching process, the team coach may consider constructing the whole workshop around the same metaphor, and in that case the introduction round should fit with the concept.

Case 2.3:   Online warm-up

Cristina worked with a team from a global consulting firm in an online team coaching session. One desire they expressed was to learn about the different people in the team. To incorporate that into the workshop, Cristina allowed space for an introduction exercise where everyone covered their camera with their hand and took it down if they wanted to answer yes to the question: "Have you ever ...?" Cristina brought some bold statements like: "Have you ever ridden an elephant?" or "Have you been on two different continents?" The team had a lot of fun, learned about one another and discovered resources about which they previously been unaware. After the initial round of about five to six questions addressed by the team coach, each team member was invited to ask a question. It was amazing to see how one of the directors asked a question about his teenage years, which most of the team resonated with and which brought the team to a feeling that they were similar.

Case 2.4:   What is your favourite Christmas decoration item?

At another workshop with the same team, Cristina adapted the process to reflect the fact that it was happening close to Christmas and everyone in the team was from a culture in which Christmas was celebrated. As the workshop was online, it was important to be mindful of the time that participants needed to react to the request. Everyone was given five minutes to search the house and bring their favourite Christmas decoration item to their computer. Once they were back, we waited until everyone was present and showed them at the same time. As we were online, it was also very simple to capture the moment with a picture.

> The scope of the exercise was not to show what items were selected, but to invite them one by one to explain what those elements said about who they were and to create a strong bonding experience. It was coupled with a breakout room where participants were invited to talk among themselves about how the story shared by each breakout room participant resonated with them and what it brought to them.

You may want to consider using some of the ideas below:

WHAT I CONTRIBUTE TO THE TEAM AND WHAT YOU CAN ASK ME ABOUT?

This is very simple: each team member responds to the question about what they can contribute to the team or what they are happy to be asked about. In online team coaching sessions, it may be useful to capture this on an online whiteboard or in a shared document so the team can refer to the results later on or even amend and extend the documents. In face-to-face team coaching sessions, each team member can write a Post-It note and the results can be collected on a pin-board or wall.

SIMULTANEOUS ANSWERS

You can ask any kind of question and invite team members to respond by either writing the answer on a big piece of paper (big enough so others can read it) or into the chat room online without pressing "enter". On the count of three, everybody shows their paper and presses "Enter" and we have the results without the team members influencing each other. This can be used in many stages of the team coaching process. At the beginning of a workshop, it might be nice to start with questions such as "Do you like the Rolling Stones?" or "Peanut butter is …"

PASSING THE PEN IN ZOOM

This is a really short collaboration exercise. The team members are asked to pretend to pass a pen to another person on Zoom and this person takes their own pen and pretends to be taking it from the person passing it. Try it … you have to announce who you are giving the object to, and the other person pretends that they are taking your pen by using their pen.

WHERE ARE YOU IN THE WORLD?

In face-to-face meetings, you can pretend the room is a map. You mark north, south, east and west, and ask team members to position themselves in the room so the map represents reality. Questions could be:

- Where did you come from today?
- Where were you born?
- Where do you live?
- Where is your favourite place?

Online, you can share a map via screen share and ask team members to annotate the screen share with their names.

USING METAPHORS AND PICTURES

Find postcards and pictures that fit with the topic of the team coaching and ask each team member to select an image that fits their current mood or their relationship with the topic. Everyone is then asked to explain why they chose this image. Online, this can be done by sharing a few pictures and inviting the team members to annotate. Kirsten's favourite search term here is "crazy dogs" (try it, you get some pretty funny results).

"GLUES CLUES"

This is an exercise for team members who know each other well and are not in horrible conflict at the moment. It's a bit humorous. What is being glued are Post-It notes. In a group of a maximum of eight participants, ask each participant to write Post-It notes for all the other participants and then stick them to the back of the chairs of the other participants or even to the backs of the participants. When all participants are done writing and gluing, everybody may read the Post-It notes that were written for them.

What you ask the participants to write onto the Post-it notes should reflect the issue at hand:

- a personal strength that I observed in you
- something about you that makes me confident that we can solve the problem together
- something that I appreciate about the way we work together
- something positive that I heard from others about you
- something you should keep doing.

For some people, this exercise is initially a bit embarrassing. At least in Central Europe, we are not so used to giving and taking compliments. When you do engage participants in this exercise, you will be rewarded by the smiling faces of the participants when they read their Post-It notes.

This exercise can work well online. The team coach needs some preparation beforehand to make sure they are comfortable with using a collaborative tool such as Mural, Miro or Jamboard. Using a Miro board, you can create several boards pre-labelled with the name of each participant. Everyone will "glue" Post-It notes mentioning what they appreciate about every other participant in the respective board. If you want to give it even more of a similar feel to the exercise in a live environment, you can upload a picture of a chair and replicate it so that each participant can "glue on the back of a chair" or insert a picture of each participant. Doing it like that in Miro allows you also to decide whether you want to keep the comments anonymous as people won't be able to trace the Post-It notes back to those who added them. In case you want to keep it simple and avoid using a Miro, simply ask participants to use the chat and send private messages to each other using the given structure.

"ONE FOR ALL AND ALL FOR ONE!"

Ask the participants to pair up. Each pair should talk about a few things that have recently been going well. The goal of the conversation is to identify four strengths that both have in common. In the next round, two pairs talk to each other and try to identify at least two strengths that the four of them share. Once this is successful, two groups of four people (eight people overall) try to identify one strength that everybody has in common. If you have an unequal group size, you can also use differently sized groups (for example three, five or seven people). You can obviously also use other encouraging questions or questions that generate hope, such as "Find things that make you confident that you can improve something" or "Collect positive remarks that you have heard about yourself from customers". The success of this exercise depends on the company and its culture – take care that this does not become too embarrassing for anyone. This exercise can easily be converted into an online form by creating different spaces on a Miro/Mural and observing how the StickyNotes are merging.

A PERSONAL SUPERLATIVE

Every participant thinks about something they think they are best at, compared with everybody else in the group – for example, "the best singer", "the best tennis player". This exercise is very short and funny, and has led to the foundation of choirs, dance clubs and tennis groups in companies. What is important for the atmosphere is that it is clear that this is not a serious competition, but that anything can be mentioned as a "personal superlative", even if it is silly. We usually start by giving our own example: "I think I am best at folding paper planes." Another variant of this is the question "What is my superpower?" which can also be accompanied by everyone drawing or creating a picture of them as the respective superhero.

You may want to consider creating a Mural/Miro space where participants can upload pictures related to their personal superlative. Be mindful of the data privacy once participants upload personal pictures: this online space should not be shared outside the team without agreement.

PRE-SESSION CHANGE

In team coaching, just like in individual coaching, you can build on the positive developments that happened between the time of setting up the meeting and the first meeting.

You can ask "What's better?" at the beginning of each team coaching step – even when you are just starting and negotiating the contract ("Since you started to think about engaging in the team coaching process, what has already happened in the right direction?"). When you start the team coaching process with individual interviews, you can ask this question at the beginning of each interview. It can be an important point in a report or it can be the start of any meeting. This question focuses the attention on progress and also clarifies what exactly should be better and what the right direction seems to be. It also creates confidence. It is often easier to start when the first step has been taken.

There are several ways to facilitate a discussion on this question.

COPING QUESTIONS

Coping questions happen when they are called for in plenary discussions or when we observe small-group discussions. It is not often a planned step in facilitation. There are rarely situations in which it is clear from the beginning that the team has to come to terms with an unchangeable structure. If at all, they happen when two teams are being merged and there are restructurings or layoffs with outplacement. In these cases, it can make sense to reserve a slot in the facilitation to acknowledge the difficulties and express appreciation for the resources that the team has already demonstrated in dealing with the difficulties.

The following forms of facilitation have shown to be suitable:

[a] *Plenary discussion.* You can ask each participant for a contribution in the plenary, answering the question "How have you managed to deal well with the situation?" Depending on the atmosphere and the team, you can then visualize the answers on the flipchart or simply listen to them.
- *Work in pairs or small groups.* Working in pairs or small groups is another possibility for answering coping questions. One of the difficulties of working in small groups or pairs is the fact that they sometimes (understandably so) ignore the instructions, "Please talk about what you are already doing to deal with the situation. Identify tips and hints that others might also be able to use", and creatively (and sadly, less usefully) redefine them to mean "Talk about all the things that are going wrong, how terribly you are suffering, and why nobody is listening to you." If you are working with pairs or small groups, it is important to be clear with instructions, maybe give a rationale and state why it is not useful to talk about how terrible things are at this point (since this is probably something that people are doing on their own time already quite a lot). However, this does not mean that it is not a bad situation or that, as a facilitator, we want to ignore the difficulty, but that looking at how people are coping might help the others. During the discussions of the small groups or pairs, it makes sense to keep an eye on what they are doing and redirect the discussions if they are not useful. Sometimes a coping question turns out to be too early and people need the time to vent and have the difficulty acknowledged – but that is very difficult to know in advance.

COLLECTING PARTICIPANTS' COMMENTS ABOUT "WHAT IS BETTER IN YOUR VIEW?" ON A FLIPCHART OR WHITEBOARD

Collecting participants' answers in the plenary is fast, and all participants can listen and understand what is important for everybody else. When you're talking about "what's better" in the plenary, the facilitator can also take care that the perception of all participants is acknowledged as valid. The things one person takes as better do not have to be the same for everyone. It makes no sense to discuss the differences in perception at this point. When you are facilitating this discussion, you can also help the group to avoid slipping back into the usual "what we think needs to be better". Online, this can easily be facilitated by writing on a slide, a whiteboard, the chat, a shared document and so on.

SMALL-GROUP DISCUSSIONS ABOUT "WHAT IS BETTER?"

You can also create small groups instead of having a plenary discussion. The day could begin with small groups going for a walk and talking about "What is better?" Each small group can take a few Post-It notes to jot down their thoughts. Of course, this exercise can also be conducted on tables or standing up. Experience shows that going for a walk takes the longest, small-group discussions with seated participants are not so long, and discussions when people are standing up require the least time. A walk should be around 30 minutes, the seated small-group discussions 20 minutes, and standing-up discussions 15 minutes. If there are several small groups writing Post-It notes about "What is better?", the answers are usually more varied than when you are working in a plenary.

Another advantage of working with Post-It Notes is that you can see how frequently an answer is given. For example, if several small groups notice that the atmosphere has improved, this perception is strengthened by the frequency. In this situation, it makes sense to cluster (sort according to topic) the Post-It notes after the exercise. It can also be useful to look at these perceived changes in the right direction with the group and talk about which of them should definitely continue. It is also very important that everybody's perception of positive change is acknowledged and validated. For example, if Mr Jones contradicts, "But I don't think our atmosphere has improved", it is important that the facilitator clarifies that not all changes have to be noticed by everyone. Every team member has their own perception and perspective, and that is the beauty of teamwork.

In such situations, the facilitator can also invite the group to continue by observing what works in order to establish their own multipartiality and appreciation for everybody's contribution: "Ah, Mr Jones, that's very interesting! Why don't you think about what Ms Smith could have observed that tells her that the atmosphere has improved and maybe also think about how you would notice an improvement in the team atmosphere? Please don't give an answer right now – have a think and observe for a little bit."

"SPEED-DATING": "WHAT IS BETTER?"

"Speed-dating" is a very nice way to start a workshop day in a fun and active fashion. This form has many names and you can also find it described as "the solution onion" in the book *57 SF Activities* (Röhrig & Clarke, 2008, pp. 61–65). You divide the group in half, with the same number of participants in each group. One group stands in an inner circle facing outward while the other group stands in an outside circle facing inward. This way, two participants are standing opposite each other, one in the inside circle, one in the outside circle. The facilitator asks the group to discuss a predetermined question for a few minutes. These can be banal questions such as "How was your trip?" or more meaningful questions such as "What in the workshop are you interested in today?" or "What has already gone in the right direction since we made the appointment for this meeting?" This way of facilitation activates participants, creates a relaxed mood and is fun. Participants can talk about important and not so important topics. You can also try and visualize the answers to the questions by distributing Post-It Notes; however, this creates a more serious mood. If the visualization is necessary or desired, you can also collect the questions after each round and put the results of the exercise on a flipchart. You can facilitate this online with breakout rooms, but it takes very good organizational skills from the facilitator to ensure you mix the pairs each time.

INDIVIDUAL WORK WITH POST-IT NOTES: "WHAT IS BETTER?"

Of course, you can also ask participants to work on the question "What is better?" individually. Each participant writes their answers on Post-It notes. Working individually is often very helpful because it gives participants time to really think for themselves. In my own experience, it is a real treasure when you can tap into the creativity and power of observation of many different people in this way. Individual work is not often used in teams or groups. It is a format that people are not used to – which is why it might not be appropriate for every situation, especially at the beginning of the workshop. It depends on the group, how important the topic "What is better?" is and the momentary mood of the facilitator.

WORK IN SMALL GROUPS OR PAIRS ON: "WHAT DID WE GET RIGHT IN THE LAST MONTHS?"

Asking about highlights in the last months is an alternative to the question "What is better?" You can ask small groups or pairs to discuss the question "What did we get right in the last months?" or "What were good moments in the previous months?" You can find a good description of how to facilitate this in Röhrig & Clarke (2008) in a contribution by Mark McKergow entitled "Sparkling Moments". Depending on the team culture, you can vary the intensity of the question. In the United States, you would probably ask, "What are you really proud of?" In Germany or Japan, you might ask, "What could have gone worse in the last months?" or "What wasn't too bad?"

Online, the team coach can prepare a Miro board guiding the team to reflect on what has been better and what they have noticed about the team with different coaching questions. The link to the board can be sent in advance to participants so they can start thinking about it and collect their thoughts. During the workshop, even if ideas were collected already on the board, some time should be allocated to the conversation about the items mentioned and what it is that the team did to get to those results – the resources they now have.

Case 2.5:   Discovery walk

Cristina was invited to facilitate a workshop for a group of teachers returning to face-to-face meetings after two years of working remotely during the COVID-19 pandemic. The sponsor mentioned that it would be important for the group to exchange their views on the difficulties brought by the previous years.

Right after the start of the workshop, after the introduction round, everyone was invited to stand up and build small groups of four to five teachers and, in groups, walk around the garden at the event location. Cristina instructed them to use 15 minutes of walking in one direction only to express all the difficulties and struggles. Once the time was over, she asked them to turn around and use the next 15 minutes in the same groups to talk about what was better, how they coped with the changes, what helped them in those situations and so on.

At the end of the walk, they were invited inside, where they could collect the useful things they did.

TEAM CHARTER/TEAM RULES

To build trust and safety within the team, and especially to support the contribution of all team members, you might want to consider inviting the team to engage in a conversation about their engagement.

Building a conversation at the start of the workshop on their best hopes about how they will work together and the values they want to bring to the process will allow the team to express elements that will be relevant to "landscape of identity".

ROLE OF THE COACH

The role of the team coach will be introduced from the beginning before the interviews take place. Nevertheless, it might be extremely valuable for the team to refresh their understanding role of the team coach at the start of the first workshop. You can also expand that and engage in a small exercise of asking the team what other qualities you should bring to the team coaching process that they have noticed during the interview stage.

Trust and safety during the workshop

BREAKS

Breaks create a wonderful moment for the team to reflect and re-engage. You may want to consider creating a schedule that allows some flexibility for breaks.

We often get the question "And what if the team asks me a question or if we drift in a different topic?" The best answer to such situations is, "Simply take a 15-minute break." It will generate enough time for the team coach to reconsider the approach and to evaluate the structure of the next activity in a way that best responds to the current needs of the team. Most importantly, it takes away the pressure of performing on the spot. Breaks are especially important online – not necessarily for communication, but for everyone's wellbeing.

EVERYONE WHO WANTS TO SPEAK CAN SPEAK

"Everyone should get the same amount of time to speak." Or at least that is what we keep on being told about how the best workshops should be run. We believe the quality of the workshop does not depend on everyone having same amount of "air-time", but rather on creating a space where everyone can feel safe and welcome to share their thoughts, knowing they will be taken seriously. Yes, some might end up talking for 10 minutes, while others do so for only three minutes. Each team member has the same chance of contributing during the time in a way that fits them.

Clearly, you will encounter team members who have the ability to talk for an extensive amount of time. In those cases, timeboxing is a great tool. If you are using an online collaborative tool, add a timer to it that will be visible to all participants. Our friend Art Pitmann uses his Zoom background for facilitation: he has a green background, switches it to yellow when someone has been talking too long and to red when they are supposed to stop. For on-site workshops, you might want to bring a speaker or simply use your mobile phone with a timer. A creative idea might be to bring a sand clock and use it also a token showing who is speaking at that moment and at the same time to timebox the interventions.

ALL IDEAS TAKEN SERIOUSLY

The Solution Focused approach is a respectful way of engaging that invites co-creation. With a Solution Focused mindset, we are already setting the foundation to take all ideas seriously and appreciate contributions (even if they seem difficult at first). As team coach, we also have the role of modelling the approach, hence it is on us to show appreciation for all contributions: We assume that every person in the room has good intentions and that the input that they are bringing is based on good reasons. Staying curious about these good intentions and asking clarifying questions will support surfacing these valuable contributions and ensuring that everyone is taken seriously.

During the workshops to facilitate the exchange of ideas and contributions, we could:

- include all team members in the breakout rooms/working groups and consider creating mixed groups
- ask for everybody's contributions: use facilitation techniques like "think, pair, share" and small groups to enable reticent people to make themselves heard
- reflect with team on how they want to work together
- model good communication – encourage good communication
- observe the team and surface it when something seems off.

Topics that are of value to the team, but that are not specifically related to the current conversation, can be added to "the parking lot". It's an extremely useful tool to keep track of contributions, topics for future workshops, wishes, changes and so on. In an online environment, simply add a frame on Mural/Miro for the Parking Lot and explain to the team what it is for. You may want to leave it also to them to add Post-It notes at any point to capture ideas without disturbing the entire group. For a workshop running on site, plan in advance to have a separate flipchart or simply a flipchart page glued to a wall/door where Post-It notes can be collected/ideas written down. Most importantly, don't be phased, surprised or offended by anything – stay in a spirit of collaboration.

Moves: Ticket office

With prior interviews

The mind map constructed on the basis of input from individual interviews represents a great starting point for defining objectives.

You might want to simply start by sharing the mind map and give time for everyone to read the thoughts collected. If you are running the workshop in an online environment, prepare a Miro/Mural/Jamboard space in advance with the structure of the workshop, including the mind map. This allows participants to have all the information in one spot and if needed at any later point, they can go back to the mind map without any troubles. If you are on site, consider whether you want to have a couple of printouts. This is especially useful if you intend to ask the team to work in pairs/groups.

Once the team has been able to review the results, you might want to invite the team to reflect upon what have they noticed, either in pairs/groups or by sharing directly with the group (if the size of the team is not too large).

A useful approach from Agile is to create small groups to discuss the topic for a set time. Once the time is up, the groups are merged, two groups at a time, with the result that at the end of all rounds you will have the entire team coming together.

Each round of merging can be used to narrow down on objectives. For example, from the first round, Group A collected three ideas, while Group B also collected three ideas. After the merger, the new group has to have three joint ideas – it might be that they vote, discuss, merge or simply come up with something new altogether.

Without prior interviews

SURVEY/POLL/VIRTUAL SPACE

In case you don't have the time, or the organization is not accepting the idea of running individual interviews prior to the workshops, you might want to consider doing a survey or a poll with a couple of scaling questions or simply create a board in Miro/Mural and invite everyone to share any thoughts they might have before the workshop. You will need to review that space regularly as there might be questions raised to which participants might expect an answer before the workshop.

Case 2.6:   Scaling instead of interviews

Working with a volunteer-based board of an NGO was a challenge in terms of time investment – each member of that board had several things on their list and finding time to do interviews was not exactly a high priority. Cristina decided to adjust the structure and create a short survey based on five elements surfaced by the president of the board. For each of those five elements, a scaling question was included along with a text space for sharing further thoughts. In that way, initial input was still collected allowing for a starting base in the ticket office phase.

The five elements were again surveyed at the end of the process to provide a space for reflection for the team on its achievements.

BRAINSTORMING

On the Mural/Miro or on the flipchart, team members can collect ideas of objectives for the team coaching process. Once the brainstorming phase is over, you will need to cluster those ideas. Trusting the team to cluster them generates a wonderful opportunity for the team to work together and take ownership of the process. Additionally, it allows for clarification around the meaning of certain Post-It notes.

Another way of facilitating the collection of ideas is to use Mentimeter/Menti (or any other similar tool). Each participant can answer a couple of questions using their mobile phone and afterwards see the collective response. This, however, has the disadvantage that you cannot cluster the items.

Plenary discussion with flipchart

Using a flipchart to visualize the discussion about goals is a quick way to clarify what needs to happen so the process is worthwhile. In the goal-setting phase, it is especially important that the team agrees on at least the general direction of the desired development. Therefore, all team members should listen to the goals of everybody else. When you are working with a flipchart in the plenary, this will happen automatically. It is important that the facilitator writes down all the stated goals. In a Solution Focused goal-setting process, you rarely have conflicting goals because you are talking about what needs to be better after the team coaching process, not about how to reach that state. In the rare case that you do have conflicting goals, the facilitator can ask for the goal behind the goal before writing anything down on the flipchart. Examples of eliciting the goal behind the goal might be:

- When you have achieved this, what will be better? What else?
- Can you explain a little bit about the background of your goal? What would you like to achieve for the team?
- What difference will it make?

Sometimes, previously mentioned goals change in this situation. As facilitator, you can then strike out the point on the flipchart and choose a different formulation.

Case 2.7:   More or less communication?

A German-American team could not agree on their goal – the Americans wanted more communication during a project. The Germans were disturbed in their work by the constant meetings and telephone conferences. So the team coach asked the Americans, "What would be better if you communicated more?" The Americans answered, "We would have more transparency. We would know who is working on what. We would be able to present the project status to our superiors more easily."

The team coach then asked the Germans: "What would be better if you had fewer meetings and telephone conferences?" The Germans said, "We would simply get down to business, do our work and could justify the project much more easily to our superiors since something is actually getting done."

"I understand," said the team coach, "So everybody wants to know the current project status, who is working on what, and both want to be able to present the project in a favourable light to their superiors."

The group replied: "Yes" and "Ja". That was a goal that both sides could work on.

The team coaching session ended with an agreement to start an experiment. The team set up a SharePoint site. Every morning, each team member entered what they were working on and how far they had progressed the day before. The SharePoint site also offered a discussion space in which people could share and discuss their ideas. Both sides put in their slides for the project presentation for their respective managements. Meetings were reduced by half and the experiment proved very successful.

Pretend feedback round

Conducting a make-believe feedback round is a very nice way to facilitate goal-setting in workshops or team coaching processes. The group pretends it is the last day of the workshop or the process, shortly before everything ends. As usual in workshops, the facilitator asks the group for feedback. Every participant states why they found the workshop especially helpful. The facilitator can visualize the replies on the flipchart; however, this can interrupt the creative flow of this method. You can also simply conduct a fictitious feedback round verbally and then ask every participant to write down their most important points on Post-It notes and stick them onto a flipchart or wall. You can then cluster the Post-It notes and prioritize them if you want. In a Solution Focused process, prioritization is not about deciding on the one and only priority that guarantees success. It is more about considering what to start with.

Letter from the future

Participants are asked to choose a future point in time and pretend they are already there. From that point in time (a positive but realistic future), they write a letter to themselves. This method was introduced into Solution Focused coaching by Yvonne Dolan (1991, p. 132). You can use this form of facilitation for goal-setting in many different ways:

- Pretend it is the year 20XX and our team coaching process was very successful; everything is just the way you would like it to be. Write a letter to yourself and tell your old self what was useful in the team coaching process. Also tell yourself what has improved and how life is for the team in the year 20XX.
- It is the year 20XX. You've won a prize for the best team and a newspaper is writing an article about you. Work in small groups and write this article.

- It is the year 20XX. Another team sees how successful you have been and would like to know what you did to make it happen. Work in small groups/in the plenary and describe your success. If you are working in small groups, you can then have half of the small groups interview the other half about how they made this success happen.

Drawing a picture

This method is especially useful when you are working with a team of creative people. Participants create a picture of their desired future – either individually or together. Afterwards, you create a gallery by hanging up the works of art. If the pictures were created individually, you can ask the "artists" to comment on their work.

More creative methods can be found under the section on the Miracle Question in Chapter 1.

- Create a problem list – turn into what people want instead.
- Rant walk/rant breakout rooms – ask people to walk for five minutes in one direction talking about what is not going well, then turn around and walk in the opposite direction talking about what they want instead, or send a message to breakout rooms after five minutes to switch to "what instead".

Moves: Preferred future

Understanding the team's and individuals' preferred future, in depth and detail, will help to deliver the best results of the team coaching process. One of the most powerful moves you can use to get this rich description is the Miracle Question.

There are many different ways to facilitate the Miracle Question in a team coaching process. It is important to take care that the description of the miracle of each team member remains uncontested and that everyone's perspective is acknowledged. If there are contradictory descriptions, the team coach might ask, "So, if this part of the miracle happens for you, what will be better?" Usually what looks like a contradictory description at first glance then dissolves into a picture that can be shared by all. The same is true for answers that may seem silly at first.

Case 2.8: The Russian countess

We were once consulting with the management team of a large Eastern European luxury hotel in a mixture between a strategy session and a management team-building event. We had asked a traditional Miracle Question and the group was working on it in small groups writing their answers on a flipchart. The atmosphere was relaxed and happy, and you could assume from the laughter that was audible behind the flipcharts that the groups were having fun answering the question. The main reason for the mirth became apparent in the ensuing plenary discussion: two out of three groups had described the following story as part of their miracle: "Countess XY is no longer sitting at the bar starting at five o'clock every day, drunk and bothering our international clients." Of course, this is not a well-formulated goal. It is specific and realistic, but it is stated negatively and not really in the influence of the hotel management. We asked the group: "So if Countess XY is no longer sitting at the bar, drunk, what is better?" The group generated answers like: "We could offer a professional bar service", "The international consulting companies could use our bar as a meeting point after work", "These companies then might also choose our hotel to host their guests or conferences." We could work on the goals stated in these answers irrespective of the presence or absence of Countess XY – which turned out not to be the decisive factor after all.

Small groups or plenary

If you encourage the group to work on the Miracle Questions in small groups, you have the advantage that everybody can describe their miracle. On the other hand, it is also very useful for the team when they hear how every team member imagines a positive future for the team. It becomes apparent that every team member wants to imagine a positive development and is therefore also likely engaged in creating it. A positive image that the team members have of each other is created or supported, which in turn is very useful for the further process. Depending on the group size, you can decide what is more important: giving each individual team member time and space to discuss a personal miracle, or sharing the miracle in the plenary.

If in doubt, we would tend to ask the Miracle Question in the plenary with the larger group. Another alternative is asking the team members to jot down bullet points individually for five or ten minutes, describing their day after the miracle. These bullet points are then shared afterwards in the plenary. You can also apply Post-It notes to the individual work, asking everyone to use black markers and write only one point on each Post-It note. You can then use a wall chart or flipchart to cluster and visualize the answers to the Miracle Question.

Another possibility is asking the follow-up questions to the miracle question one after the other. You start with: "How are you going to start realizing that the miracle has happened?" and ask the participants to write down their answers on Post-It notes. You then asked the plenary: "Who else will notice that the miracle has happened?" You can then create a stakeholder mind map on a flipchart where each individual branch is a person or group of people who will notice that a miracle happened (Figure 2.2).

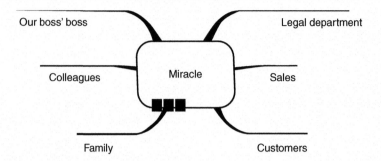

Figure 2.2 Stakeholder map.

You then create small groups, each of which works on the signs that will tell one stakeholder group that the miracle must have happened. One group might work on what their families might notice, while the other might work on what their colleagues will notice, and the next might work on what the legal department will notice. They all collect their answers on flipcharts (or pieces of flipchart paper if you do not have enough flipcharts). These flipcharts are then hung up on the wall and read by everyone. Usually many answers are created, which makes it necessary to start a process of prioritization. This can be facilitated by using sticky dots or votes. Scaling is also a relatively simple way to prioritize the answers. For each flipchart, you could ask: "On a scale of 0 to 10, where 10 is the morning your stakeholder groups realize that the miracle must have happened and 0 is the opposite, where are you now? What is already working well? What would be a next small step?" Online, you would simply use a digital whiteboard rather than flipcharts.

Miracle board

There are many creative ways to facilitate the miracle question. It is fun to describe a desired future together, and this mood can also influence the method of facilitation. When you are working with a "miracle board", you draw three lines on the flipchart to create six spaces which are then used to create "scenes" or "pictures". Small groups or individuals start by drawing the last image: the morning after the miracle. It is very useful to give the instruction that the image should show the team acting, doing something the morning after the miracle; otherwise, you run the risk that the description of the future has nothing to do with the daily reality that the team desires after the miracle – for example, we all won the lottery, the aliens have landed and have solved all our problems. The pictures before the last picture should show moments that are a bit like being on the way to the miracle situation. The first image should be a real incident from the team's past that was like the miracle, such as a "forerunner" of the miracle. After drawing the flipcharts, they are hung up in the room and the participants have time to look at them. Afterwards you can move on to scaling. Online, just use digital whiteboards with prepared spaces for the scenes.

Role-play in the future/videos

The basic idea of the "miracle board" is that team members create a rich and vivid image of the desired future, then go back to the first sign of the miracle that happened in the past. This basic idea can also be implemented with other media. The participants can role-play significant moments or shoot short video sequences. Especially when you are working on a strategic new orientation or when there have been significant changes in the team, this method can be really useful to store the results of the miracle question as videos and keep them accessible for a while – for example, on a shared server or hard drive. Technically, this has become rather easy – most participants use smartphones, which are capable of recording short video sequences with sufficient quality. Apple and Microsoft computers usually come with free programs that you can use to edit the videos. The group doesn't necessarily have to be together physically to do this – everyone can shoot their own little video and you can then invite the group to edit into a whole video, or the video can be a recorded virtual meeting (a bit boring, but why not!).

Pinboard-timeline

Kirsten once developed a really simple visualization of the miracle question for a workshop. The basic idea is the "timeline". Create a long stretch of flipchart paper on the wall by gluing four or five flipcharts together at the short end. Start with the description of the miracle at the end of the timeline. Everybody can jot down the most important elements of their miracle with markers on Post-It notes and stick them onto the last flipchart, labelled "miracle". When you are facilitating this, take care to ask about concrete signs of the miracle: "How will you notice that a miracle has happened?"

In larger groups, you can also assign different perspectives – for example, part of the group describes how the customers will notice that a miracle has happened and the other part describes how top management will notice it. The different perspectives can be visualized by different-coloured Post-It notes. After sticking the miracle Post-It notes to the end of the timeline, you can work back to the present and describe the incidents in which signs of the miracle are apparent. You can also reserve one or two flipcharts for the past, where the group is invited to write down incidents that already were a little bit similar to after the miracle; this gives them confidence that it is possible for the team to take steps in the direction of the miracle. Online, you use a whiteboard, Mural or Miro instead.

A fictitious meeting

Holding a fictitious meeting in the future is a shorter way of facilitating the Miracle Question. The team imagines the miracle has happened and they are holding the meeting in the future. The team members can either play themselves in the future and talk about what they appreciate about the new situation, or they can take the roles of important stakeholders and reflect on the wonderful development of the team from an outside perspective. The latter variant is very useful for strategy development processes. It is also quite useful to take care that the answers are somewhat realistic.

Visualizing the fictitious meeting in the future can be a little difficult – you can record the meeting on video or audio, then summarize or visualize afterwards; however, this is a lot of work, takes time and the answers are not available immediately. Another possibility is asking an assistant to jot down the most important points on the flipchart or using Post-It notes. On occasion, I have simply recorded the most important contributions by typing them quickly into my computer and sorting them later with the group by showing them via data projector. Here, the online version is much easier – you can record the session, then note the most important points by watching it again.

Press conference in the future

The team collects all the stakeholders who would notice progress. If you have a large team, you ask small groups to prepare what the respective stakeholder group would notice. In smaller teams, you assign one stakeholder group to each participant, give them a few minutes to prepare and then hold a press conference, pretending that it happens in the future and all has gone well. The team coach plays the journalist asking Solution Focused questions such as, "Wow, what a wonderful success! Stakeholder group 1, what are you noticing about this success? What impact did it have on you?"

In the virtual space, you can record the session and transcribe it. Face to face, recording and transcribing might be a good idea, or you could have another coach present who visualizes the most important ideas that emerge.

Going for a walk

Sending the participants for a walk in groups of two or three is very simple way of facilitating the Miracle Question. Most often, participants appreciate being able to get up and move. Often, when you go for a walk, you also have more creative ideas than when you are stuck in a conference room. For visualization, ask the group to take markers and Post-It notes, or simply ask people to report on their ideas and write them down on the flipchart when the group returns.

Writing an article

You can invite the team to write an article about their success in the future. They could split up into small groups and each group writes in the style of a different newspaper: *The Times, Washington Post, National Enquirer, The Sun, The Daily Mirror, The Financial Times* and so on.

There are plenty of other facilitation techniques. We will list some more ideas, but what you choose will always depend on what best fits the clients:

- Working on creating a metaphor for the team together
- Creating a joint picture of the team using newspaper clips, pictures or a vision board
- Writing a piece of code (suited to IT companies)
- Campfire conversations (goes very well if you create the space to reflect that either in Miro with some pictures and the structure, or on a site connected to team-building activities)
- Exploring the desired future by engaging in "Suppose that …" types of activities: "Suppose you have received an award for the best team; Suppose you have been recognized as …; Suppose you are doing a press conference on …; Suppose someone talks about you in a book – what would they say?"
- You may also want to draw inspiration from Agile coaching and do a retrospective in the future.

Case 2.9:   A miracle award

Working with the board of an association created by coaches to support refugees, it was natural for Cristina to invite them to imagine that they had been nominated by ICF Global for an award.

The team members were invited to think about what they would like to be mentioned in the ICF presentation of who the team was as an NGO and how the organization contributed to refugee relief using coaching. It was a wonderful space for them to start considering how their current vision needed to be adjusted.

Moves: Successful past

Once you have defined the desired future, the team needs a way to transform that into something tangible and reachable. This is where scaling questions can be very useful. They allow the team members to measure where they are on their path to the desired future and represent a measurable perception of progress, as you can come back to the scale throughout the team coaching process. The location on the scale is not so relevant, as it opens up the conversation on all the times that the team succeeded in achieving their goals.

Scaling walk

The scaling walk illustrates the scale in the physical space. You take one corner of the room to be the 10, the other a 1 or 0. (Katalin Hankovszky lets each person pick a different spot in the room as their 10. This way, nobody can know where the others are on their scale.) Participants position themselves physically on the point on the scale at which they see themselves at the moment. The ensuing questions can be accompanied by movements. If you are talking about what is still working or what is going well, you can ask the group to look towards the direction of 0. If you are talking about the effects of a next step, everybody in the group can actually take a step forward. Usually, the individual team members are quite distributed on the scale. This way you get natural small groups, which can then discuss the following questions together. You can use pinboards or flipcharts to visualize. One flipchart could have the heading "What is still/already working well?" and the other "Next steps". The "Next steps" flipchart is usually quite suitable for clustering and determining areas that need to be talked about to advance a step on the scale. Online, you don't use a flipchart, but prepare a digital whiteboard.

Exercise 2.1: Scaling walk for self-coaching

Why don't you try a scaling walk when you are facing a problem by yourself? Position 10 is somewhere in the room and exemplifies the solution which you want to have. Put yourself on the 10 and contemplate what exactly is different at a 10. Then step onto the point where you are now and think about what tells you that you are already there and not at 0. Then take the next step in the direction of 10. How will you notice that you are one step ahead? Who else will notice and what will that tell them?

Case 2.10:   Scaling walk in training situations

A pharmaceutical company had discovered that its sales reps were having difficulties talking effectively to "key opinion leaders" – in their case, important medical doctors, professors and heads of research institutes. However, to place a highly effective new medication, it was important to convince these "key opinion leaders". The new product had many advantages for patients and the patent for the old medication of the same company would soon expire. Several sales reps had argued successfully that patients should be shifted to the new medication, but other reps were having more difficulties. The pharmaceutical company therefore wanted to conduct a workshop to increase competence and exchange best practices.

We used the scaling walk at the beginning of the workshop. After goal-setting, it was clear to everyone why it was so important to push the new medication. The personal targets of the reps were aligned with the company goals and the incentive structure had been adapted. Everyone was also convinced that the new medication offered many advantages for the patients.

We had a large room for 25 participants. Everyone positioned them-selves on the scale from 1 to 10, with 10 being "I like to talk to key opinion leaders about our new product and I know exactly how I can convince them of its usefulness and effectiveness" and 1 "the opposite". We then asked the participants to form a line and walk from one end of the line (the participants who had no problems talking to key opinion leaders) to the other end of the line (the participants who were less confident about their skills). This way, we had small groups of par-ticipants who were mixed between more confident and less confident people. There was also one group where everybody was sort of halfway confident (and, of course, the scale only told us about the confidence, not about the actual skills).

These groups of around four people wrote on Post-It notes what was already working for them. We then clustered the answers on pinboards. It became quite clear that many exchanges of best practices had already taken place in the small groups, and everyone had increased their com-petence and confidence. Our next question to the same groups was, "How will the key opinion leaders notice that you are one step ahead on the scale?" We also clustered these answers, and it became appar-ent that there were several topics that could usefully be worked on in small groups. For example, there was one group on "a summary of relevant studies" and one group on "How can I convince people when I know that my medical expertise is far below that of my conversation partners?"

Although we did not have any deeper knowledge of the subject mat-ter of "How can I convince key opinion leaders in medicine?" we were able to help the participants answer all important questions. Every rep had advanced one or two steps. We were lucky enough to be able to conduct a follow-up day a few weeks later, when participants reflected their experiences together. We also conducted a scaling walk and were very happy to notice that the whole group had significantly moved in the direction of 10. This was also an impressive confirmation for the people who had hired us.

Plenary discussion with flipchart

You can also facilitate a scaling question with the whole group using visuals on a flipchart. You take one or two flipcharts and hang them up horizontally. You draw a long line in the middle of the flipcharts and add numbers 0 (or 1) to 10. Yvonne Dolan uses this visualization for the scale in her individual sessions. She draws an arrow instead of the line to signify that even after 10, development is possible. After you have drawn the line on the flipchart, the participants take sticky dots to mark their positions. If you want an anonymous process, you can hang up the flipcharts in a different room, behind a pinboard, and so on. The participants then stick their dots onto the scale during a break when nobody else can see this happening. The subsequent questions can be asked in the plenary or in small groups. Scaling can very easily be integrated in any online facilitation tool as you can create a line and allow participants to add Post-It notes to mark where they are. To make it more personal, you may want to consider inviting them to create their own avatar that they can use throughout the exercises and place that on the scale. Working digitally, you have the advantage that you can create the possibility of anonymous contributions.

Raising your hand

If you have a very large group and it is not practical for everyone to move around – be it to the location of the flipcharts or in the form of a scaling walk – you can also ask the participants to indicate their position on the scale through a show of hands. Raising your hand up as high as possible indicates 10, and lowering your hand as far as possible indicates 0. Online, you would take "the top of your screen" as a 10 and "the bottom of your screen" as a 0 and participants can move their hands in the video to indicate where they are now.

Humming

If you are working with large groups and on topics that make it difficult for participants to be open about their assessment, you can ask the participants to start humming when you call out a given number. Humming is not as obvious as raising one's hand, and the whole process is usually fun and lightens the mood.

Highlights from the past

Allowing the time for the team to spend exploring the successful past can be facilitated in multiple ways:

- Ask the team to split in small groups and do partner interviews of the past successful events. You might want to prepare cards or notes with Solution Focused questions that can help them guide the conversation towards collecting what is it that they have done to make it a success.
- Create a timeline with the entire team of past highlights either on a flipchart or online on a Miro/Mural. As this will be a plenary exercise, you might need to ensure you get everyone to share.
- *Small group cascade:* each team member collects highlights individually, then they form groups of two and share those; then the groups merge one more time into groups of four and then eight. Throughout the rounds, collect adjectives that describe the team based on those successful events.

Resource gossip

This type of exercise can be used as a warm-up exercise, as a catalyst for collecting ideas on the successful past and as a closing round for the team to generate ideas about what each team member can do more of.

Participants are invited to sit in a circle or in small groups. One participant sits in the middle while other are invited to "gossip" about their colleague in the centre. The "gossip" is focused on positive traits. Different questions can be used:

- What are things that X did today that you want to see more of?
- What did X do in the last year/month/week that impressed you/that had a positive impact on the team?
- What do you appreciate about X?

If you are running this in an online format, use a board in Miro/Mural to simulate the structure and ask the participant who is sitting in the middle to close their microphone and camera while others are sharing.

Case 2.11:   In spite of everything, what went well?

Cristina was invited to facilitate the meeting of a group of teachers from Bavaria responsible for all secondary school subjects. They were a team of teams, as they were only coming together to consult, but each had their own objectives at the subject level.

The sponsor asked that a conversation around the COVID-19 pandemic was accommodated to better prepare them to move on. Therefore, Cristina invited them to reflect upon the things their colleagues did during that time that supported the team and created a positive and empowering atmosphere. To match the time constraints, each participant received three pages where they could write down their feedback for the team members with whom they were working. After 15 minutes' writing time, they were invited to exchange papers.

The feedback from the participants was that they were reminded of the small actions they took, and they had not been aware that they were so much appreciated.

Moves: Gift shop

In the "gift shop" the team coach invites the team to consider experiments, actions, anything that they would like to do after the session in order to facilitate their growth. Usually, teams will have their own methods of planning and accountability structures. Today, most teams use software such as Asana, Trello and Jira – our advice is to use whatever they are using. Here are some tips for facilitating the emergence of "post workshop experiments".

Decision-making

It is quite useful to make sure as facilitator that the people who are given action points or to-dos by the team are also willing and happy to take them on and that the team leader agrees. It is important to clarify within the team coaching process what can be decided by whom (you can find more about this in the section on clarifying the contract.) If it is not clear whether a possible decision is within the power of the people present, it is better to err on the side of caution and ask, or give the team the task of asking whether this is within the scope of their decision-making power. Otherwise, it can be really frustrating if the team decides upon measures that cannot be carried out due to overarching concerns. The same is true for decisions about the use of resources: the owners of these resources need to agree or be asked to agree. For example, the team can think that hiring an intern would solve many of their problems and may start planning steps to get there. If there is a company-wide hiring freeze, however, this will not help. This is the same with travel arrangements or projects that tie up hours of your own time or that of other teams.

Prioritizing

Creative teams sometimes generate a plethora of ideas for possible actions. Of course, every suggestion is welcome as an idea; however, you can sometimes not implement everything that is being suggested. The facilitator is asked to help the team to prioritize. We use traditional tools for prioritizing – although, of course, we know that it is never completely discernible which action will have the greatest success. On the other hand, you have to somehow agree on what you will try first. It is best to leave the choice of prioritization method to the group. For that, it is quite useful to explain ideas to them quickly and clearly.

EISENHOWER MATRIX

You create a matrix or a four-field diagram of "important–not important" and "urgent–not urgent" and ask the team to assign every suggested action to a space in this matrix. Visualization on a flipchart using Post-It notes or on a digital white-board is quite practical.

Case 2.12:   Prioritization with Eisenhower

As Cristina was working with a small project team, it became clear that team members were very innovative and willing to think further and expand. This led to them creating plenty of to-do items that were simply lying around creating frustration among the team members. Cristina raised this observation with the team members and engaged in a conversation around what needed to be adjusted in their way of working. It was clear that simply prioritizing tasks was not providing the desired outcome.

Hence, an Eisenhower matrix (Figure 2.3) was introduced to bring in that second dimension of "urgent–not urgent". This created for the team members a realization that they needed a different system to monitor their tasks. Asana (project-management software) was only bringing them the list of topics in the order of prioritization, and it was not matching their creative style of working.

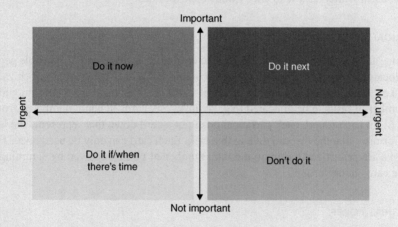

Figure 2.3 Eisenhower matrix.

SHORT-TERM/LONG-TERM SUCCESS

You can also sort the suggestions by determining whether they can be implemented quickly and promise short-term success (quick wins) or take more time but might have a lot of impact.

VOTING

Asking the group to vote on which steps to take first is a very quick way of prioritizing action points. In order to prevent a situation in which someone is unable to identify with the result because none of their suggestions were voted in, you can give every team member more than one vote per suggestion. You can visualize that by giving every team member a number of sticky dots.

SYSTEMIC CONSENSING

"Systemic consensing" (Paulus et al., 2022) is a method of collecting ideas and then evaluating them on the basis of how much resistance there is to each of them. This does not sound like a Solution Focused exercise, but it works really well in cases where there is no one great solution and all solutions have drawbacks. It works when you need to compromise. Each team member allocates a number of "strength of resistance" (for example, 0 – no resistance; 1 – would be okay but small resistance; 2 – not okay, medium resistance; 3 – no way, huge resistance) to the individual solutions and the results are added up. The solutions with the lowest resistance numbers are then discussed again. Online, this is very easy to do as you can use a whiteboard with anonymous contributions.

PRIORITIZATION POKER

Once all tasks have been defined, they have to be prioritized and responsible people allocated to them. A playful way of accommodating that is by using prioritization poker. Each team member has a set of cards in their hand up to the maximum number of tasks to be allocated (e.g. six tasks, six cards in hand, numbered from 1 to 6). In each round, each participant can put a card down that represents the level of priority that they would give to that task. Each card can only be used once. Then tasks are prioritized based on the total number of points received by summing up the cards in each round.

T-SHIRT POKER

On a flipchart or virtual board, draw the shape of a t-shirt in XS, S, M, L, XL sizes. Tasks are added to Post-It notes and all participants are invited to read the tasks and prioritize them. Of course, some Post-It notes will be moved between different t-shirt sizes as each participant can move them. Some will stabilize on a t-shirt size while for others a conversation will be needed to get the team clarifying the tasks and their understanding of the importance of each task.

Working on topics

When you are coaching a team and there are several topics that need to be covered, the team needs to decide the order of priority and how they would like to tackle the topics. This is one of the few points where a team coach might enter into thinking about the content of the session and their interdependencies. Sometimes there is a natural sequence of topics. Take the example of the old "NASA Game" exercise, where teams are asked to rank items of supply according to their usefulness after a plane crash in the desert. If the team decides to stay where they are and not move (the right decision, just so you know if you are ever in this situation), material for building shelter would rank much higher, for example, than if they decided to march through the desert (not advised). In team coaching, this could be that the team needs to decide on roles and responsibilities first before starting to work on topics, or they need to decide on a strategy before they can move into more tactical issues.

This also influences what can be dealt with in plenary and what can be delegated to small groups. It is best to ask the team about the interdependencies of the issues (as you cannot know this well as a team coach) and to find a good sequence together. This may also be done in preparation for the team coaching together with a small project group of the team.

When you have decided which topics need to be discussed first and by everyone, you can then move into working with smaller groups or breakout rooms. Here are two ways in which you can help these working groups be successful:

- *Create a briefing for the small groups.* If you ask the plenary to create a short briefing for the small groups, you will increase the likelihood of acceptance for the results of the small group work. Take a flipchart or digital whiteboard and ask the plenary, "What is important for this small group to take into account?" Take five minutes for the creation of the brief for each small group. If there is no time, you can also put the flipcharts in different spaces in the room or in different corners of the digital whiteboard so everyone who wants to contribute to a small-group topic but cannot join can provide their input.
- *Offer a structure and/or brief facilitators.* To make the discussions as fruitful as possible, ask for volunteers from the team before the team coaching session and do a mini-facilitation training session with them. Teach them the Solution Focused structure of "ticket office, preferred future, successful past and gift shop" so they can guide the discussions away from blamestorming and keep them constructive.

You might also offer the small groups a "facilitation guide" by way of a structured flipchart or a prepared digital whiteboard with Solution Focused questions:

- *Ticket office:* What would you like to achieve in today's breakout sessions? Check: is this goal in your influence, feasible, positively described (presence of something not absence of something)
- *Preferred future:* If we achieve this, what difference would it make to the respective stakeholders? Draw a mind map with the stakeholders and what they might notice?

- *Successful past.* On a scale of 0 to 10, where 10 means that you have already achieved your goal, where are you now? What is already going in the right direction?
- *Gift shop.* How would you and the stakeholders notice a step up on the scale? What will you propose as solutions to the plenary?

When they report to the plenary, ask the plenary for comments and invite them to agree on experiments (rather than feeling that this will be forever).

Implementing and accountability

As a team coach, you can also assist the team in creating structures that will make a successful implementation or experiment more likely. You can invite the team to consider what gives them hope that this will work or ask them for other ways to stay on track (even if there are glitches along the way).

KANBAN BOARD

An easy way to document what is happening in a team is the so-called "Kanban" board. It can be virtual or physical, and consists of a space with three slots: "to do", "doing" and "done". The individual tasks can be placed on (virtual) Post-It notes and whenever someone decides to take care of a "to do", they write their name on the task and move it to "doing" and then to "done" when it is completed for all to see.

INDIVIDUAL TASKS/HOMEWORK/EXPERIMENTS

If the action points are something that can be worked on individually and assigning specific tasks with due dates and resources is not workable (e.g. when the topic is "creating a better work atmosphere" or "showing more appreciation for each other"), you can ask individual team members to state what they would like to "start doing" or "do more of" in the future. In some team coaching sessions, participants are also asked about what they would like to stop doing. Solution Focused team coaching can do without that question since for us it is about what needs to happen rather than what people need to stop doing. After telling each other what they would like to start doing or do more of, team members can write down their actions on the flipchart or the facilitator can take on that task. You can also facilitate this step by asking everybody to write their actions on index cards so they can take them back to their offices as a reminder.

PETER SZABO'S IMPLEMENTATION INTERVIEWS

At the 2012 SOLWorld conference in Oxford, Peter Szabo demonstrated a nice method which can contribute to people actually implementing what they have planned. This method is especially suitable when the implementation plan focuses on things you know you should really start doing but that somehow just do not happen.

To begin, every team member answers two questions that are written down on two different pieces of paper:

- Question 1: What would you like to implement in the near future?
- Question 2: Tell a story about a time where you managed to implement or started doing something that wasn't easy at first.

The group then pairs up. In the first round, both partners tell each other their success stories without mentioning their implementation project from Question 1. After the partners have finished telling their success stories, they tell each other what was helpful or inspiring about the other partner's story. In the next step, everyone finds a new partner. First, one of the two reports their implementation project. The other partner answers: "I don't know if this has anything to do with your project, but I have a story for you."

The person then tells the success story that their previous partner shared in the previous round. If they know anyone in the group who has a similar story or can share hints that could help with implementation, they then refer the partner to that person.

The partners then switch roles.

In the end, both exchange what they learned from these conversations and how this supports them in actually implementing what they have planned.

THE "S3" METHOD

In a lot of meetings when the "action planning" stage is near, you will see a lot of people looking at the ceiling. People will share sentences that start with "someone sometime should ..." and no one actually picks up those tasks. This is how the S3 method started.

Place all the tasks that "someone should do sometime" on Post-It notes/virtual Post-It notes and ask participants to read them. Then encourage everyone to choose the tasks they want to take on and commit to doing them. At the end, there will still be some tasks left. For all of those, create a conversation about why they were perceived as important to be done but no one wants to commit to them. Maybe they weren't important after all or there are not enough resources. The main thing is to figure out what might happen to them: revise, drop, get more resources ...

CONFIDENCE, BENEFITS AND APPRECIATIVE FEEDBACK

Asking about how confident participants are that the measures they agreed upon (or the results of their team coaching) will lead to the desired improvement is another important element in Solution Focused team coaching. When we ask this question, we are sometimes surprised about the answers. As coaches, we might be very confident that the group has identified action items that are likely to lead them to success, but the group or parts of the group might not be at all confident. It is best not to over-complicate situations such as these by starting a process of interpretation about how this occurred – for example, by assuming that there are "hidden agendas". Of course, we know that "hidden agendas" exist, but we do not pay much attention to them. We try to create a framework in which everything that can serve to improve the situation can be stated in a respectful way.

Creating this framework also includes asking people who seem distant or not engaged what can be done to make it possible for them to join in. Sadly, there are groups that have already had to experience several processes for development or even coaching processes that were not useful. Their confidence that something can be changed by engaging in such a process is understandably very low. They have learned that they have to play along in order not to create any negative attention, but they do not believe anything will change. Asking such groups how confident they are that something can change – either at the beginning or end of the workshop – can be very useful. If the answer is "We are not very confident", then we would deal with the situation as if we had asked a scaling question. We would ask what, if anything, gives them at least a little bit of confidence and then go on to ask what needs to happen so they can have more confidence that a positive change is possible.

Case 2.13:   A useless presentation

A large supplier of automotive parts asked us to offer a presentation coaching to a few of its important employees. The participants were technical specialists and middle managers. They were all between 30 and 40 years of age, motivated and friendly. Our feeling was that the coaching was going very well and that everybody had made a lot of progress in their presentation skills. At the end of the first day, we asked them how useful this had been for them and how confident they were that they could use what they had learned. We fully expected enthusiastic answers. You can imagine how surprised we were when we heard that the participants had really enjoyed themselves but that they had no confidence that they could use any of these skills in their daily lives. Quite flustered, we asked whether there was something that was at least a little bit useful and, much to our dismay, we received no answer. Of course, we were not able to hide our disappointment. The participants must have felt sorry for us and said this was not our fault, but that the presentations they were used to giving were based on a very different procedure. In their presentations, they were only using the so- called "one-pager", a presentation with only one slide that contained all the necessary information. Most presentations happened over the telephone or in meeting rooms, where everybody was sitting down. Our wonderful exercises and coaching conversations on structuring and designing PowerPoint presentations, on dealing with stage fright and exuding confidence, were very interesting but not applicable in their organization. In this moment, we realized that we should have been more thorough in our contract negotiation with the learning and development department and also with the group. We believed that we knew what a business presentation was – and thinking you know is almost always a mistake. Had we been more thorough in our approach and practised Solution Focused "not knowing", we would have been more to the point with our presentation coaching. Luckily, we had asked the question about the confidence and usefulness in the middle of the coaching. We could therefore use the second day to work on "one-pagers" and the presentation situations described by our participants.

CONFIDENCE SCALE

You can use a confidence scale with groups just as you can with individuals. You ask what makes the team confident that change will happen and what could make the team even a little bit more confident. The question works exactly like a scaling question and can be facilitated in the same way. If you scale confidence at the end of the workshop, you usually do not have a lot of time left, so working in the plenary is the most practical way of facilitation. The more time you have after the confidence scale, the longer forms of facilitation you can use because you can work with the team's answers afterwards.

CONFIDENCE SNOWBALL FIGHT

The confidence snowball fight was described by a Solution Focused colleague on Facebook. He had finished the team coaching process with a group, and many useful changes had been achieved. The last workshop in this longer process took place during a cold and very snowy winter. The colleague asked the group to write down everything that made them confident that the progress they had achieved could be maintained or even built upon on pieces of white Xerox paper, one comment per sheet. The participants wrote their answers, crushed the papers into paper snowballs and had a very fun snowball fight. After a while, everyone collected the snowballs that were lying around and read the comments from the snowballs they had collected out loud.

POSITIVE PARANOIA

Ben Furman and Tapani Ahola (1992) coined the term "positive paranoia" for this hope- and confidence-generating experiment. The background for this experiment is that teams and other groups like to focus on what does not work and overlook all the positive things that are already leading them in the desired direction. Furman and Ahola work with teams to the point at which the desired goal is clear and well formulated, and they have a sense of hope and have identified first steps. They do not create a large action plan or follow-up plan because that way you risk someone not doing what they have promised to do and then the attention of the team reverts to focusing on what is not working.

Instead, the team receives the task of observing closely what is already going in the right direction. Whenever a team member notices that somebody has carried out a task or is behaving in a positive way, they secretly put a small sign (e.g. a paper flower, a glass gem) on the desk of the person who has acted in the desired way. This experiment sounds a little bit silly and it might remind people of the little pictures or gold stars that their elementary school teacher used to indicate that they had done their homework well. However, what is important here is focusing the attention of the team on what is working – whichever way you manage that. It is well worth thinking about ways of could be establishing this direction of observation for the team that are in keeping with the team's culture. One idea is to use coffee tokens for the cafeteria.

RESOURCE GOSSIP OF THE COACHES

When you are working with a team of coaches, you can use "resource gossip" to give appreciative feedback to the team and increase their confidence about the possibility of change. The group of coaches pretends to be gossiping about their observations of the team while the team is listening. Of course, this is not the usual gossip, but resource gossip. Therefore, the coaches talk about all the things they have observed that make them confident the team will reach its goal. You can do this live or even in teleconferences where the coaches are talking and the team is listening in. If possible and useful, you can also involve other stakeholders – for example, customers or other departments with which the team works – to listen in on or share their observations of the changes in that conversation.

ATMOSPHERE/BENEFIT DIAGRAM

The perceived benefit of the team coaching process and the confidence that it will have positive results for the team are closely connected. We therefore like to ask the team how useful they think the process has been long before the end of the process. On the one hand, this helps us to correct things that might have gone wrong. On the other hand, the team feels strengthened in their ability to control the process and be taken seriously. We usually create a flipchart with a matrix. One axis is labelled "benefit" and the other is labelled "work atmosphere". Participants can anonymously make a cross at the appropriate point for them, where they see the process as being at the moment. We then ask what has already been useful or beneficial and what was good about the work atmosphere. We take care not to just fish for compliments for us as facilitators, but try to invite the team to observe what they have contributed to the benefit and positive atmosphere of the process. Obviously, we also ask what if anything could be done to improve both.

SECRET MISSION

Everybody promises to do something secret for the team between sessions; in the follow-up sessions, people guess who did what for the team.

Case 2.14:   A conflict disappears

Kirsten was invited to coach a team whose members were describing their atmosphere as tense and unfriendly. There were many conflicts, and the team did not feel like a team at all. The contracting happened in a team meeting with all team members, which Kirsten was able to join. To make use of the (rather long) time between contracting and the actual team coaching workshop, Kirsten suggested the "secret mission" to the team members. Everyone was supposed to secretly do something for the team until next time they meet.

Weeks later, in the workshop, Kirsten met a team that had changed completely: people were laughing, sharing stories – it was amazing. As a first exercise, Kirsten handed out a piece of paper to each participant and asked them to write down their name on top of the page. The pages were then handed to the next participant, who noted down what they thought the person whose name was written on the paper did for the team. There were things like cake magically appearing on a Friday; someone had created a secret email address from which they sent appreciative comments to the team mailbox. Everybody felt very happy to be recognized and the conflict evaporated into thin air.

IMPORTANCE OF FOLLOW-UP

Scheduling a follow-up session has many advantages:

- The team has a natural deadline for tasks.
- They have the possibility of seeing their development in action.

- They can celebrate their achievements.
- They can take stock and agree on what comes next.
- They can tackle things there was no time for in the first workshop.

A follow-up session can be shorter and structured quite simply by first looking at what has worked (see the section on "pre-session change") then by a new round of goal-setting (see the section on "the ticket office").

Liberating structures

Apart from the possible "moves" described above, we would like to mention an interesting resource that you can use when you are preparing for a team coaching session. *The Surprising Power of Liberating Structures* is a book with a selection of 33 alternative structures for facilitating meetings and conversations, curated by Henri Lipmanowicz and Keith McCandless. The basic idea of this collection is that there are five main "microstructures" that we use in organizations and groups:

- presentations
- managed discussions
- status reports
- open discussions
- brainstorms.

The problem with these is that they are either too constraining (in the case of presentations, managed discussions and status reports) or too loose (in the case of open discussions and brainstorms). Liberating structures, on the other hand, are routines designed to embrace distributed control. They include a fairer, larger number of people in shaping the next steps. The benefits connected are innovation, inclusion, participation, clarity, purpose and fun. Their use can be adapted during online and offline team coaching.

Liberating structures are simple and anyone can lead them easily. Once you have experienced one, it is very easy to start experimenting. All the instructions of how to run liberating structures are on the website (www.liberatingstructures.com) and in the book. On the website, select the Liberating Structures menu tab and pick one. You can read the purpose at the top and then skip to Step 5: Sequence of Steps and Time Allocation. There is also an interesting app for Apple and Android that can help you choose the right frame for your purpose. Most frames are easy, pragmatic and practical, and you can use them for different purposes in different phases of team coaching.

References

Dolan, Y. (1991). *Resolving sexual abuse*. New York: W.W. Norton.
Furman, B., & Ahola, T. (1992). *Solution talk: Hosting therapeutic conversations*. New York: W.W. Norton.

Lipmanowicz H., & McCandless K. (2014). *The surprising power of liberating structures.* New York: Liberating Structures Press.

Paulus, G., Schrotta, S., & Visotschnig, E. (2022). *Systemisches konsensieren: Der Schlüssel zum gemeinsamen Erfolg (6., überarbeitete Auflage).* Holzkirchen: DANKE-Verlag.

Röhrig, P., & Clarke, J. (2008). *57 SF activities for facilitators and coaches: Putting solutions focus into action.* Cheltenham: Solutions Books.

Chapter 3

Special team coaching formats

Abstract

This chapter explores special team coaching formats, such as Agile coaching, Agile retrospectives, shadowing, regular supervision, Solution Focused reflecting team, tetralema and team-building.

Agile coaching

A special format of a team coaching is the one performed in an Agile environment. Before we explain how this format can be run, we need to quickly clarify what an "Agile environment" is for all those who are not familiar with this approach and what it means in the real world. This will help also to outline the difference between an "Agile coach" and a "coach".

An Agile environment is a company (or a team or organization) that supports Agile project management, an environment (born in software development but currently adopted also in other industries) based on four basic pillars. which we also described in our section on the "cousins" of the Solution Focused approach in Chapter 1:

1 Individuals and interactions over processes and tools
2 Working software (or results) over comprehensive documentation
3 Customer collaboration over contract negotiations
4 Responding to change over following a plan

A company (or specifically a team) based on this culture normally accepts and promotes change, innovation and process improvements. Some of the most important practices are based on short working increments called "sprints" and working collaboratively.

The basic unit of the Agile environment is the Agile team, a small group of people assigned to the same project or effort, nearly all of them on a full-time basis. A small minority of team members may be part-time contributors or may have other

DOI: 10.4324/9781003370314-3

responsibilities. The notion of a team entails shared accountability: good or bad, the outcomes should be attributed to the entire team rather than to any individual.

The team is expected to possess all the necessary competencies, whether technical (programming, designing, testing) or business (domain knowledge, decision making ability). Roles and responsibilities do not matter as much as results: a developer may test, perform analysis or think about requirements; an analyst or domain expert can suggest ideas about implementation, and so on.

In this kind of environment based on the relevance of the team working, team coaching is a deeply important practice, and it is linked to the role of the Agile team coach. An Agile coach helps organizations, teams, and individuals adopt Agile practices and methods while embedding Agile values and mindsets. The goal of an Agile coach is to foster more effective, transparent and cohesive teams, and to enable better outcomes, solutions and products/services for customers (Scrum Alliance, 2021).

The main differences between Agile team coaching and "professional coaching" can be described as follows:

1 Like any other coach, the Agile team coach uses questions and frameworks to help the team to find their way to solve problems, gain clarity around specific situations and achieve goals. Differently from "professional coaches", Agile coaches have a specific agenda when working with a team: they are interested in helping the team to become more effective, responsive and adaptive.
2 During an Agile team coaching session, the focus of the team coach is on aligning teams with the Agile principles and values. Their support is also based on their experience, which means Agile team coaches can not only use the "coaching" tools, but can also become mentors or teachers if required.
3 Normally, an Agile team is a cross-functional team, created to solve a specific problem or issue. When an organization wants to develop an Agile mindset, it has to eliminate the divisions between the different parts of the organization so the team needs to be formed by people from different parts of the company in order to learn how to create value for the customer.
4 The focus of a team coaching can also be the internal dynamics of the team. In order to improve their results, the main focus of an Agile team coach is the impact of the team on the organization; in this way, the team can measure its performance.
5 During an Agile team coaching process, the Agile team coach has to push the team towards a deep comprehension of the customer's point of view, data and metrics, and continuous improvement. The link between these three aspects will be the central discussion of every session and the Agile coach will push the teams to ask themselves, "How can we perform better?"

Finally, we need to remember that there are five different types of meeting in the agile world and each type is used for a different goal. These are explored below.

Kickoff meeting

The kickoff meeting takes place at the beginning of a project and focuses on people and their interactions. It is also called the inception or chartering workshop. It is the alignment meeting where all aspects of the project boundaries are considered and in which all project stakeholders participate. In this meeting the team members get to know each other and share their common purpose and objectives. Working agreements are often established to set the working modalities of the team.

There are three basic elements of the kickoff meeting:

- *Setting the purpose.* The purpose of the team's work is to provide inspiration and make sense of their activities, not only from the team's point of view, but also and above all from the point of view of the end customer, and to know what measurement criteria are needed.
- *Create alignment.* If team members did not know each other before, it is clarified what skills each one can bring to the project, or what skills are useful that they would like to learn. Alignment is also generated when creating common rules and setting project goals.
- *Understand the context.* This element is important as interactions between team members are a key part of a successful project, as is collaboration with third parties inside or outside the company. The creation of an interaction map makes visible the boundaries and interactions the team will have with any other departments and stakeholders.

Real-time planning meeting

This is the first project meeting that focuses on what to do and how to do it during an iteration. In Scrum, it is called "sprint planning". After the time-boxed duration has been established, the goal of the real-time planning meeting is to gain complete knowledge of the work and activities to be done, set a starting date, create focus on the project and agree what is required.

Starting from the value to be delivered to the customer, the team prioritizes the activities and provides a time estimate. To do this, the team must have a deep knowledge of the customer and be able to locate the information they need. The focus of the meeting is encapsulated in these questions:

- What do we do?
- How do we do it?
- How much can we achieve in the given time period?
- Are we all committed to the results decided together?

Daily meeting

The daily team meeting takes place standing up, every day at the same time, in the same place and with all team members present. It lasts a maximum of 15 minutes and serves the team members to align themselves on day-to-day developments or to resolve impediments in case someone needs help from the team. In Scrum, it is also called a stand-up meeting and is quite prescriptive as it is very software development oriented. However, teams working on different projects with a large timeframe or working by processes hold this alignment meeting once a week or at different times, depending on the team's working mode.

The questions the team asks in this meeting are:

* What have we done to date?
* What will we do during the next iteration?
* Are there impediments? What are they and what do we need to overcome them?

If questions arise that do not involve all team members, but just a few people, those who have to resolve them continue the meeting without involving the whole team.

Check meeting

At the end of each iteration, the team shows the increment to check its validity. It may be a minimum viable product or results on the process or results on a change that is shown to the end customer, or to the product owner, or to the sponsor, or perhaps it is the team itself that checks its performance. The focus is on the result produced, what can be accepted, whether it corresponds to the definition of "done" and what needs to be changed. Based on the feedback from the customer (external or internal), the priorities are redefined in the next iteration and will be discussed in the next real-time planning meeting.

A check meeting is precisely for sharing the work done, aligning the project and resolving any impediments. The team, the Agile coach, the product owner and the customer are present.

Retrospective meeting

This meeting is totally dedicated to reviewing what the team has been able to achieve in a specified timeslot, call a "sprint". Agile retrospectives can be used for many things, not only for Agile teams, which is why we are offering a whole chapter on this approach.

Agile retrospectives

One of the formats of the team coaching specifically used in the Agile environment is the retrospective meeting. It is based on the last principle of the Agile development, which says: "At regular intervals, the team reflects on how to become more effective, then tunes and adjusts its behaviour accordingly." The Agile manifesto makes it clear that, in order to best live the Agile values, teams should meet regularly to check in and make adjustments.

The retrospective meeting involves the team and the Agile coach, and has a variable duration – usually between one and two hours, depending on the length of the cycle and the time the team has decided to give itself for this type of meeting. It is a time when the team devotes its attention to analysing and reviewing together what happened during the previous iteration. There are various types of retrospective meetings in the Lean Agile culture:

- the retrospective held at the end of a project cycle, where the results are analysed and a presentation is prepared to the leadership team to explain what worked, what didn't work and what the team needs in order to overcome the impediments and improve performance
- those held at the end of each sprint in the Scrum methodology, in which the time is prescribed by the length of the sprint
- those established by teams working on processes to decide on improvements to the value stream, which take place at the end of each trial.

No matter which Agile methodology the team is adopting, the focus must be placed on *how* the team members work together and how relational issues are addressed, along with any conflicts, improvements in the way of working in terms of processes, practices and tools. In practice and in a nutshell, the retrospective meeting can be compared to a coaching session in which the team focuses on the learnings from previous actions and focuses on the experiments to be implemented in future actions.

If necessary, the rules that the team gave itself during the kickoff meeting are revised or added to improve the way the team members work together. The retrospective meeting is a time when the members exchange feedback and the Agile coach gives and receives feedback from the team.

Once the team has decided, based on experience, on the time needed for the retrospective meeting, the meeting is time boxed – that is, within the time that has been predetermined – and the Agile coach is responsible for the facilitation process and time. The coach then proposes a method and timeframe, taking care to warn the team of the time the meeting is taking. One simple and widely used method, among many, is to have the team work on a whiteboard divided into three sectors to identify:

- What worked?
- What did not work?
- What can we do better?

Everyone writes their Post-It notes in the appropriate sector. The Agile coach asks the team to cluster them – that is, to group them by similarity – then starts the discussion.

The Agile coach's presence is crucial to keep the time, keep the focus on the "how" and make sure the most important needs are addressed. The coach invites team members to review the rules and bring any concrete actions to try out in the next cycle. In fact, by the end of the retrospective meeting, the team has to decide on the next steps to be taken and it is good practice to have a list of specific actions and behaviours to adopt in the future.

A successful retrospective meeting has significant characteristics:

- *Safe environment.* This is essential to allow people to bring their best contribution to the meeting. Any shadow on psychological safety undermines the possibility of collaboration and destroys the ability to build trust, to realize the conditions for constructive disagreement and to give honest and direct feedback. A climate of security and trust is one of the characteristics of Agile teams.
- *Effective feedback.* Part of the responsibility of the Agile coach attending the meeting is to make sure that feedback is shared in the right way. Effective feedback simply reports what has been observed without adding personal or interpretative comments. For example, if a team member wants to draw attention to the punctuality of a colleague, they should not write "You are distracted and late", but "You arrived after the start time of the meeting". That is, it is always necessary to separate the behaviour from the person for feedback to be effective and to avoid establishing defensive behaviour. Therefore, also avoid asking "why?" questions
- *Address all issues.* When the two previous characteristics are present, team members can address all issues, even the most uncomfortable ones, the real relational issues of a team, the ones that are difficult to talk about and that need to be facilitated by the presence of the Agile coach. Solving these issues can often make the team significantly better.

Shadowing

Sometimes the team would like an "outside perspective", from someone who can observe how they are working together. This observer should then provide recommendations about areas for improvement and comment on what is already going well. In Solution Focus, we don't believe in "objective" observers. Every "observer" changes the situation. However, these requests exist and most often they can be shifted into an activity that is both useful and compatible with a social-constructionist approach.

In Solution Focused shadowing, we would start by a traditional "ticket office" – what might be different after the activity, what might it lead to? With the answer to this question, the things that the team wants observed most often become clear. Examples might be "How are our discussions, are we productive, are we running in circles?" or "How inclusive are we of everyone's ideas?" The coach can then ask about observable signs: "What will I be seeing that will tell me that you are being productive (or inclusive)?" By describing in detail the kind of behaviour the "shadower" might see, the team is already focusing their attention on the rich details of their preferred future, which in turn will make this future more likely.

During the shadowing, the observer then simply has to note all the instances in which they see the desired behaviours and who did what. The "feedback" strengthens the team. In cases when the opposite of the desired behaviours happens, the team coach might describe this to the team and ask them what they would like to be doing differently next time.

What is important, again, is that the team coach makes very clear that this is only their perspective and that what they saw may or may not be the relevant instance for the team.

With many meetings now happening online, recording meetings is quite easy. Another really great way of helping a team improve their collaboration and performance is to create a recording of a normal meeting and invite every team member to watch the recording. They are tasked with finding their favourite moment and their least favourite moment in the meeting. In the team coaching session, they are then asked to present the favourite moment and let the others know what they appreciated about it. For the least favourite moment, they are asked to say what exactly they would want to happen instead. In this way, the team can learn to "shadow" itself and start learning from its own performance.

Regular supervision

Team coaching and regular team supervision share a few characteristics, and the line between team supervision and team coaching is blurry. Many teams in the social sector are required to take one team supervision session every month.

Team supervision has a slightly different focus from team coaching. It can have a stronger aspect on quality assurance and case supervision/best practice sharing than team coaching often does. Table 3.1 may help to clarify.

Table 3.1 Differences between team coaching and team supervision

Team coaching	Team supervision
Coach does not need subject matter expertise.	Supervisor may need subject matter expertise if quality assurance is a key factor.
Functions:	*Functions:*
• Supporting team to collaborate well • Supporting to maximize potential • Supporting high performance	• Restorative function (helping team to take care of wellbeing and mental health) • Quality assurance function (case supervision can be included) • Supporting team to collaborate well • Supporting to maximize potential • Supporting high performance

Table 3.1 is an attempt to provide some guidance about when an engagement may be called "supervision" and when it should be called "team coaching". In reality, there can also be cultural issues in play. "Supervision" is the name you might hear in the social sector, while "coaching" might be the name of the engagement in business. Whatever the name, a Solution Focused team coach or team supervisor will have to check what the team, sponsors and other stakeholders would like as their preferred outcome of the engagement. Once the outcome is known, a suitable name can be found for the engagement. And even that should be influenced more by what the clients prefer than what is the "right" name according to any academic definition.

Regular team supervision is usually short – maybe two hours every four to six weeks. The supervisor could still start the whole engagement by interviews with the team, sponsor and stakeholders, but it is not very likely that they will be able to do interviews before every two-hour session. As there is also regularity to the process and the sessions are mandated to take place, the team will not always have "a topic" for the session in our experience, which can be a bit tricky for both the supervisor and the team.

It is really helpful to start a year-long engagement with interviews to collect topics that can be tackled if there is nothing more pressing. Having a repository of "useful things to discuss" makes regular supervision more fun and more fruitful. If interviews are not possible, the first session could be used to generate ideas for the whole process. The team supervisor might also send the team an online survey in preparation for the supervision session with questions such as, "Suppose we have a really great session next week, what difference will it make?" or "Suppose next session is really useful for you, what might we have talked about?"

The regular team supervision can use all the moves from Solution Focused team coaching, depending on what the team wants. The structure can be a walk through the gallery, just as in Solution Focused team coaching. Table 3.2 presents a structure for Solution Focused team supervision which we have found to work. Again, it always depends – don't just take it and run with it, but instead adapt it to your team and circumstances).

It really helps for the team supervisor to make some notes on each session:

- What were the goals?
- How were they related to the overall goals of the process?
- What was the outcome?

The coach might use a session in the middle of the year to take stock and make sure the process is going as well as it can. It may also serve as a reminder of all the development the team has gone through. Successes are easy to forget! Using the last session to review all achievements is also a good idea to generate motivation and pride in the team's work together.

Table 3.2 Structure for Solution Focused team supervision

Time	Activity
00:00	Welcome What's been better since last time we spoke? What went well?
00:10	**Goal setting** • Present survey results and decide (vote, etc.). • Suppose these two hours are really useful, what will you take away?
00:20	**Slot 1** Example for a general topic (e.g. "How do we deal with critical parents in our school?") • Ticket office: formulate good common project (e.g. we will have found out how to ...). • Preferred future: what difference will it make, who will notice, how, stakeholder map. • Successful past: scale. • Gift shop: scale +1, action planning/agreements.
01:00	**Slot 2** Example for a case supervision using an adapted reflecting team process (e.g. in my group, Bianca throws tantrums and I don't know how to deal with it): • Case donor explains case. • Others ask clarification questions. • Case donor turns around or switches off camera. • Others give one element of appreciation each ("What impresses me about case donor ..."). • Others provide questions for case donor to think about (not to answer right now), ideas, own resonances, learnings they have had. • Case donor turns around and mentions what was significant and where they are now. • All think about how this discussion has also helped them.
01:45	**Harvesting results** • Collecting learnings. • Collecting actions. **Feedback for next session** What worked well and what might we do even better next time?

Solution Focused reflecting team

The Solution Focused reflecting team is a process that helps teams to allow the solution to surface with the help of the team's collective intelligence. The way in which this process is usually performed creates an atmosphere of mutual respect to support positive problem-solving. This tool was developed by Harry Norman. for more information, see Norman (n.d.).

Development projects often lead teams to tackle complex issues. These teams rarely start out with all the answers to the problems they are trying to solve, and regularly encounter barriers to achieving their intended outcomes. This tool offers an opportunity to listen to colleagues and use their expertise.

There are six phases in the Solutions Focus reflecting team approach:

1 *Preparing.* The person who wishes to receive help (the presenter) comes to the meeting with a specific request.
2 *Presenting.* The presenter outlines the situation to the team. The team listens attentively without interrupting and lets the presenter finish.
3 *Clarifying.* The team asks specific questions to understand the situation more clearly, such as "What are you aiming to achieve?", "What signs will tell you that you are making progress?", "What have you already achieved in relation to this?", "What are the first signs of progress you would be pleased to notice?", "Who can support you in this?" and "How can we help you in this conversation?" The presenter replies after each question.
4 *Affirming.* Each team member tells the presenter what has impressed them the most about how they are handling the situation. Or they engage in "positive gossip" together about what has impressed them. Positive gossip simply entails saying positive (kind, encouraging) things about someone in the third person. So, for example, "Mary has done a great job organizing this meeting and bringing together these two actors who were not aware of one another's existence." The presenter listens silently to each item of positive feedback and says, "Thank you" at the end.
5 *Reflecting.* The presenter retreats a little from the group and the team members take it in turns to go round the table and offer one item of appropriate input at a time. If one person has nothing to offer, they say "Pass" and this cycle continues until everyone has said all they want to say or they run out of time. Inputs may build creatively on each other. The input offered at this stage includes anything each member considers relevant. This can be technical input, advice, reflections, metaphors or other forms of input. While the team is reflecting, the presenter remains silent and listens. The presenter may want to take notes.
6 *Responding.* After the reflections, the presenter responds briefly to what has been said, thanks everyone and (usually) sets their next step.

Tetralemma

Matthias Varga von Kibéd and Insa Sparrer (2005) developed an interesting possibility to work with teams that are confronted with having to take a decision: the tetralemma. It is derived from Indian logic and focuses on solving the perception of a dilemma with two diametrical poles (e.g. taking on a project–not taking on a project) and generating more than these two possibilities. Here is our variant of working with the tetralemma.

We create a constellation of five different positions:

1 the one
2 the other
3 both
4 neither of the two
5 the fifth non-position "none of this but also not this".

Each corner of the room can represent one of the four positions marked by a flip-chart, a piece of paper on the floor or other markers. The team first walks into the first corner and describes, for example, why they absolutely want to take on the project (the one), what the advantages are and who would profit.

Then everybody moves to the opposite corner and describes (the other): why the project should definitely not be taken on, what are the disadvantages, and who would benefit.

From the third position in yet another corner, the team members look at "the one" and "the other" and reflect on what "both" could mean: in our case, for example, the things that are important to the team irrespective of what they decide, being able to manage their daily priorities professionally and looking good in front of other departments.

From the fourth position, "neither of the two", the team looks at all the other three positions. The team might think about alternatives that would also achieve the goals that became apparent on position three: taking on a different project, describing the successes of the team, the company blog and so on. The fifth non-position is not a position in the room. The team walks around together and reflects on what else all of this might mean.

On the fifth position, you often develop interesting conversations and insights far beyond the solution of the issues at hand.

If there is no room, you can also use a flipchart to draw the different positions, use toy figurines or take four chairs and ask one person to sit down on each chair as a representative for the respective position. The fifth element stays standing and can walk around. The representatives of the positions on the chairs talk from their positions and the rest of the team listens. Afterwards, the team summarizes what were the most important and interesting insights that came up in the discussion.

This approach can easily be used in a virtual environment as well. The different positions can be created via the breakout rooms and the fifth position, the final one, can be run directly in the plenary. You can also create an online whiteboard with the four corners and a separate space for the fifth position. There are solutions like www.wonder.me that allow a team to move avatars in different corners of a virtual space. Virtual reality is also starting to move into the coaching space so it remains to be seen what impact that will have.

Team-building

Most traditional team-building exercises can be turned into effective Solution Focused exercises by using a few hints and tricks, which we describe below. There are only a few that cannot really be used in Solution Focused team-building, as they are inherently deficit and explanation oriented.

What is not suitable?

Solution Focused approaches to team coaching are always resource oriented. It is about helping participants to discover strengths and possibilities, resources they were no longer aware of possessing. After a Solution Focused exercise, participants are positively surprised about themselves – whether because of the content they discovered or because learning was fun and easy. The good working relationship between coach and participants is a result of this dynamic. In a few older coaching concepts, you still find exercises that aim to demonstrate the team's incompetence in order to strengthen their motivation to learn. For example, in a train the trainer session for team trainers in which we once participated, the trainer established the rule that from now on all decisions of the group would have to be 100 per cent consensual. The aim of this rule was to demonstrate to the team that consensual decisions are very difficult and indeed almost impossible. As was to be expected, the group got stuck in very frustrating discussions and wasn't even able to agree on when to take breaks. Afterwards, the trainer elaborated on the reasons for this failure. Most participants had already experienced such situations before, so there was not much information gained. The frustration level was immense, and the team's relationship with the trainer was so disturbed that a few participants left after this exercise. If there is one advantage of demonstrating incompetence, it is the clarity with which a problem appears (or created). We think this clarity can be achieved much more easily without disturbing the working atmosphere and thereby the willingness of the participants to change or learn.

A Solution Focused approach creates a good working relationship between coach (facilitator, trainer) and participants quickly. It also consciously helps construct positive and supportive relationships between the participants. Exercises that endanger these working relationships are hard to turn into Solution Focused exercises. All coaching components that produce conflicts or serve to make one participant lose face also fall into that category. In one team coaching, for example, a participant always came in late after breaks, yet the other participants tolerated his behaviour. It was only when the coach mentioned this phenomenon that the group learned that the participant had been instructed by the coach to be late in order to demonstrate the dynamic of unpunctual starts. The goal of such interventions is often to show what is "really going on" in the team. The root cause of the problem needs to be identified and eradicated once and for all. There is a clear linear causality between "the problem" (and the team member who is seen as the problem) and the solution (which is usually getting rid of the problem). In Solution Focused team coaching, the goal of the intervention would be elicited differently: by asking the Miracle Question, exploring exceptions from the problem or resources of the team and defining small steps into the direction of the goal.

Similar ideas also form the basis of so-called "instruments" for team diagnostics or personality diagnostics or personality typologies. The team has a problem. The team coach therefore starts looking for the root cause (more or less scientifically): all team members fill in a questionnaire to determine their personality type – for example, the DiSC profile, the Myers-Briggs Type Indicator, their team roles. The results show where to find the real problem of the team and how it might be solved – for example, by adding another team member with a complementary personality type. These kinds of interventions are especially difficult to combine with a Solution Focused approach when the instruments applied are not taken as typologies (such as DiSC or Myers-Briggs) but are misunderstood as diagnoses of static personality characteristics. The Solution Focused approach assumes that change always happens, which makes it difficult for us to work with instruments that posit unchangeable personality cores.

For the Solution Focused team coach, working with personality profiles looks like a detour via a presumed root cause of the problem. However, it is still possible to follow up such an intervention in a Solution Focused way. You might ask, "What does the typology analysis show are the advantages and resources of your team?", "Where do these resources show up in your daily life?", "If you assume that XYZ is missing from your team – how have you been able to cope?", "On a scale of 1 to 10, where you with regard to …?" This way, the personality diagnostics can provide a useful invitation for a conversation in the team or individual coaching.

Another word of warning: some typologies – such as, for example, "Integral Coaching" or "Spiral Dynamics" (Beck & Cowan, 2006) – assign a development level to each client. There is a globally determined path of development – almost like a path to salvation – and the desired development of the client or the team is predetermined. Assuming a predetermined, globally and eternally valid path for development for every person is a philosophical or religious stance that you can take; however, it is very far from assuming that every case is different, that you work on what your client wants. In Solution Focused coaching, we elicit the goals of the clients and do not assume that they pre-exist somewhere.

When we are working with colleagues who come from approaches that seem incompatible with our view of coaching, we try to acknowledge their good intentions to be helpful to their clients. Someone who represents "Spiral Dynamics" or Jungian personality types is not a bad coach or a bad person. They might be helpful, but they are not Solution Focused. Especially when working with HR departments, we have often experienced situations where a fruitful collaboration is possible even when coaches espouse different approaches; the key is accepting the differences and remaining curious about them.

What is suitable?

Many traditional exercises and team coaching tools can be used for a Solution Focused learning or change process: exercises from outdoor training, games or team exercises suitable for a seminar room, structured role-plays, exercises with observer feedback and so on.

Strategies for transformation

There are basically two ways of turning exercises and tools into Solution Focused exercises. You can start from the Solution Focused process and enrich its elements with exercises, or you can take exercises that you know from a different context and turn them into Solution Focused exercises.

If you want to change an exercise in a Solution Focused way, it makes sense to look at the different phases of the exercise: What do you need to take care of when you are introducing the exercise, when you are carrying it out and when you are debriefing it so that the exercise can be useful for the clients?

INTRODUCTION/BRIEFING

There are a few general success factors for introducing team activities – for example, clarifying the goal of the exercise so that participants feel safe and convinced that it is a good use of their time or announcing the structure and timing of the activity. Here are a few additional hints for directing the focus of participants on resources and success factors when using activities in a Solution Focused way.

When you are introducing the activity, you can ask the whole group or individual participants to observe what is already going well during the activity. You can distribute observer sheets or assign targeted observation tasks focusing on individual factors to get useful and positive feedback. It is about identifying what works and not what does not work. Of course, we still know that the context of an activity is very different from the context of daily work. However, if something goes well in an activity, it can be a first small sign that this is also possible in the daily life of the team.

DELIVERY

When the activity is carried out, every team member should feel safe. Nobody should have to fear embarrassment or loss of face. Of course, as a team coach this is not always completely under your control. Sometimes you have obnoxious participants who like ridiculing others. In this case, it is important to de-escalate the situation. If you want to talk about it, you should be able to appreciate everyone's perspective but also show that a different way of communicating has better results for the team atmosphere.

> ## Case 3.1: Welcome to the jungle
>
> Kirsten was conducting team coaching with a group of trainees. Among them was a girl who did not seem very popular. Whenever she said something, two other trainees rolled their eyes. The exercise was about finding a path through a grid marked on the floor as a team as quickly as possible. In order to protect the unpopular girl and create a better learning atmosphere for everyone, Kirsten was looking for a way to busy the eye-rolling trainees so they would no longer have time to roll their eyes. She decided to give them the role of referee, which did not leave any time for them to do anything else. Later, we were able to use the example of the grid exercise to talk about how appreciating everyone's contributions is important, no matter what our personal relationship with them might be.

DEBRIEFING

The focus of the discussion is also crucial for the debriefing – we concentrate on the demonstrated skills, resources, generated ideas and "aha moments" of the participants. This means that the debrief, or solution, comes from the participants themselves. Just as in individual Solution Focused coaching, where you only know which question you asked when you hear the client's answer, you can also only say what an activity was good for after it is complete. For this reason, it makes sense to start the debrief with very open questions such as, "What did you notice?" or "What did you discover during the activity?" We do our best to choose activities that can create a specific effect or ask questions which direct our clients' focus in a specific direction, but it is really our participants who have to tell us what progress they were able to make in an activity.

In the second step, we pose appreciative questions about the resources that were discovered in the exercise: "Who contributed to the solution?", "What did they contribute?", "What do the activities say about our strengths and resources?", "What would you like to keep doing in daily life?"

Since we do not assume that the context of an exercise and the context of daily life are the same, it is necessary to plan a transfer of learning from activities into daily life. This can be facilitated by asking about where the resources that were discovered already show up: "Where have you noticed something similar in your daily life?" or by asking about how what was learned can be transferred to a different context. You can also work with scaling question: "Where were you on a scale of 1 to 10 regarding topic XYZ during the activity?", "Which number would you give yourself in your daily business life?", "What is already working well in daily life?", "How would you notice that you reached one step higher on the scale?"

References

Beck, D., & Cowan, C. (1996). *Spiral dynamics.* New York: Wiley.

Norman, H. (n.d.). *Solution Focused reflecting teams – SFRTeams* https://sfwork.com/solwo rld/downloads/SFRTeamPrimer02.pdf

Scrum Alliance (2022). *State of Agile coaching report.* https://resources.scrumalliance.org/ Article/state-agile-coaching-report

Varga von Kibéd, M. & Sparrer, I. (2005). *But on the contrary: Tetralemma work and other basic forms of systemic structural constellations.* Heidelberg: Karl Auer.

Chapter 4

What kinds of teams can you coach?

Abstract

This chapter highlights the specifics of different teams, what to take care of, what may be different and how to coach these teams. Topics covered are executive teams, shop-floor teams and teams of teams. Two important sectors for team coaching are explored: teams in the educational sector and teams in hospitals.

Introduction

We don't value categorizing teams too much; our ethos has always revolved around particularities rather than generalizations. The following should be taken merely as a potentially helpful heuristic rather than as a description of how "all teams are like that". You may find teams in the educational sector that are much more like executive teams and shop-floor teams that are completely different from your expectations.

Executive teams

The stance of a Solution Focused team coach is to engage in a collaborative conversation for the benefit of the team. In the case of executive teams, the main hurdle might be ensuring a collaborative approach as the entire team needs to take time and engage.

Contracting with an organization for an executive team coaching process will require the buy-in and commitment of all members. As the team coach is usually brought in by one of the members of the leadership team, obtaining the buy-in also means the team coach is seen as impartial and as responding to the entire team.

Executives are human beings, too – so should it really make a difference if your clients are C-level executives? Not really. And we should not put people into boxes: there are many different kinds of C-level executives. So please take the following with a grain of salt. We will share what our personal experiences of

DOI: 10.4324/9781003370314-4

some specifics of executive coaching are. You might have completely different experiences.

Let us start with a positive: C-level executives won't like wasting time. When executives commit to a coaching process, they usually want to use their time wisely. They want to see outcomes, development and signs of progress. Therefore, once they have committed to the process, they are engaged and a joy to work with.

Case 4.1: Executive team coaching

Usually, Cristina works with regular workshops of three to four hours' duration. In this case, the executive team was under enormous time pressure and had many responsibilities as the organization was growing rapidly. The structure needed to be adjusted to working for two hours every month.

It was very little time, but it was the only way to get the team together. The objective of each workshop had to be very clearly defined so the team could make progress and serve its own development.

The entire process lasted ten months, with a strong focus on the vision and long-term strategy of the organization. At the follow-up meeting four months after the end of the last workshop, the team was very grateful for the emergent process and that they had discovered how to adjust their way of working to respond to their changing industry.

There is different knowledge available about what coaching is

In our experience, it is crucial to find out what the client already knows about coaching. Many executives we have met were a bit unclear and were expecting more of a mentoring or sparring process. We clarify and define coaching before we start, and ask whether they are interested in "coaching". That does not preclude them forgetting halfway through, so it is best to have the definition present more than once.

Coaching may not be what they want

When you explain that coaching is about asking questions and about clients developing their own solutions, executives sometimes perceive that this has little benefit for them. They are used to developing their own solutions and usually are really smart people who are aware of their solution-finding processes. Coaching may not be the best option for them. However, some do need an honest conversation partner who is not enmeshed in the hierarchy of the organization. In these cases, we have sometimes re-labelled what we are doing as "sparring". You can be very sure that the client would never take on board one of our contributions just because we said so – full responsibility is with the client. However, since executives do not have a lot of people to whom they can talk openly, this may be an invaluable service.

The clients do not seem to prioritize the process

Executives are usually very busy people. Their schedules change constantly, priorities shift and they are not always in control of their own time. They might have to cancel or postpone sessions frequently. Don't take this as a sign of a deteriorating coaching relationship (and if you are unsure, ask). Make sure you have your cancellation policy clearly communicated and otherwise be flexible. Personally, we like working on a retainer basis – we are sure of being paid and can roll with what life throws at us.

You feel like you have to prove yourself

A person in "high places" can feel intimidating. However, an intimidated coach is not very useful. You may not be the best coach in the universe, but you are the one who is there – so stop feeling intimidated! We think the best advice we can give here is to get to know your clients as people. Jump over your fear and into the coaching relationship.

Trust may be difficult

Many executives find a lot of people want something from them. It is smart to be a bit cautious and not trust everyone at first sight when you live in such a world. In our experience, it can take a while for executive clients to open up. Treating your client as human beings and showing up as a human being yourself are the best remedies in our view. Don't take reservation personally – it makes sense for them!

Working with executive teams brings some additional challenges:

- Interviews might be difficult to organize as that require additional time.
- There is a need to maintain neutrality and ensure the role of coach for any team member is not mixed with the role of team coach.
- Don't get caught in politics and don't let politics get in the way of the team coaching.
- Be aware of the emergent nature of the business, which could make the team coaching process change scope on a continuous basis.
- As the team is formed of leaders, the topics might be more strategic than operational.

- Are you a team coach or consultant or mentor? The executive team might expect a mixture of roles and that needs to be clarified from the start.
- The team might expect the team coach to understand everything completely – remember that you are not meant to be an expert in the specific industry.

With a thorough contracting phase and constant contact with the team, the process can bring significant results to the executive team.

Shop-floor teams

Most team coaches have an academic background and come from the middle or upper-middle class. They are mainly white women in their fifties (our observation, not based on any statistic). Shop-floor teams are usually made up of lower-class non-academics, who are likely to be more diverse in their ethnic background. The team coach is assigned higher privileges by society than the clients, and the dynamic that can ensue can strengthen unhelpful narratives and weaken the relationship between coach and clients. Also, ways of communicating may be different. In our experience, shop-floor communication can be quite clear and direct, and does not shy away from open criticism. There may be (probably well-founded) reluctance to engage in a "woolly" or "aloof" team coaching exercises led by someone who is very different from the team. The team may feel that the team coach does not understand their reality (and is probably right in assuming that).

Bridging this divide is not easy. Our usual Solution Focused ways of contributing to a good relationship – speaking the language of our clients, holding them in positive regards, stressing their resources and skills – may seem patronizing and disconnected. We have found that good contract clarifications are key. We need to clarify the goals of the team members and listen closely to what they want. Asking them what the team coach would need to do to support them and sticking to the role they will let you take is important. It is also helpful to look for connections wherever you can find them – for example, a joint love of sports, music, small talk about daily events.

Kirsten has worked with quite a few shop-floor teams and has really enjoyed it. When reflecting on "what worked", we think it is her sense of humour, her ability \ not to be fazed by anything that happens and her authenticity. She does not pretend to understand or be the same, but she does not let that stand in the way of honest connection. She is grateful for the honour of being able to work with each team and is curious about team members' lives and work. If tensions arise due to class differences, she can surface them without making them stronger by reverting to categorization. The discussion stays focused on how she can support the team. Yes, it can be a nasty divide, but bridging it is one of the most important challenges of our time and it can only be done with humility and an ability to let go of our assumptions and learn from one another.

Team of teams

As already discussed, it is important to understand the distinction between team and group as this might have an impact on the process. At the same time, it would be useful to notice whether there are actually multiple teams inside, as each team might have its own objectives and sometimes those objectives might be contradictory.

Coaching a team of teams requires understanding the overall scope of the process and what the best hopes for the joint process might be. The team coach could be interested in conducting interviews with the team leaders and maybe with some of the team members from different teams.

When we look into facilitation tools, a process for a team of teams would better be served by tools specific to coaching large teams – Kitchen Table Conversations, Fishbowl, World Café (see Chapter 5).

Particularity of the team of teams process resides in the following aspects:

- *Contracting.* Is the coach supposed to work only with the entire team to facilitate the communication, or is it the role of the team coach to engage in separate processes also with each team separately?
- *Scope of work.* This is mostly around the interaction between teams, communication and creating a joint vision.
- *Desired future.* Substantial time needs to be allocated to creating this vision.
- *Successful past.* This might need to be looked at from the perspective of the various teams.

The Galveston Declaration (see Chapter 1) offers valuable principles that can be put to use in the context of team of teams:

- Acknowledging that there are multiple "truths" as each team might consider their "reality" more complicated and complex
- Facilitating the emergence of new identity – that of the joint team
- Inviting all members to entertain change – each interaction will generate change and each team member can amplify positive change
- Noticing resources and possibilities – the scope of successful past of the team would be around noticing the resources the team of teams has to work together and generate positive change.

When working with a team of teams, the team coach should be aware of the potential that the role of the coach might be more to facilitate the process than to coach.

Educational sector

Kirsten has a lot of experience coaching in the education sector, mainly in Germany. There are a few specifics to the educational sector that are worth mentioning (although these may be completely different in your country).

Schools live in a rich map of stakeholders. As providers of education, they are usually fulfilling a few different roles at the same time: educator, administrator, social worker, counsellor, assessor, evaluator, door-opener and door-closer. Most teachers started in the profession because of their love of supporting young people and in daily life they are being frustrated by many of the other roles. This is a resource and an obstacle at the same time. Team coaching can always come back to asking about how the young people may notice an improvement – that is the goal everyone is after. On the other hand, when there are too many non-related activities that teachers have to complete, the frustration level can be quite high.

At least in Germany, schools are not particularly well funded. Teachers and administrators have a large workload and taking time to step back and reflect is not an obvious choice most of the time. The extra work that is created by the team coaching process may not be welcome. When Kirsten first started working with schools, she was surprised at how long things took. But when she realized that the team only had very little time outside of teaching to discuss and implement improvements, she understood. It makes sense to learn about meeting structures and available time for implementation of results before entering into a team coaching process in a field where those involved are already overwhelmed. Otherwise, the team coach comes in bright-eyed and bushy-tailed, full of enthusiasm, only to be disappointed later on, generating cynicism among the team along the way.

Hospitals

In the group of the trainers and coaches of SolutionsAcademy we have an experienced trainer and coach, Gesa, who usually works in the hospital environment. Carlo had the chance to interview her on the use of the team coaching in this very special environment. One team she supports is a team of midwives who are already experts in their work in supporting newly graduated midwives grow in their roles and become more experienced.

Gesa uses the team coaching approach in two different ways. The first is a mix of team coaching and team training. In the first part of the meeting (normally it is a one and a half-day format), she coaches the team to define the attitude every midwife has towards the task of supervising the new graduated on a scale from 0 to 10, then she helps them to define what they already know about this activity. After this, she lets the team define the most important aspects that can be discussed during the meeting to make the team coaching as productive as possible for themselves. By doing this, they define the contents of the day that should be discussed, redefined and reviewed, and they define how they want to do it as well (plenary discussion, small groups, individual reflections and plenary, role-play). If they understand that they are missing some important information on a specific item – for example, giving feedback – Gesa asks them for permission to share a part of the content and then lets them decide how they want to practise it together.

The way Gesa uses the framework of the team coaching is extremely productive, helping the midwives to reflect on what they already know about themselves and to choose autonomously and responsibly the topic about which they need further information.

The second way of using the framework is the follow-up to this first meeting, after some time. During this second moment, Gesa lets them decide the agenda of the meeting (normally half a day), based on the experience they have gained in the meantime, transforming the team coaching to a team supervision session.

There is also a third (less used) way she uses the team coaching approach: to create (or refresh) the teamwork between doctors and midwives. With the goal of helping them to raise their level of collaboration, she creates a space where they can get to know each other better and can discuss new way of collaboration.

Based on Gesa's experience in this very delicate environment, she advises us that great care is required in the creation of the contract agreement. Due to the high level of hierarchy present in some environments, the coach needs to be very precise in researching the different possible stakeholders of the different teams and activities to avoid excluding any of them and generating unhelpful situations.

Another specific need of this environment is linked to the high number of rules due to the health restrictions that must be taken into account when the team starts to generate new ideas and behaviours. The coach has to support the team to reflect on them and encourage them to "remain within the lines" in generating the solutions in order to avoid wrong expectations.

Chapter 5

What size should the team be?

Abstract

Teams can range from two to a much larger number of team members (usually not more than 15). This chapter introduces you to working with large groups and small teams. For large groups, the Solution Focused versions of Open Space technology, or Bar Camp, World Cafe, Kitchen Table and Real Time strategic change, are delineated.

Large groups

Usually, teams are no larger than 15 team members. However, sometimes a team coach is asked to work with whole departments, entire schools or even a whole start-up together. This is when some knowledge of large group facilitation comes in handy.

Open Space/Bar Camp

The Open Space method was created by Harrison Owen (2023). He was interested in the functions of myth, ritual and culture and founded a consultancy, H.H. Owen and Company, to help companies in transformation. His main focus is the "power of self-organization". Legend has it that Harrison Owen's idea for Open Space emerged when he noted that participants at a conference were more engaged during the coffee breaks than during the event itself. He began structuring an entire conference in such a way that participants felt free to propose topics and discuss them only if they were interested in them, which tied in well with his ideas about self-organization. He imagined that if a group was united by passion and interest, it would be able to self-organize and achieve its goals.

The work is based on five "principles" and one "law". The principles are:

1 *Whoever comes is the right person.* The decisions that are made during the work are the work of those who are present. It is therefore pointless thinking about

DOI: 10.4324/9781003370314-5

who could have come or who should have been invited; it is much more useful to focus on those who are actually there.

2 *Whatever happens is the only thing that could happen.* In a particular situation, with certain people and discussing a certain topic, the result that will be achieved is the only possible result. The synergies and effects that can arise from the meeting of those people are unpredictable and unrepeatable, so whoever facilitates an Open Space meeting must relinquish control of the situation: trying to impose a result or a work programme is counterproductive. The facilitator of an Open Space conference must have total confidence in the abilities of the group.

3 *When it starts is the right time.* Given the creative aspect of the method, it is clear that there must be a beginning and an end, but the creative learning processes that take place within the group cannot follow a predefined time pattern. For example, deciding to take a break at a certain time can prevent a dialogue from coming to an end, thus losing information or ideas that are fundamental to the realization of the project.

4 *Wherever it is, that is the right place.* The space is opening everywhere all the time. It is important to be conscious and aware.

5 *When it's over, it's over.* If more time is sometimes needed than planned, the opposite also happens. If, for example, two hours have been allocated to deal with a certain topic, but the discussion runs out faster than expected, it is pointless to keep repeating oneself – much better to devote our time to something else.

The only law governing an Open Space meeting is the law of two feet: if participants find that they are neither learning nor contributing to activities, they are asked to get up and move to a place where they can be more productive. That is, if a person is having a conversation about a topic and does not feel they can be useful, or is not interested, it is far better for them to get up and move to another group where they can be more useful. This attitude should not be interpreted as a lack of politeness, but rather as a way of improving the quality of work.

An Open Space meeting proceeds as follows:

1 Opening circle (agenda co-creation process at the start, without the facilitator helping/synthesizing/suggesting/reducing topics). Each person who thinks they have a topic for discussion should write it down on a card, then stand up and present it to the plenary group, making sure that the person who proposed the topic is certain they care about it and does not think someone else should do it. When the topics have been exhausted, each proponent should attach their card to the noticeboard. Once this is done, everyone can observe the various topics that have emerged and decide which group they wish to join.

2 Facilitator's explanation of principles and law (calling them guidelines, invitations, whatever).

3 Multiple conversations, which ideally happen around the same big space and across time (without the facilitator helping those groups). The groups formed

will be self-managed and might produce, once the discussion topics have been exhausted, a report that, together with those of the other groups, will form the instant end-of-work report.

4   Closing Circle (comment and reflection). At the end of the day, there is a closing session, or an update session if the Open Space is spread over several days. There is no need for any particular formality, everyone sits in a circle again and the facilitator asks if anyone would like to express their opinion on the work done and what they intend to do in the light of the facts that have emerged.

The Open Space can be an effective tool, but it should only be used if particular conditions are met. Otherwise, it not only becomes ineffective, but is also a waste of time and money. It normally works in a situation that involves:

• a serious and real problem to work on (business burning issue)
• a high degree of complexity
• multiple points of view
• widespread conflict
• the need to find a solution immediately.

However, we can also list some of the most important factors that result in a successful Open Space meeting:

• Select the environment carefully and make sure you check the rooms – hotels *always* want to stuff more people in one room than is feasible for an Open Space: you need a bigger space as the plenary room and more "little" spaces for the multiple meetings planned.
• Explain the process in the invitation and explain the rules well on the day.
• Use an "agenda wall" with prepared Post-It notes.
• Make sure people know what they want before you start facilitating (e.g. by having them pair up and coach each other on that).
• Feedback wall: you can prepare facilitation and note-taking guidelines for the small groups.

The role of the facilitator

Facilitating an Open Space is very different from any other facilitation experience and the desire to have control over events must be put aside. The facilitator must first define the time and space, launch the topic to be discussed and set out the law and the four principles. When the group is arranged in a circle, they must "open the space" by entering the centre. They take the floor to present the topic to be discussed and explain that the blank wall in the central room represents the work program and that it will be constructed on the spot and by the participants themselves.

It may seem that, once the initial explanation phase is over, the facilitator has completed his task; however, this is not the case. The facilitator must always be present – obviously physically, but also mentally, focused and always available. They must convey confidence and tranquillity, always telling the truth to gain people's trust. Finally, they must be capable of not attempting to control events in order to bring them to a point they decided upon in advance; such an attitude would lead to the certain failure of the Open Space meeting.

Facilitating the Open Space format online needs to be accompanied by a board in Miro/Mural where the schedule and structure is visible to everyone and each space is linked back to the agenda. Each session is facilitated in a separate breakout room. If you want to add a more authentic feel to the Open Space you can consider creating an immersive space on platforms such as Spatial (www.spatial.io)

Case 5.1:   Team coaching for strategy

During his past experience as a facilitator, Carlo applied this framework in a team coaching with the goal of defining the guidelines for the future development of an Italian branch of a corporation in the chemical industry.

The main goal was the definition of the strategic guidelines of the development of the branch for the next five years. The CEO of the company, a wise and far-sighted person, asked Carlo to facilitate the team coaching session, choosing to involve a big part of the company in this definition, instead of "simply" asking the board of directors to take the decisions. His goal was to invite everyone to participate in the creation of those guidelines. It meant involving more than 60 people in a large team coaching session, creating the right space for free discussions about the different point of view and summarizing everything at the end of the day.

The event was organized in the plenary hall of a hotel near the headquarters of the company and the invitations to all the people involved were sent out one month before the meeting. The invitation contained a carefully crafted message clarifying the importance and the goal of the meeting, the explanation of the relevance of the presence of all persons involved and the guidelines for the event. It also contained the non-exhaustive list of some topics that should be discussed during the day and the call anyone who wanted to share their ideas about them.

On the day of the event, 16 people came forward and presented their ideas to the plenary group. An agenda was created and everyone was given the opportunity to attend the discussions in the various designated breakout rooms. In order to ensure that those presenting the topics also had the opportunity to take part in other discussions, each topic was repeated twice at two different times and in two different locations. During each discussion, the presenter of the topic recorded notes about what emerged on a flipchart and, at the end of the two presentation sessions, was tasked with producing a couple of sheets of paper on which to note down the salient points that had emerged. In the next round, all presenters had to post the sheets produced in this way in the plenary room, leaving time for everyone to read them.

The final round consisted of free discussion of the results at five round tables, placed in the centre of the plenary hall, at which everyone was free to sit. At the end of the discussion, each table would produce a flipchart with its three most relevant guidelines from the entire day, which would be analysed and developed by the board of directors.

World Cafe

The World Cafe is an effective method for engaging in informal, lively, concrete and constructive conversations on issues relevant to an organization or community. It is based on the principles developed by "The World Cafe" (https://theworldcafe. com), but the format can easily be adapted to different situations and needs.

This format allows many people to dialogue together, develop a shared understanding of the situations being addressed and converge on initiatives that unite. It is a practice that fosters dialogue, knowledge transmission and mutual influence between people.

The guidelines

- *Clarify the context.* Identify from the outset why you are bringing people together. Knowing the purpose of the meeting will help you consider which participants should be involved and which elements are important to realise the purpose.
- *Create a hospitable environment.* Create a space that provides security and encouragement. When people are at ease, they think, listen and speak in the most creative way. Consider very carefully how the invitation and the physical space (ambience and furniture) help to create a welcoming atmosphere.
- *Explore questions that matter.* Discovering and designing questions that are important to participants are an area where your depth and attention can produce significant results. Your cafe can develop around a single question or around several questions in a logical progression through various shifts in dialogue.

World Cafes are an exploration and discovery of important issues and a search for effective solutions.

- *Encourage everyone's contribution.* As team coaching facilitators, we are increasingly aware of the importance of encouraging participation, but most people don't just want to be there – they want to actively contribute and leave a trace. It is important to encourage everyone to share their ideas, perspectives and proposals; at the same time, it is appropriate to give freedom to those who want to participate simply by listening.
- *Connect diverse perspectives.* The opportunity to move between tables, meet different people, actively contribute your thoughts and connect the essence of one's discoveries to continuously expanding circles of ideas is one of the distinctive characteristics of the World Cafe. Participants bring ideas and themes to the different tables, exchanging perspectives and significantly increasing the possibilities for discovery and of surprising new insights.
- *Listen together for insights and deeper questions.* Through the practice of shared listening, attention to themes, recurring patterns and insights, we begin to feel a sense of connection with others.
- *Gather and share collective discoveries.* After several rounds of conversation, it is necessary to start a conversation involving the group as a whole. This offers the opportunity to connect general themes and questions that are now present.

The World Cafe process

1 *Setting.* Create a "special" environment, most often modelled after a cafe – that is, small round tables covered with a checked or white linen tablecloth, butcher's paper, coloured pens, a vase of flowers and optional "talking stick" or similar item. There should be four chairs at each table (optimally) – and no more than five.
2 *Welcome and introduction.* The host begins with a warm welcome and an introduction to the World Cafe process, setting the context, sharing the Cafe etiquette, and putting participants at ease.
3 *Small-group rounds.* The process begins with the first of three or more 20-minute rounds of conversation for the small group seated around a table. At the end of the 20 minutes, each member of the group moves to a different new table. They may or may not choose to leave one person as the "table host" for the next round, to welcome the next group and briefly fill them in on what happened in the previous round.
4 *Questions.* each round is prefaced with a question specially crafted for the specific context and desired purpose of the World Cafe. The same questions can be used for more than one round, or they can be built upon each other to focus the conversation or guide its direction.
5 *Harvest.* After the small groups (and/or in between rounds, as needed), individuals are invited to share insights or other results from their conversations with

the rest of the large group. These results are reflected visually in a variety of ways, most often using graphic recording in the front of the room. (World Cafe, 2023)

Kitchen Table

A kitchen table conversation is a way to conduct one or more conversation in an informal and relaxed but productive way. The methodology was introduced by Rick Wolfe and Lisa Francis-Jennings (2019) in their book *Innovation at the Kitchen Table*.

The strengths of the Kitchen Table resides in creating a space for conversation, active listening and sharing different perspectives with multiple stakeholders in the room. The general law of those conversations is that there are no right or wrong ideas and everyone's contribution is equally important.

The setting is created by arranging the space to show that everyone is to be taken into account. The middle table is for selected stakeholders/experts/decision-makers and is surrounded by multiple round tables. Depending on the topic and number of facilitators available, it might be useful to allocate a flipchart to each table. In preparing for the event, the team coach needs to invest significant time in ensuring that those who will be seated at the main table are confident and understand the process and what is required from them.

Rick always recommends that you make sure the entire group invited to the kitchen table receives a clear invitation in advance, and that the process is explained one more time at the start of the event. The workshop is opened by the host (team leader, HR, CEO, etc.) to set the stage and explain the context of the topic, and the mandate over the process is handed over to the team coach (mostly acting as a facilitator).

Assuming a process run in an organizational setup, the process is generally divided in the following main moments, lead by a facilitator:

1 *Middle table input.* Those seated at the middle table are invited to share their perspective on the first question raised by the facilitator. Each person has a couple of minutes to share without responding to what the others seated at the middle table are sharing.
2 *Conversation and active listening.* Once the initial thoughts have been shared, each participant from the main table is invited to join one of the side tables. Their role is to listen and capture the perceptions/thoughts/ideas/concerns raised at that particular table. Each table is invited to explore the remarks that were made before at the main table and bring in their input. (As the participants from the main room have been prepped before, they will know they can't interrupt the conversation at the table and they should stay in their active listening role.) The facilitator needs to keep an eye on the time and ensure everyone knows the schedule.

3 *Summarizing at the main table.* Once the time allocated for conversation at the side tables is over, the participants from the main table are invited to return to their places. The facilitator invites them to share what they heard was important or being shared at the tables they attended. It is important to ensure they keep in mind that they should not switch to providing a response or explanations to the remarks that were made; their role is to surface the valuable input that was being offered.

4 *Repeat.* If needed, you can repeat the steps above one more time in case there are further ideas that need to be clarified.

5 *Next steps.* Once all opinions have been captured, the facilitator can support the participants at the main table to identify main ideas/next steps that can be extracted.

After the event, a debrief session should be conducted with the team. The team coach would bring the notes and summary of results from the kitchen table and engage further with the team to transform them into actionable steps.

Selecting the participants to join the main table might sound like a dreadful thing. Hence, it is important to have prior conversations with the team/HR/sponsor to explain the process and identify that most useful representation at the main table and have enough time with those individuals to prepare them.

The role of the team coach or the facilitator is crucial to this method because they have to be able to create engaging but not leading questions for the experts and for the participants, as well as pick up interesting threads and expand them on other tables, and manage disagreements so that they can stay in a healthy and productive place in the discussion.

Case 5.2:   Kitchen Table

In one of the sessions from a team coaching course, after introducing the Kitchen Table conversation methodology, one participant approached Cristina as she was eager to introduce the Kitchen Table in a team coaching process that she was planning. Here is what Mihaela found useful from using the Kitchen Table in one of her team coaching processes:

Kitchen Table conversations were a tool that was used in team coaching interventions when an organizational system was going through leadership changes, when we wanted to define a new vision but also when we wanted to observe the dynamics between the roles and personalities of the members involved in this system.

Thanks to the working scenario that the tool proposes, the team coach can focus on the observation of the relationships between the participants, on the level of openness existing in their dialogue, on the level of interest and personal contribution to the clarification of the chosen topic and finally on the observation of the interference of the organizational context in the communication and decision patterns practised.

In this particular case, there was a team of teams coming together as a leadership team and two functional teams. For them, it was important to consolidate on the progress they made and clarify the company vision and, most importantly, the way they wanted to interact with each other.

Kitchen Table was used to support the team in clarifying these topics by allowing the middle table to be populated with the leadership team and in the room was every team member. The team coach took the role of the facilitator and guided the teams through three rounds of questions to explore them.

One of the realizations from using Kitchen Table conversations was that the process allows for exchange of ideas, everyone being listened to and engaging with the scope in mind. The other element that was important related to addressing diversified topics and capturing a multitude of ideas and at the end having clear take-aways.

Solution Focused real-time strategic change

Real-time strategic change is an organizational development method from the 1980s with elements that can be used effectively in team coaching. The special focus of real-time strategic change, as the name implies, is decisions and even project work happening in real time. We have long been in favour of workshops in which actual work happens, rather than meetings in which people meet to distribute work that takes place once someone gets around to it (or not). The topics of real-time strategic change are usually fundamental challenges, a new strategy, reorganization and reorientation – in short, anything that is fundamental and needs action soon.

The phases of real-time strategic change meetings are quite similar to the Solution Focused gallery (there seems to have been something in the air in the 1980s, with many future-focused approaches emerging from that period):

1 Goal setting and current status
2 Future vision
3 Generating options
4 Project planning and actions.

In original real-time strategic change, Step 3 is "problem analysis and diagnosis". For reasons you will understand by now, we relabel that step "generating options".

Here are some options to facilitate a Solution Focused real-time strategic change:

1 Goal setting and current status:
   • Talk by management: What is difficult about the situation and why do we need action?
   • Goal-setting in small groups/plenary (e.g. with Post-It notes): If we successfully spend two days on this, what will tell us that it was worth our time?
2 Future vision:
   • Work in small groups: Suppose we manage this challenge, what difference will it make?
   • Stakeholder map: Suppose we are successful, who will notice?
   • Talk by an organization that already mastered this challenge.
3 Generating options:
   • Scaling with the whole group: On a scale of 1–10, where 10 is our future vision, where are we now? What is (still) working?
   • Discussions in departments/teams: On a scale of 1–10, where 10 is our future vision, where are we now? What is (still) working?
   • Scale +1: Suppose we move one step higher on the scale, who will notice what?
   • Open Space facilitation: In order to reach our vision, what do we have to discuss? Definition of projects and presentation of projects
       At the end of the "generating options" phase, the organization or team ideally has a whole list of ideas. After this phase, the team takes a break during which the decision makers review the ideas and make concrete decisions on what they want implemented. They create concrete work packages for the team.
       When the team comes back, the decision makers present the way forward and give their rationale as to why they think the ideas they chose are suitable for the moment.
4 Project planning and actions: The team now gets together in the appropriate groups and starts planning the projects defined by the decision-makers. Ideally, there is enough time to start working. As everybody will still be in the same room or in close proximity, it is easy to communicate to other groups if changes need to be made.

The whole process is then followed up after a few weeks.

The role of the team coach here is more one of a facilitator and process designer than a coach, and it may be worth mentioning this to the team. There are situations in teams and organizations where something urgent arises – a crisis or new development – and team coaches may be asked to support the team in these situations. Rather than the team or organization having to get used to someone new (such as an organizational developer), team coaches might use this approach. In the follow-up, more traditional team coaching topics, like a reflection on what went well and how the team could perform and collaborate better next time, might take place.

Small teams

Coaching a small team means you may want to take into consideration few important factors that make such an engagement a slightly different task from coaching a large team. In our experience, the following factors play a very important role in ensuring you offer the best value as a team coach to a small team:

1 Asking questions or/ and speaking out in a small group may be particularly challenging for some people, so your task will be to make them feel safe expressing their opinions and encouraging everyone to contribute equally.
2 Small teams allow great flexibility – as a coach, you will have more flexibility to adapt to the needs of each participant and get to know each team member personally.
3 Interpersonal dynamics in a small team is more likely to be self-managed by the group over the duration of coaching.
4 Small-team coaching offers space for flexible delivery – if/when the need arises to meet, you can organize a coaching session within a short period of time, either in person or using commonly accepted virtual means (remembering confidentiality).
5 Small-team coaching offers the team members greater space to deeply engage in the process and benefit from the setting this provides.
6 Timing might be something to consider. With larger teams, any exercise/activity takes time. With small teams, it might be that you work through the agenda very quickly, so be prepared to work on further topics once you are done with the initial structure.

These factors are important and, once you take them into consideration, we encourage you to think about how you can apply Solution Focused moves as a way to tap into the power of small groups and to encourage participants.

Case 5.3:   Coaching a team of two

Coaching a team of two? Would that work? Yes, it would work just as well.

Cristina had the opportunity to work with a very small team of two people for six months. They would meet every month for a two-hour session and work on a certain topic in line with their objectives defined at the start of the process.

One time, both came to the session completely overwhelmed and finding it difficult to engage. After 30 minutes, it became clear that the initial structure of the workshop was not matching their needs, so Cristina suggested they go back and strengthen the team feeling and their desire to work together. As a team of two, there were challenging times ahead to balance the workload. And the sense of belonging to a team was definitely needed. At the end of the two hours, even if the structure of the workshop had to be defined on the spot, both left with a stronger feeling that they could count on the other person to help pull through.

References

Owen, H. (2023). *A brief user's guide to Open Space Technology*. https://openspaceworld.org/wp2/hho/papers/brief-users-guide-open-space-technology

Wolfe, R. & Francis-Jennings, L. (2019). *Innovation at the Kitchen Table*. StratAffect.

The World Café (2023). World Cafe method. https://theworldcafe.com/key-concepts-resources/world-cafe-method

Chapter 6

Difficult situations

Abstract

Team coaching is not without its difficulties. This chapter offers you an exploration of the most important difficulties you may encounter as a team coach: negative participants; negative groups or mandated teams; attacks on the coach; endless chatter in the team coaching; situations in which no one wants to speak. The chapter covers dealing with strong emotions, as well as a situation where the team wants to use a diagnostic instrument (which is counter to the Solution Focused philosophy, but does happen). The chapter also describes several methods of helping a team resolve conflict: steps to conflict mediation; a description of how to use "time to think" and definitional ceremonies from narrative practice. Topics of diversity and inclusion are explored through a Solution Focused lens.

Introduction

In this chapter, we describe a few difficulties that may arise when you are facilitating team sessions. Of course, these only occur very rarely; however, it still makes sense to think about how you might deal with them should they happen. Allow us a word of warning: especially when you have not run many team coaching sessions, you might focus your perception too much on what may go wrong and on all the difficulties you foresee for the session. This will result in you becoming more anxious, increasing your perception of any small difficulty and blowing it out of proportion – not a good way of creating good conditions for yourself and the team. So read our remarks on how to deal with difficult situations and pack them into your emergency kit, then immediately forget that there might be difficult situations ahead. This way, you are prepared, as well as relaxed, and looking forward to your next team coaching session.

Difficult situations or participants?

In Solution Focused thinking, no participant is "difficult". As mentioned above, we interpret any behaviour of a participant as an offer of cooperation. Naturally,

DOI: 10.4324/9781003370314-6

every once in a while we perceive a participant as bothersome. Sometimes a participant also seems to disturb the group. As a team coach, we then have to reframe our perception and ask ourselves what the positive intention behind the behaviour we perceive as "bothersome" or "disturbing" might be. Sometimes we have to help the group or the respective participant discover what they need or what needs to happen so the environment can be transformed into one that no longer makes it necessary for anyone to be "bothered" or "disturbed". The question we primarily use for such interventions is "What instead"?

- From difficult situations to difficult participants.
- Difficult participant = perception of resistance.
- Between the noses and not between the ears.

Negative participants

Some participants are very critical toward a team coaching process – or team coaching processes in general. They do not believe anything useful can come out of it. With this kind of expectation, they often seek confirmation in the session. No suggestion is good enough, and every activity is suspected to be a waste of time even before the participant has tried it.

Case 6.1: The negative engineer

Kirsten was facilitating a strategy process for an international engineering company. The most important stakeholders were invited to think about their future communication strategy. Participants were from many countries across the globe. She started by goal-setting: "What needs to happen here today so that coming to this workshop was worth your time?"

Everybody answered the question – except for a German engineer who said that what the participants had come here to do had been fixed in the agenda and the invitation. He was not in the mood for "games" – the new communication strategy was far too serious a matter. When Kirsten asked what needed to happen for him instead of "games", he answered that he needed to see us working seriously on what we had come to do and that not a lot of time should be lost with facilitation blah blah, etc. She asked how he would recognize "serious work", but that was too much for our German engineer. He did not want to comment further. Kirsten asked him whether we could continue with the planned process, and he agreed. The rest of the group was very enthusiastic and happy with the process; only our engineer was not joining in.

Kirsten asked herself what he might need to be able to participate more energetically – in other words, what was important to him. Since he had not wanted to respond when she had asked, this was a bit difficult to guess or to find out. She also did not want to focus all her energy on a "negative participant" and thereby take that energy away from the rest of the group. Luckily, Kirsten remembered that the participant was an experienced professional and adult who probably had good reasons for his behaviour. So she continued working with the group and ignored the grumpy remarks from the corner in which the engineer had placed himself for the time being.

Kirsten used a coffee break to start a conversation with him. She confirmed that it was also important for her to have an effective and efficient day with the group. Kirsten said that she had heard him say very similar things – for example, that he wanted an efficient and goal-oriented process. They might, however, have different ideas on what exactly that was – which again is quite normal for people who are meeting for the first time. And – to Kirsten's surprise – he agreed. Kirsten asked him to be patient and bear with the process for a while, and also to alert her when we were going off track or doing something that made no sense, as well as to make suggestions about how to improve. She told him it was important for any group to have someone in it who did not fear expressing their opinion and who was critical of the process to improve it. Over the course of the day, this man was able to make a few very interesting and helpful suggestions, which were used positively by both Kirsten and the group.

Giving critical participants the task of being critical participants is sometimes a good chance to help both them and the group to profit from each other. On the one hand, you change the perception of the coach from "what a bother" to "they have an interesting way of showing their cooperation". On the other hand, the critical participant feels that they have been taken seriously and their needs and concerns have been appreciated.

There are a few traps here, however. Sometimes what we are doing actually does not make any sense. We might not have understood what the team wants and what their concerns are. Maybe we missed crucial information, or the organization or HR department forgot to tell us something that was important to the team. Or maybe we did not listen well enough. In these situations, you have to go back to ground zero and think from the beginning. Don't see the "reframe" of a "difficult" participant as a "facilitation trick", but as a sincere quest to find out what can be useful to the team at any given moment. And if what is useful is not what you planned to do, you have to be flexible and change the plan.

Another trap can be that there are sometimes very different interests of team members represented within a team. It may be that this results in a situation in which it makes more sense for one participant to sabotage the process instead of collaborating on a solution. We do not want to say that it is a good idea to start a team coaching session with this focus – this too easily turns into a self-fulfilling prophecy. In our experience, it makes sense to go back to goal-setting when you feel there are no overlapping interests in a team coaching session. Ask the group: "If this workshop is worth your time, personally, for each one of you, what will be better as a result? What else?" It might be useful to have everybody write down their answers on Post-It notes individually before asking the plenary. You only continue working with the group when you can find a goal that is worth the time for everyone in the room. The worst that can happen is that the group discovers there are not enough congruent goals to go on – and this is a valuable piece of information. We would then go back to the HR department and the team leaders (if they were not present in the session) and ask what would need to happen to obtain more congruent goals for the team. We might be able to clarify or even change the framework conditions in the organizational environment.

Negative groups – mandated teams

Sometimes the team coach has the impression that the whole group is negative. This happens very rarely when you can clarify what the needs of the group are in interviews with each group member. The cases in which we were confronted with a "negative" group are exclusively from situations in which someone else – and not the team – generated the idea that a team coaching or training session was called for and the team did not agree.

Case 6.2:   Yet another change

At the beginning of her career, Kirsten was asked to take over presentation training and coaching sessions for a sales team. Their boss had asked one of Kirsten's network partners and had talked very negatively about their "complete lack of presentation skills". Her network partner did not know that this boss was known for his temper tantrums and overly critical attitude. He was very unpopular in the organization because he consistently regarded only himself as competent and saw everybody else as a "complete waste of space".

The network partner – unaware of all this turmoil – called Kirsten and asked whether she could run these relatively standard presentation training and coaching sessions for the sales team as he had too much to do. At the start of her career, Kirsten was very happy about such an easy and substantial piece of work, so she agreed. She assumed there had been a meeting to clarify the process with the HR department and maybe even individual representatives of the sales team. Hence, she entered the first session with naïve confidence.

Imagine her surprise when she arrived and looked into a round of stony faces. One participant said, "Now let's see what kind of entertainment our boss has provided this time!" People started laughing sarcastically. "Do you know how much presentation experience each and every one of us has? There is really nothing you can teach us or coach us on."

Kirsten was flabbergasted and the participants probably realized how uncomfortable the situation was for her. This might have eased the tension a little bit. Surprised, Kirsten asked, "So what makes your boss think that you need a presentation training?" More sarcastic remarks ensued: "When you ask our boss, we probably need training to wash our hands." Kirsten sighed: "Oh, I'm sorry – then we are all really at the wrong event." Maybe her unpremeditated sigh made the participants drop their weapons in surprise about her honesty. They started complaining about their boss and told her it was very difficult to deal with his inability to see their competences. Kirsten could very much empathize with them since she was in a very similar situation herself at that moment. After a while, the group had vented their frustration and Kirsten asked them how they usually dealt with the situation productively.

There were the first signs of a willingness to work together, and the atmosphere became significantly more productive. One participant said, "There is really no use complaining. We cannot cancel the session, neither can our coach – we would all be in big trouble. And really, it is not the coach's fault." They continued by negotiating about what might happen in the planned sessions so we would not be wasting everybody's time. The team said they were interested in giving and receiving each other's and Kirsten's feedback on their presentation skills in real presentations they were planning. They also wanted her to use video to record and analyse their presentations. They had successfully formed a secret alliance for learning in spite of the circumstances.

After a few sessions, Kirsten asked the group whether they wanted to give feedback to their boss on the consequences of his overly critical behaviour. However, nobody was confident that this would change anything for the better. The only positive effect she was able to achieve for the team was that she was able to give honest positive feedback on their commitment and performance as presenters to the organization.

It is sometimes really hard to see "negative" behaviour as an offer of cooperation, but things can become a lot easier if you do. A "negative" group is at least open and honest, and makes it possible for the team coach to start communication about what is needed. The biggest trap in such a situation is for the team coach to take the behaviour of the team personally. Even in the unlikely case that the team coach has made a mistake, has not understood what the job is about or not taken concerns seriously enough, it is still better to find out about it before venturing into a session than afterwards in the evaluation sheets. You do not run the risk of spending several days with something that makes no sense at all.

We feel strong responsibility when we are taking up the lifetime of our clients with our team coaching measures. If you have 10 people in a two-day/16-hour workshop, you are taking up 160 hours, which is 6.66 days in someone's life. We really do not want to waste them. When you are dealing with "mandated teams" – that is, teams sent into a team coaching process by their boss or by the HR department and who do not see any need for it themselves – you can use the same tools as when you are working with individual clients. It is important to find out what the clients want to achieve if it is not what the original requestor wants. A useful question for these kinds of situations was developed by Mark McKergow (Jackson & McKergow, 2002): "Who is a customer for what?"

In contrast to coaching sessions with individual clients, different team members can have varying degrees of willingness to work on a useful goal for the coaching session. It is very important to be sensitive and to take care not to lose a participant. If you are too fast, you can lose those who see no need and have no interested in coaching; if you are too slow, you lose the people who have already been able to grasp a sense of the situation. In the worst case, with people who cannot see why they should be in this session at all, we have asked them to look for a space in the room they could use to work on other things rather than getting bored and boring everybody else. When possible, we asked the HR department or the original requestor of the session to agree (without giving individual names). If it is not possible to ask for permission, we would always opt to let participants use their time in whichever way is most useful for them rather than wasting everybody's time. It takes courage, but nobody has ever criticized us for it after we have explained the situation.

Other possible difficulties

Attack on the coach

Over decades of experience as a coach and team coach, it has only happened twice that participants could not alleviate their frustration other than by attacking us as coaches. The tone was very aggressive, and the main concern seemed to be to prove that the coach is a complete idiot. It is very hard to keep calm in such situations, reduce your own stress reaction and concentrate on the offer of cooperation that is obviously not there. Even in such a situation, it really helps to remember that you are not a complete idiot and that you are in the same boat as the participants.

Case 6.3: The coach as idiot

Mr Grabert was grumpy. Again, such a useless, stupid coaching session. His whole desk was full of important work. It was shortly before the end of the fiscal year, and his bonus depended on his ability to close an important deal before that. Maybe there was a way to shorten the session if he could curb the coach's enthusiasm. He entered the workshop room with a frosty demeanour. Many of his colleagues were already there – Grabert was sure they would also appreciate a shorter (or no) session. After the team coach had welcomed everybody, the following dialogue ensued:

Team coach: I looked at the minutes of our last coaching session ...
Grabert: Oh, yes? And did you understand anything? My impression was that you did not. Admit it – you have no clue when it comes to our business. You are just a hired training girl in a suit ready to cash in on your daily rates.

Exercise 6.1: The coach as idiot

Think about what you would answer in such a situation – however it might have arisen. Identify at least seven possibilities so that you are prepared if you ever get into such a situation. Rest assured, though, that such a conflict in the vast majority of cases has nothing to do with your qualification as coach, but rather is a result of difficult interactions that occurred previously. Remember, you might not be the best coach in the world, but you are the only one who is there.

Here are our seven possibilities:

Counter-attack

What? A counter-attack by a Solution Focused coach? You cannot be serious! Did we not just say that it was all about cooperation? Yes, it is about cooperation; however, there are business cultures in which the Solution Focused "Aikido" method of gentle and productive interaction is perceived as too soft and is not taken seriously. A team coach who cannot stand their ground when attacked in this way will have difficulties achieving a productive result. In these few cases, a counter-attack can make sense. The important thing is to return to cooperation very quickly. This is almost like a ritual, a duel: everybody shows their weapons. After it has been established that the other is a worthy opponent, and you belong to the same class of serious thugs, you can go on to plan the next robbery. When we were running a conflict coaching process in Dubai, the group told us that a first step in solving a conflict situation could also be to start yelling and shouting at your opponent. They thought this behaviour would create respect and the willingness to cooperate. Of course, this is not our preferred solution, but if called for, why not? In our case this strategy could play out like this:

Grabert: Oh, yes? And did you understand anything? My impression was that you did not. Admit it – you have no clue when it comes to our business. You are just a hired training girl in a suit ready to cash in on your daily rates.

Team coach: Mr Grabert, if comments like this really impressed me, I would probably really have no clue about your business – do you have another one?

Columbo method

Many over-40 readers will know Peter Falk as Inspector Columbo. The character is an absent-minded homicide cop who solves many cases by feigning to walk out the door after he is done questioning a suspect. The suspect lets down his guard and thinks the interrogation is over. Inspector Columbo turns around, still pretending to be absent-minded and confused, and asks one question that will decide the case. This is why feigned confusion is called the "Columbo Method". This method works especially well because it offers an alternative to the instinctive "fight or flight" mechanism that often kicks in when we are in stressful situations:

Grabert: Oh, yes? And did you understand anything? My impression is that you did not. Admit it – you have no clue when it comes to our business. You are just a hired training girl in a suit ready to cash in on your daily rates.

| *Team coach:* | Uh-hum, yes. I also really like my suit. Now I'm a little bit confused. What does all of that have to do with our minutes? |
| *To the other participants:* | Let's go on, shall we? |

Answering with a question

The traditional method used in Solution Focus is to step back and ask about the goal or those who may have coping questions.

| *Grabert:* | Oh, yes? And did you understand anything? My impression is that you did not. Admit it – you have no clue when it comes to our business. You are just a hired training girl in a suit ready to cash in on your daily rates. |
| *Team coach:* | I am really sorry you feel this way. What could we do under the given circumstances so that this is worth your time? |

The question of competence or incompetence of the team coach is not discussed.

Conflicts take precedence

In European systemic consulting, there is a saying: "Disturbances take precedence!" We do not think this is really the case. When you adopt this adage, it is all too easy to focus on all the factors that make a successful coaching process difficult. Nevertheless, it is not the adage itself, but the systemic process that coaches suggest, that is very useful. The behaviour of the participant is labelled "a disturbance in the interaction" and not classified as a form of aggression. A "disturbance" is much less dramatic than a conflict and takes up much less attention. It is simply normal that human relationships and interactions are sometimes "disturbed" and not running smoothly.

Grabert:	Oh, yes? And did you understand anything? My impression is that you did not. Admit it – you have no clue when it comes to our business. You are just a hired training girl in a suit ready to cash in on your daily rates.
Team coach:	Oh – it looks like we're having a bit of a glitch in the process. Actually, I wanted to discuss the goal of this meeting with you, but this doesn't seem to be the right thing at the moment.
To all participants:	It seems to me that it would be useful to look at this glitch before working on the results we want to come away with. Would that be okay with everyone? Mr Grabert – what is important for you at the moment?

What is still working well?

A Solution Focused way of dealing with such "disturbances" or "glitches" is to look for exceptions and resources. There is obviously little confidence that something can happen in this coaching session that is useful for the team. A prerequisite for using this Solution Focused way of dealing with such a situation is recognizing and acknowledging that the process or relationship isn't working smoothly at the moment.

Grabert:	Oh, yes? And did you understand anything? My impression is that you did not. Admit it – you have no clue when it comes to our business. You are just a hired training girl in a suit ready to cash in on your daily rates.
Team coach:	Oh, I'm really sorry – our collaboration doesn't seem to be working very well at the moment, does it? However, I do think if anything is to come out of this session, we have to collaborate and come to a productive working relationship. It would really help if we all are confident that we can achieve something useful today.
To everybody:	Would it be okay if we started by spending some time on this?

The team coach then takes a flipchart and jots down a scale of 1 to 10. 10 means the team is very confident that this team coaching session will have useful results and 1 is the opposite. The team members now rate their confidence by posting sticky dots or marking a cross on that scale anonymously (the team coach looks out the window during the process).

Team coach:	Let us first look at why some of you are not a 1. What is already happening in our coaching session – something that I am doing or something that you as a team are doing, that gives you confidence that this can be useful?

These answers are collected on a flipchart. Afterwards, the team coach elicits answers on what X+1 would look like. What would need to happen so that the team can be a little more confident that the results of the process will be useful? Again, it helps to create one flipchart for what the team will be doing if it is more confident that something can come out of the sessions and what the coach will be doing when the team is one step higher on the confidence scale.

What was that all about?

Very seldom, there will be cases in which you have situations where one participant in the workshop isn't able to behave in such a way that the other participants to not feel extremely disturbed by their behaviour. This does not happen often, and in our case it has never happened in business situations. We do know these kinds of situations from our work with high school students and workshops for unemployment agencies. Our experience transferred to our example could look like this:

Grabert: Oh, yes? And did you understand anything? My impression is that you did not. Admit it – you have no clue when it comes to our business. You are just a hired training girl in a suit ready to cash in on your daily rates.

Team coach: Mr Grabert, what was that all about? You're obviously not willing to collaborate constructively here. Do us all a favour and go back to your office and work on something that is useful for you. I suggest we meet with your boss and the HR department later on to agree on how we should proceed afterwards.

The seventh method

The seventh method is "It always depends ..." Continue thinking about what kind of solutions you would feel happy with and how you could feel comfortable in difficult situations. I'm sure you will find your very own "seventh method".

Endless chatter

Sometimes you have people in workshops who talk a lot. Their motto seems to be: "Everything has been said but not by everybody." Therefore, they busily repeat what has already been said or illustrate points that have been mentioned previously with their own lengthy examples that nobody is really interested in. The other participants begin to roll their eyes and become annoyed. Sometimes this kind of behaviour can even get on the nerves of the most patient team coach.

It is important to differentiate two things: Is the participant getting on your nerves only? Then it might be best to mentally take a "patience pill" and remind yourself that work is sometimes work. If the participant is getting on the nerves of other participants or even the whole team, then it might be helpful to launch an appreciative attempt to rein in the chatter.

All methods that deprive the chatterbox of their audience are usually useful: small-group work, peer work or individual work. We have created especially good experiences with cascading groups: you pose a question, and everybody thinks about the answer individually first. Next, you condense the most important aspects of your answer together with a partner. Then you form small groups of four people who write down the most important results on a maximum of three Post-It Notes.

We don't think exposing the chatterbox in front of the group or making them lose face makes sense. Sometimes it is useful to spend time with such people during the break and listen to what they have to say. It also helps to remind yourself that some people learn by verbalizing what they think. Usually, chatterboxes do not have negative intentions – they want to contribute and help people have fun, and they think their discoveries are important and want to share them. We have also found that recognizing the expertise of the chatterbox can help. We have asked them during the break whether they would mind holding back what they have to say to give other participants a chance to think for themselves or to generate answers since they seem to need more time.

The aquarium

Sometimes you are confronted with the opposite problem to the chatterbox. You enter the room as a team coach, and one by one of the participants start arriving. They do not say anything except for a mumbled "morning". The answers to any questions from the team coach are short and there are long breaks in the conversation. You feel like you are sitting in a goldfish bowl among the fish.

Exercise 6.2: We have ways of making you talk

At this point, you already have considerable skills in devising possible reactions. Invent at least four ways of activating the participants or helping them to contribute.

Pair work or small groups

Devise a really good question and ask the participants to work on it in small groups or pairs. Tell them beforehand how to document the result: on Post-It notes, in a role-play or on the flipchart.

Paradoxical silence

The team coach takes up the language of the team, stops speaking and from now on continues working non-verbally using gestures and mime. Here they write a question and a number of minutes on the flipchart. They then signal using mime that now everybody should start working on this question individually. If a participant starts to talk, the coach signals that they should be quiet. After a while, everybody will probably want to start talking.

Patiently count to 300

Patiently accepting that there is silence is not always easy. However, it can be a good method to warm up the group. Usually, the silence is not the problem. The problem is that the coach starts thinking about why the group is silent and gets entangled in their own interpretations of the silence. Counting to 300 is sometimes more useful than trying to entertain the group or "fill" the silence.

Ask what the matter is

You can simply ask why everybody is so quiet. It might be that yesterday was the night of the annual company party, an important football game was lost by the local team or there are other reasons why everybody didn't sleep well. Maybe there is also an important reason that you can deal with in the team coaching session.

Dealing with strong emotions

"The whole world is a very narrow bridge and the main thing is not to be frightened" is a beautiful old Jewish saying. Human beings have strong emotions when something is important to them. We do not ignore this fact in Solution Focused work: emotions simply happen, and they belong to any process. The difference from traditional work is that we do not focus on the expression of emotions. They are simply there and, in most cases, they do not get in the way of the work. Insoo Kim Berg is said to have mentioned in a conversation with a woman who was very sad and could not stop crying, "You know, it is possible to cry and think at the same time." So if somebody becomes emotional in a few workshops or somebody is angry or sad, then your main task as team coach is not to be frightened and to keep focusing on the good in the working relationship: the goal, exceptions and resources. It is very helpful to have an attitude of "it is completely normal that you feel this way – these things happen."

Case 6.4:   Anger and frustration

Everything in the company was going downhill. Salaries were no longer as good as they had been. The food in the cafeteria had gotten worse. The company was hiring more and more temporary people and was giving out fewer and fewer normal contracts. Those in the leadership team of this company were fed up with everything. The last thing they wanted was a coaching session to think about how to lead their people. During the whole day, they kept talking about how it was really impossible to lead people well under these kinds of conditions. They were simply upset.

After the whole group had started another round of complaining, Kirsten asked the team whether they should plan some time to talk about "leading in difficult situations". She was very surprised to hear that they were not at all interested in talking about this topic. They all thought this would not change anything. The conditions of the company were dictated by economic circumstances, and they would not be able to do anything about that. Kirsten asked the team how they might deal with this instead, and how the session could explore their understandable, yet not very productive, desire to have time to complain every once in a while.

In the morning, there had been discussion about how team members noticed when they have a good team leader. One answer was that the leader would take time to listen to them and acknowledge and recognize their concerns and complaints. They had named this "Sometimes being a wailing wall". It was then agreed that a team coaching session could also be used to express frustration, complaints and concerns about the situation, and that it would be useful for them if Kirsten acted as their "wailing wall". She should simply listen patiently and remind them to return to more productive issues after five minutes.

The team wants to use a diagnostic instrument

Before we go deep into this part, we need to know why we are putting the request of a diagnostic from a team under the category of "difficult situations"? In what way is this request a "difficult situation"? Normally it is not, and there are so many diagnostics that are able to measure different dimensions of a team: the level of trust, the level of conflictuality, the way the members prefer to communicate, the "personality identity" of a team and the kind of predominant culture representing the team ... and each of them can be a powerful way of representing a specific aspect of the team dynamics.

So why do we consider that request a difficult situation? In order to discuss it, we need to remind ourselves of the "benefits" of having a diagnostic. Here are some of them:

- They can create a common understanding of the problem or of the starting situation.
- They can "justify" the current situation of the team and the related problems.
- They can help to validate some assumptions (*This is the reason we don't trust each other ... we are in the earliest stage of the team ...*)

We also need to reflect on those other thoughts: how can we be sure that "all" the situations make reference to those described in the diagnostic? How can we be sure that all the teams in a specific stage of their life can observe a lack of trust? How can we be sure that all individuals in every team can be described as the diagnostic is describing them? And finally, what happens if, after having used a diagnostic, every member of the team has different ideas to solve the problem, including the exclusion of some "non-suitable" people?

A good question here might be "In which way can the description of the problem, with the help of an external diagnostic, really help the team to identify a solution?"

As Solution Focused practitioners, we believe that:

- every situation is different
- the change always happens
- the client is the expert of the situation
- the client has all the resources to face the situation.

Based on that, we should believe that the team has everything that is needed to find the solution and that the client (the team and each team member) is the only one who "really" knows what is useful about the situation. So why do we need to use an "external" tool?

Normally, the need for a diagnostic is related to a form of "measurement" of the progress that a team can make towards the goal and is generally requested by the team lead or HR. If this is the case, in the initial stages of the project we could let those people reflect on which kind of indicators they think they can support and that represent the progress of the team. During the stage of the individual interviews, we can also ask the team members to reflect on what types of indicator might be useful for them. At the end of our round of interviews, we should obtain a rich grid of the most representative variables.

This set of variables can be used in all the stages of the team coaching process:

- during the workshop, to "scale" the future perfect and to assess the current situation as they perceive it
- between the workshop and the follow-up, to evaluate their progress by themselves, periodically
- during the follow-up, as a measure of the progress they have reached and to spot the most fruitful actions they have performed
- at the end of the project, to monitor the systems of the work the team has performed.

Conflict in the team

Fundamental considerations

When conflicts arise in the team coaching process between team members, or if the conflict is the reason for the team coaching process, the first important question concerns who might be the best people to start solving it? If you separate the conflict parties from the team and try to solve the conflict with these parties, you are signalling that the rest of the team members have nothing to do with it. Both conflict parties are identified as "the problem".

If you try to solve the conflict with the whole team, you run the risk of having the conflict parties lose face in front of the whole group. An isolated conflict that does not have a lot to do with the whole group can also steer a great deal of energy and attention away from what is important to the group. It is difficult to say which procedure is best. In any case, it is important to keep these possible dynamics in mind. As with any team coaching process, it is very important for the team coach to stay multipartial in conflict situations.

Every team member should be able to assume that the team coach is on their side. This is easiest if the coach can sympathize with the different perceptions and does not try to judge them: it is what it is. The coach should try to speak the language of all conflict parties. They may need to invent language that gives every conflicted party the feeling that they have been understood. The team coach listens especially carefully for possible joint goals, exceptions and resources. In Case 6.5, conflict at the end of the team coaching session helped the team to reach an even better solution:

Case 6.5:   Life is not a piece of cake

Ms Miller felt that she was being treated unfairly. Ms Faber always got the more interesting projects. Ms Faber mainly had to deal with IT (databases and project documentation). Ms Faber had promised to receive training from Ms Miller to be able to deal with these kinds of tasks. However, that training had not happened in the last two years.

The team coaching process was about developing strategies for the next year, deciding who would work together with whom and what priorities should be. During the whole process, Ms Miller had not talked about her desire to do something other than databases and project documentation. She seemed a bit shy but positive and interested in results. When the tasks and responsibilities were being distributed at the end of the workshop, everybody simply assumed that Ms Miller would continue to deal with documentation and databases. When she realized this, she lost her temper.

Ms Miller: Yeah, sure, me again. Right. Great! I will probably be spending the rest of my life programming stupid databases just because everybody else is too lazy or stupid to learn how to do this. Ms Faber – you have been promising me for ages that you will let me show you. I am fed up!

Ms Faber: Ms Miller, you know well that I did not have any time to get trained on this. Do you think we like looking into your sour face when we ask you to program a database for us? It's not that life's a piece of cake!

Chef:	Ms Miller, Ms Faber – that's really not what we are here for!
Team coach:	Just a moment. Let me see if I got that right: Ms Miller, you would like us to take into account that you want to do other things than just database programming when we assign tasks, right?
Ms Miller:	Exactly, but ...
Team coach (interrupts):	Okay, good. Ms Faber, if I understand you correctly, it is important for you to recognize that all team members do things that are not their favourite tasks and that everybody should be a good sport and not get on other people's nerves with their bad moods.
Ms Faber:	Yes, correct and Ms Miller is ...
Team coach (interrupts):	We have about 1.5 hours left. I do not think that we have time here to talk about what went wrong in the past. But we can take care to see that it will be better for everybody in the future. So please excuse my interrupting you a bit brusquely. If you are interested, we can talk about what happened between the three of us if you want. But now let's use the remaining time to think about a way of distributing tasks that everybody is happy with, okay?
Ms Faber and Ms Miller:	Of course ..., you're right ... I'm sorry ... the main thing is that we will find a better solution for the future.
Team coach:	So the way we just suggested to distribute the tasks does not seem optimal. What about the other team members: would it be okay with you if we spent some time thinking about which criteria tell you that the tasks have been distributed well. It would be nice if everybody could have fun with most of the tasks assigned to them, wouldn't it?
Team:	Sure ... yes, okay , you're right.
Team coach:	Mr Boss, are you okay with that, too?
Boss:	Well, our previous solution doesn't really seem to work anyway.
Team coach:	Then let's get down to business. We have been working with scales the whole day. Let us first define what a 10 of

a good task distribution is. Then let's see what we already have and then continue thinking about what the steps would be for an even better task distribution. Okay?

Team: Okay, let's roll!

Team coach: Let's spend 45 minutes on this and then we have another 45 minutes for more task distribution.

Team: Sure.

Team coach: Please take five Post-It notes each and write down five criteria that tell you that you have a good task distribution in your team. How would you know that your task distribution is at a 0 on the scale?

The team worked for 40 minutes and found that many of the criteria they had for a good task distribution (oriented to the competencies of each team member, clarity of priorities, information routes in case of changes and so on) had already been fulfilled. What was not working yet was training each other and standing in for each other in case of absences. Also, the team members did not yet dare to talk about what they liked doing and what they did not like doing so much. It seemed that Ms Miller's outburst had opened up the possibility for the whole team to talk about personal preferences. The team was very happy with the new solution.

Team coach: I am very impressed with how you want to take care of each other in this team. It is not only important to you that you do your work in a professional way and that you distribute work fairly, but you also want to take care of individual preferences. Thank you, Ms Miller und Ms Faber, for enabling us to have this discussion. If you had not talked about this, the result would not have been as effective.

Steps of conflict mediation

Just as in team coaching sessions, conflict mediation never follows the exact same process. The process always has to be adapted to the concerned individuals and there is no pre-described sequence of steps. It sometimes happens that you need to take a loop back to the step that you had already talked about previously. The topic of Solution Focused conflict mediation is dealt with comprehensively in Fredrike

Bannink's (2010) wonderful book *Handbook of Solution-Focused Conflict Management*. Here are some possible steps, which you will also find discussed in this or in a similar way in her book.

Establishing and maintaining a good working relationship

When you are dealing with conflict, it is especially important to establish and create a useful working relationship – not only between the coach and concerned parties, but also between the conflicted parties themselves. This is sometimes not easy. Feelings have been hurt and communication is obstructed. It is hard for the conflicted parties to regain confidence that a good solution is possible. Drama and conflict are almost magical magnets for our attention. Remember the last time you had a serious conflict and remember how difficult it was to think about anything else? It was as if the thought of the conflict eclipsed all other thoughts you might have had.

Apart from the normal Solution Focused possibilities for creating a good working relationship, such as normalizing (meaning it is completely normal for everybody to feel what they are feeling in this moment), Fredrike Bannink (2010) has developed another method. She calls it the "Māori method". Apparently, it is customary in Aotearoa New Zealand's Indigenous Māori culture that every participant in the meeting gets a chance to speak up once at the beginning of the meeting. They can speak as long as they want, but then they have to sit down and cannot reply to anything that is being said until the round is finished. This leads to everyone saying only what is really important to them. Also, people tend not to say anything too offensive because other people could react to this and they would then not be able to defend themselves. A Solution Focused way to use the "Māori method" is to ask: "What do you need to speak about here today so that you can have a productive and future-oriented conversation?"

Goal – goal behind the goal

"What is better for all conflicted parties when the conflict has been dissolved?" Using this or a similar future-oriented question, we try to find out what the world of the conflicted parties will look like when the conflict has disappeared. The question serves to turn the attention of the conflicted parties to things that exist outside the conflict. It generates hope that a life without the conflict is possible. This can only work if we can describe what would be there instead. Other questions could be:

- Suppose your conflict was solved, just like this – what would that look like? What would be possible then that is not possible now? What else?
- Imagine … you go home after this meeting. The meeting was very useful for you. So you go home and you do whatever you plan to do for the rest of the day. Sometime in the evening, you get tired and go to sleep. In the middle of the night, a miracle happens, and the miracle is that the conflict has disappeared into

thin air ... just like that. Since you are sleeping, you do not know that a miracle happened – and nobody tells you, either. How would you start noticing the next morning that miracle must have happened? Who else will notice? How? What will they notice? What will you be doing differently? What else?

- When your conflict is solved, what will be better? What exactly? What will be better for you (Party 1)? What for you (Party 2)? What do you think will be better for Party 1? What do you think will be better for Party 2? ... And when this happens, what else will be better?

Afterwards, you can start by setting goals for the coaching process at hand: "What needs to happen here today so that we can take a small step in the right direction?"

Exceptions and resources

Once you have elicited the goal behind the goal, you can start discovering exceptions and resources. You can either do that by using a scaling question, where 10 is somewhere between reaching the end goal after the miracle (if people already have a lot of confidence), or as small as "it is a little bit more likely that you can take a small step in order to start working together again."
The next questions could be:

- When was the last time that the situation was a little like after the miracle?
- How high was that on the scale? What became possible for you?
- What exactly did Party 1 or Party 2 do in this moment? What did each of them contribute?
- There was a time before the conflict – how was your relationship then? What exactly did you do when it was better?
- How did other people notice that it was better? What else?

Next steps

At the end of the mediation process, the parties agree on experiments, actions and first or next steps that could lead to an improvement.

Experiments

Experiments offer good possibilities for the parties to venture gently into a new reality, which includes hope for better collaboration. Sometimes it is not easy to imagine that healing a work relationship is possible (and even possible quickly) after so much excitement and conflict. The parties in conflict sometimes feel like a quick solution signifies a failure to recognize that there was a lot of suffering during the time of the conflict. This is why, as a coach, you should try to go slowly and never express more confidence than the clients themselves.

Here are some interesting experiments:

- Observe closely and notice everything that goes in the right direction. Please report these instances to the coach in the next session – this is necessary because we have to find out exactly what you want instead of the conflict.
- Throw a coin every evening – heads means that you will conduct yourself the same way as you always do, tails means you will behave as if the miracle had already happened.
- Whenever you see that the other party is doing something they should continue to be doing, put a small flower on their desk.
- Make an attempt to say something positive about your colleague in front of others at least four times next week. The special challenge is that you have to mean it.

Agreements and actions

When both parties are no longer extremely emotionally involved and are confident that the conflict can be solved, both can make contributions about how they want to behave in the future so a conflict like this is avoided or the existing conflict is solved.

To start the discussion you could ask:

When you are looking back on this time two years from now and everything went in a way that you can actually be proud of yourself and how you conducted yourself, what will you be saying then about your attitude and your behaviour during this time?

The coach asks both parties what their plan is for improving the situation and asks the other party whether they agree or there is anything else that they need, and vice versa.

Case 6.6: The files are in a mess

Team coach: I think we are now clear about how both of you would like each other's behaviour to be in the future. Ms Rutter, you are at a 4. Ms Andres, you are at a 5. Suppose both of you are one step higher on the scale. What will you be doing then that you are not doing or doing less of today?

Ms Andres: I heard Ms Rutter say it is important for her that she can find everything when somebody calls. I could take the last 10 minutes of my work and try to put everything back and write a quick note for Ms Rutter.

Team coach:	Ms Rutter, what will you do when you are step higher on your scale?
Ms Rutter:	Instead of getting terribly upset when I cannot find something, I will write a text message to Ms Andres asking her where I might find it.
Team coach:	Ms Andres – does this work you, if Ms Rutter writes you a text message in these cases?
Ms Andres:	We can at least try it. And also, I can influence this. If I do not have time to put everything back or to explain where I put things, I will get more text messages. At least it is worth a try.
Team coach:	How confident are you on a scale of 0 to 10, where 10 means you are very confident, that this can bring an improvement and you can actually implement this step?
Ms Andres:	A 6.
Ms Rutter:	Also around a 6.
Team coach:	What makes you confident?

The next steps and agreements should be things that both parties actually want to implement and that make both parties confident that they can lead to an improvement. Talk is cheap in these circumstances. It is very important to find something that helps the parties to move out of the perception that the other person is only doing things to bother them. In these situations, it is also possible to ask what will happen if the parties do not stick to their agreements and design a strategy for how to get back on track. This way the parties can prepare to deal with setbacks without questioning the success of what has already happened.

Exercise 6.3: De-escalation

Ben Furman and Tapani Ahola (1992) developed a very nice exercise for teams that are often in conflict situations with other teams. This exercise contrasts the "normal" or usual behaviours of teams that team members often display when they are in conflict with other people, who then become "the enemy", with a more constructive way of dealing with inter-group conflict. You can suggest this exercise when you see a similar dynamic happening.

First split the group into two small groups. Group A leaves the room and thinks about the faults of Group B. Group A then enters the room. You facilitate the following typical dialogue (maybe supported by a visualization on a flipchart). The objective is to simulate the typical escalation process and a conflict – try to have fun with the group in role-playing the road to conflict.

Here is the process:

1 Group A blames Group B for something.
2 Group B denies it.
3 Group A finds examples to support the blame.
4 Group B blames these examples on the conditions and/or the environment.
5 Group A develops an explanation for the unprofessional behaviour of Group B.
6 Group B develops an explanation about why Group A accused Group B so unfairly.
7 Group A threatens Group B with consequences.
8 Group B threatens Group A with consequences if they don't stop accusing Group B.
9 Group A leaves the room.

While Group A is outside, you explain to Group B how you can react constructively to criticism, whether justified or not. Again, you can write down these points on a flipchart.

1 Listen.
2 Express empathy – maybe even say you are sorry.
3 Ask what the other group wants instead.
4 Negotiate.
5 Agree on a first step.

Group A comes back to the room. This time, Group B reacts constructively. This conversation is normally much calmer and is more goal-oriented. Most of the time you do not have to say much about why it makes more sense to react to criticism as was demonstrated in the second example.

Time to think

Time to think is a title of American writer Nancy Kline's (1998) book *Time to Think*. She explores the idea of a thinking environment, which is critical to constructive communication, connection and action. There are two important lessons from this book: that the quality of the thinking we do impacts the quality of our action afterwards; and that the way we treat each other while we think impacts the quality of our thinking.

As coaches, we want to create space and conditions in our team coaching work that will help people to think well for themselves. Nancy Kline (1998) identifies ten ways that are most reliable elements of such an environment. We present them here, as these will help you to agree on and partner within the framework for the work you are doing with your clients:

1   attention – listen with respect and without interruption
2   equality – treat others as peers; give equal time and attention; maintain boundaries
3   ease – creates connection, so offer freedom with no rush and/ or urgency
4   appreciation – genuinely acknowledge other people's qualities
5   encouragement – encourage new ideas, move beyond internal competition
6   feelings – allow them to happen, acknowledge them but don't let them cloud your communication and thinking
7   information – offer facts and information, dismantle denial
8   diversity – welcome diverse thinking and identities
9   incisive questions – remove assumptions and challenge our limiting beliefs and preconceptions
10   place – create physical environment that nurtures thinking and shows people they are seen, valued and heard.

We often practise these points in our coach training and constantly think of creative and nurturing ways to use them in our coaching work. You may want to explore this concept as part of your partnering with the team you will coach. Get everyone to improve their thinking skills, prepare and get ready for the coaching work and facilitate the achievement of the solution in the process.

One way of using "time to think" in conflict resolution to help the parties listen to one another goes like this:

•   Ask the question: "What is your freshest thinking about … ("how to solve this", "what is happening", "what people really need", depending on the situation).
•   Pair the group up into diverse pairs and ask one partner of the pair to speak for five minutes while the other listens attentively and says nothing, apart from maybe asking: "And what else are you thinking about …?"
•   Switch listener and speaker.
•   Ask the group back into the plenary. Every participant can now speak for two to three minutes, answering the question, "What is now your freshest thinking?" The main thing here is not to pretend that participants did not listen to one another. It is about what emerges in the moment.

Enabling conflict parties to listen to one another is powerful and often a great step toward a resolution.

Pressing the pause button

We know that sometimes people get so frustrated, angry, emotional or simply stuck and unable to respond that it threatens to escalate the situation and/or prevent a constructive resolution. In such situations, we often offer a strategy called "Pressing the pause button". In a nutshell, this is a strategy to pause the conversation which will give the parties to the conflict space and time to reflect, think, gather thoughts and then respond in a way that addresses everyone's interests and needs.

We encourage you to describe the technique and agree on its use with the team at the very beginning of the coaching process. You need to explain its purpose and the process of application:

1   When any party of the team coaching group feels they need time to think, they either signal it verbally by using commonly agreed words – for example, "I need time to think" – or by using commonly agreed non-verbal cues – for example, non-violent hand gestures such as putting the hand on heart or head. What is important is that everybody agrees to respect this. Once someone signals this need, the conversation stops immediately.
2   Agree on a time limit for the "time to think". We advise no less than 20 minutes and no more than 24 hours.
3   Once the "time to think" starts, your team members should be encouraged to spend this time doing whatever they need to return to the process in a constructive way. It can be doing something self-soothing (e.g. stretching, listening to music) or reflecting on how to respond to the other team members (e.g. reflecting on their own beliefs, values, desires).
4   Check in. After the agreed time, you should check in with everybody to see whether they are ready to come back to coaching and conflict resolution. If someone is not ready, agree the time interval for the next check in.
5   Resolve the conflict. Once everyone is ready to return to the process, proceed with the coaching, revisit the disagreement and resolve it in the most effective way possible.

We all know that conflict resolution is not the easiest coaching conversation you will have. We also know that empowering people to enter the process with the tools such as "time to think" provides them with a simple, yet extremely effective, tool to navigate the conversation in a respectful, constructive and focused way. We encourage you to add this technique to your toolkit.

Definitional ceremonies

In conflicts, the parties involved often initially focus on the past: what happened, who did what, what was so stressful about it? "Definitional ceremonies", a structure from Narrative practice (White, 2004, 2007), make it possible to take this need of the parties involved into account and at the same time contribute to mutual understanding and the resolution of the conflict.

They can be used mostly at the beginning of a conflict coaching session, but also repeatedly in between, when the participants focus on past difficulties. Definitional ceremonies are suitable for conflict coaching with two participants or for situations where two or more groups are in conflict. They require tact and the ability to listen carefully to what the participants want, even though they may initially only express what they no longer want.

"Definitional ceremonies" are particularly suitable in situations where people want to have an emotionally positive relationship with each other after conflict resolution – such as when dealing with team members who work closely together or leaders in an executive team.

In conflicts, many participants are not only concerned with a "solution" – that is, what should be different after the conflict. During the conflict, evaluations and identity attributions of the respective other person have often arisen, which stand in the way of a further relationship. If, for example, project member A feels that another project member B is constantly passing off A's ideas as his own, A may conclude that B is an egotistical narcissist. You don't like to work with such people, even if you agree in conflict coaching that in the future B will say who he got the idea from. "Re-authoring" makes it possible to find one's way back to a more understanding cooperation without having to descend into the "depths of the problem".

In the following, we describe the steps of using "definitional ceremonies" for conflict resolution in teams.

In the initial situation, the parties meet to resolve a conflict between them that has lasted longer and goes deeper. The title of this meeting could be, for example, "conflict coaching" or "mediation". At the time of this meeting, all conflict parties should be at least cautiously interested in resolving the conflict and willing to talk. It may be necessary to conduct a preliminary interview with each party to determine whether and how a joint discussion can be conducted.

"Definitional ceremonies" can also be appropriate spontaneously in conflict coaching sessions when things surprisingly "heat up". Then it is probably useful to get agreement from both parties to change the focus – for example, by saying, "I have a feeling that something is very important to both of you here. Would it be all right if I asked you about it for a moment?"

We follow this structure most of the time:

1 Explain procedure, obtain permission, clarify sequence.
2 Strengthen listening skills of Person B.
3 Interview Person A about what is important.
4 Interview Person B for "re-telling".
5 Interview Person A about Person B's "re-telling".
6 Possibly arrange a next meeting.
7 Interview Person B about what is important.

8   Interview Person A for "re-telling".
9   Interview Person B about Person A's "re-telling".

If there are more than two people, you might either ask Group A and Group B to speak (if there are two opposing viewpoints), or ask A, B, C, D, etc. to speak in turn.

Phase 1: Explain procedure, obtain permission, clarify sequence

Acknowledge that there are different points of view:

> It seems to me that you have different perspectives on what happened. It's normal that we all have different perceptions. At the moment, however, it seems to make your cooperation difficult.

Explain your proposal for how to proceed:

> I would like to suggest that we spend some time together exploring your perspectives and motivations. In doing so, I would first have a conversation with Person A, with Person B listening. Then I would interview Person B and finally Person A again. Then we'll take a little break and I'll ask Person B afterwards about their views and motivations, with Person A listening. That way, you don't have to respond right away to what each other says but can focus on getting to know each other's perspective and motivations.

Get permission to do this:

> Could you imagine such an approach being useful, or is there something else you'd like to do right now to take a step forward here?

Clarify which of the two parties to the conflict will be interviewed first:

> Would it be okay if we started with Person A and Person B listened first?

Phase 2: Strengthening Person B's listening skills

Invite Person B to focus on listening and understanding. To do this, it is useful for Person B to put themselves in the role of someone who listens in an understanding, appreciative and supportive way, and to describe beforehand in some detail how this person does this, so they can draw on these resources. To do this, you can ask, for example:

*   Is there someone in your life who often listens to you in an understanding and appreciative way?

- How can you tell that this person is listening to you in an understanding and appreciative way?
- What else?
- When you are listened to in such an understanding and appreciative way, what becomes possible for you in this situation?
- What else?

Depending on the openness of the parties to the conflict, this conversation can be held right away. If the situation is very tense, you can start asking these questions without B openly responding to them. The main thing here is that B does not listen in his role as a party to the conflict, but with as much appreciation and openness as possible. In difficult conflicts, you can also ask the listening party to simply pretend to be the person they know always listens well.

When B feels able to really listen, begin interviewing A. Person B sits off to the side or perhaps looks in another direction – not interacting with you or A in this process. As a coach, however, you still have B in the corner of your eye. If you notice that Person B is beginning to listen as a party to the conflict, you can pause briefly and ask what Person B needs to get back into the role of appreciative and understanding listener.

Phase 3: Interview Person A about what is important

Say, "I would like to talk to you about the things that brought you here and that you would like to change. Person B will listen to us appreciatively and understandingly, as she has described, won't they?"

Person B reaffirms. "Person A, the fact that you want a change indicates to me that something about this is very important to you. Can you tell me what is important to you about this?"

As a conflict coach, you listen carefully to Person A's description here, but interrupt when Person A begins to accuse Person B.

The whole conversation should be about what is important to Person A, why it is important and how it became important to Person A without addressing Person B's behaviour.

Follow-up questions might include:

- Is there a moment for you in your life where you discovered for yourself that … is so important to you?
- Then what was that like?
- Why is that so crucial to you?
- What do you want to accomplish for everyone on the team with this?

Phase 4: Interview Person B for "re-telling".

In this phase, you talk to Person B and ask Person A to listen as appreciatively and understandingly as Person B did previously.

Explain your approach:

Now, I don't want to ask you to just tell me your impressions, but I'd like to ask you questions that I hope will be helpful – would that be okay?

For example, ask the following questions:

- Person B, in listening with appreciation and understanding, what most attracted your attention?
- Do you remember the words Person A used when talking about what was important to them?
- Was there anything that touched you or to which you can relate yourself?
- What did the conversation between Person A and I trigger in you?
- Has anything changed for you as a result of listening?
- If so, what has changed as a result of listening?

Phase 5: Interview Person A about Person B's "re-telling"

- Person A, in listening with appreciation and understanding, what most attracted their attention?
- Do you remember the words Person B used when they talked about what it triggered in them or what they can relate to?
- Was there anything about it that touched you or to which you can relate yourself?
- What did the conversation between Person B and I trigger in you?
- Has anything changed for you as a result of listening?
- If so, what has changed as a result of listening?

Afterwards, it is good to take a short break. Then the roles change and Person B tells what is important to them, while Person A listens with appreciation and understanding.

Further procedure

After both interviews, the conflict parties have usually developed more understanding of each other, and each knows what is important to the other. On this basis, possible solutions can then be discussed that take all this into account.

Case 6.7:   We are not talking! Never again!

During an executive coaching session in a project management company, where Kirsten coached the management level below the CEO using 360° surveys, it emerged that the board member responsible for sales and business development and the board member responsible for the core business – namely the execution of projects – were no longer talking to each other. Even when they were in the elevator with each other, they didn't talk. They considered each other incompetent and hopeless cases. However, for the continuation and further development of the company, it was crucial for the management team to establish a common strategy and agree on which and how many projects should be acquired, and that an overview be created of what would be handled when and with which employees.

In principle, both parties involved, with whom Kirsten had already had individual discussions as part of the 360° coaching, saw it in the same way. There was a fundamental willingness to sit down together, albeit grudgingly.

The meeting started very cautiously. Both parties shook hands, sat down and said nothing at first. This gave Kirsten the opportunity to explain her idea of how to proceed. This broke the ice and they both agreed to give it a try. They agreed that the younger board member responsible for sales and business development should start the interview.

Kirsten first asked the project director about the most appreciative and understanding listener in his life. In this case, she didn't want to know exactly who that was – the mood was still too tense for that and she could imagine that it would have been too much of a challenge at that moment to open up like that. However, the project director was able to think of a specific person and also confirmed that he was good at putting himself in that role. It was particularly nice that he remarked, "If we can't manage to really listen to each other here today with you in the room, we might as well not do it! I certainly want to try as best I can."

In the interview with the chief sales officer, it emerged that it was important to him to value all employees in the company equally, regardless of hierarchy. He enjoyed the exchange, quick decisions and uncomplicated procedures. As an example of why this was important to him, he recounted an incident from his previous job where exactly this kind of behaviour saved the company.

The project manager had a few "yes, buts" written all over his face as he listened, but then said during the "re-telling" that he had been particularly impressed by how enthusiastically and joyfully his colleague had spoken about working with the employees. He also saw the company as being more like a tanker than a speedboat. He would find it difficult but would like to start thinking about how to change that. He was even able to make some self-critical remarks in the direction of his own contribution to the sluggishness of the company.

The sales director was visibly relieved to hear this. He was surprised by the flexibility of the project board member and very much appreciated his openness at that moment. For him, the consequence was that he could now much more easily imagine looking for solutions together.

After the break, Kirsten spoke with the project manager. He was very concerned about planning and calmness in the staff. He told me about an incident with another board member who had occasionally accessed the employees of the project board directly without consulting them. This had even led to a young family man feeling compelled to cut short his family leave just to finish something that would have taken time. It was important to the project board to protect its employees here.

This was also met with appreciation and understanding from the sales executive. We ended the meeting at this point. In subsequent meetings, the two clarified responsibilities, processes and how to communicate urgency to each other without rushing. One particularly nice side-effect was that the idea of each other's lack of competence seemed to have evaporated.

The concrete description of what is important to a person, and where and how this person learned this, is important because it allows one person to understand the views and motivations of the other party to the conflict. The approach described here comes from Narrative practice. One might think that the question "Why?" is not part of the Solution Focused repertoire. The difference in problem-solving approaches here is not the absence of the question "Why?" but the fact that the analysis of the reason for the conflict is omitted. Both the Solution Focused and the Narrative approaches, in their invitations to talk, focus on the rich and, above all, concrete description of what is desired and what is already there. The "mixed technique" presented here does not just ensure a future improvement of the situation, but also a better understanding between the conflict parties in the future. The rather unhelpful explanations of the past (e.g. "He's just incompetent") are replaced by more helpful explanations (e.g. "He just had to be quick, so there was a bit of chaos").

Diversity and inclusion

Team coaching processes can include elements of diversity and inclusion. As both are increasingly important topics in today's world, it is useful for a team coach to be versed in the issues and the ways in which organizations aim at dealing with them.

In social-constructionist team coaching, we know that no team operates in a vacuum. The dominant narratives and ways of distributing privileges, rights and duties to different groups of people always influence what happens in a team. The ways these are distributed also influence the relationship between team coach and team (see the description in our section on executive teams and shop floor teams).

We have a preference for equitable and fair treatment of all, and at the same time know that viewing the world "equitably" is almost impossible given the web of different dominant stories in which we are all ensnared. If a team coach is read as white and middle class, they might experience privileges and responses to the ascribed privileges that they did not intend to take advantage of or communicate. Yes, our coaching assumption of multipartiality and as few assumptions as possible help, but it is not the whole solution. Systemic racism, sexism, homophobia and so on exist, and closing our eyes is not an option.

But how can we help teams when issues around diversity and inclusion arise? This book is too short to go into depth – a whole book should be written about this! But here are a few, non-encompassing, potentially helpful ideas.

The dominant narrative can be "externalized" so the whole team can become aware of it and start acting in solidarity against it. Rather than speaking about a man who "is a chauvinist", the team could speak about "someone who got recruited into the worldview that ..." Rather than hurling angry accusations against one another, the team might become aware that everyone is ensnared in these dominant stories and neither negate their impact nor enter into blaming each other. This does not mean hurtful behaviour gets excused or responsibility is relegated to "society", but it makes a lot of difference if someone hears "I know you are not a person who ... However, when ... happened, it played into the story of ... as ... What I'd prefer is ..."

Kirsten was able to interview Loretta Ross for the ICF Germany podcast on her concept of "calling in" instead of "calling out". The podcast is published on January 8, 2021, at Coachfederation.de/podcast. She advocates "calling people in" instead of "calling them out" on their mistakes. "Calling in" happens with love instead of anger.

She recommends the following strategies:

- Start with self-assessment: are you calm enough, are you not feeling too hurt to have the conversation?
- Ask yourself what is it that you would like the person to change.
- Make sure you are skilful enough to have the conversation with love.
- Talk to the person in private, not publicly.

- Stay calm.
- Use a non-threatening starter phrase: "I don't think I understood what you were trying to say … " or "Everything was going well in this conversation and then the temperature changed. Can we go back and find out what happened when the temperature changed?"
- Ask for the change in an understanding way: "I used to call people [insert the offensive word], too, but I have learned that they prefer to be called [better term], so now I use that word."

One of the prerequisites here is not to assume the worst of people but assume that they have good intentions but might not be educated enough about what offends others.

Of course, groups who are experiencing discrimination are not responsible for the education of the privileged group – it is the responsibility of the dominant, privileged groups. The team coach can help raise awareness and also help to create an atmosphere of listening and understanding the intentions.

Another issue may arise if a team coach notices structures in the team or organizations that actively counteract equality, diversity and inclusion. The team coach must then decide whether they would like to support the organization.

References

Bannink, F. (2010). *Handbook of solution focused conflict management*. Toronto: Hogrefe.

Furman, B., & Ahola, T. (1992). *Solution talk: Hosting therapeutic conversations*. New York: W.W. Norton.

Jackson, P. Z., & McKergow, M. (2002). *The solutions focus: The simple way to positive change*. London: Nicholas Brealey.

Kline, N. (1998). *Time to think: Listening to Ignite the human mind*. London: Cassell.

McKergow, M., & Jackson, P. Z. (2002). *The solutions focus: The simple way to positive change*. London: Nicholas Brealey.

White, M. (2004). Narrative practice and exotic lives: Resurrecting diversity in everyday life. Adelaide: Dulwich Centre.

White, M. (2007). Maps of narrative practice. New York: W.W. Norton.

Chapter 7

Continuous development as a team coach

Abstract

This chapter walks you through the steps of becoming a team coach through education and further development. You will learn how you can chose your initial training and how to continue with reflective and deliberate practice to improve your skills as a team coach. We cover team coaching supervision and provide an overview of the most important possibilities to gain an accreditation or certification as a team coach.

Initial training

Using the language of metaphor, we don't believe you can build a stable and solid house without proper foundations. As a coach, you partner people in conversations that change their life. We strongly believe that building your knowledge, collecting your theoretical and practical experience, practising in safe and supportive peer spaces and getting high-quality training, mentoring and supervision are key to you becoming a great coach.

Your initial training is a major stepping stone in building your ability to coach masterfully, impactfully and ethically. That is why it is so important to select a program that offers high-quality training and an opportunity to experiment and practise with diverse group of people and under the watchful eye of experienced practitioners and great tutors.

As the team coaching area has become an extremely dynamic and growing area within coaching, we encourage you to select the training that offers you the following elements:

- theory (with the model and philosophy that is best aligned with who you want to be as a coach)
- practice (in and out of class)
- peer learning (in and out of class)
- mentoring – both individual and group
- supervision.

DOI: 10.4324/9781003370314-7

Reflection

Reflection is key in building our self-awareness and nurturing our growth as humans and coaches. We invite you to create your own habit of self-reflection as well as reflection with your peer groups, mentors and supervisors. Looking back and reflecting on our work is an extremely valuable experience that allows us to evoke our awareness of our abilities, strengths and potential areas for growth.

We find this quote really powerful: "The ability to reflect on one's actions so as to engage in a process of continuous learning" (Schön, 1983).

Reflection can take place at different moments in time, and each time it may serve your growth slightly differently.

We see reflective practice as something you do on a continuous basis and not simply as a snapshot/a block of time in the calendar that needs to be used to think about something. The important element of reflection is extracting learnings; otherwise, it remains only as thinking time. Each moment of reflective practice needs to be seen through the lens of defining a purpose for that activity – perhaps better understanding the way you approached an event, discovering new way of doing something, exploring your thoughts or feelings in a certain moment from a team coaching workshop.

There are plenty of reflective practice models that can be used and adapted to team coaching, including the Solution Focused approach called SOLUTION. It is up to you to identify the method that best suits you.

SOLUTION reflective practice

This approach is based on the desire to step away from perception that reflective process needs to be a cumbersome process or that you need to approach it as something that only happens in a strict manner. SOLUTION has the purpose of creating a space to reflect upon a session linked with your objectives for the reflection, be it to learn more about the situation, how to bring more of your competencies, how you want to present as a team coach and so on.

Hence it starts with:

S – from "Suppose this reflective session is useful to you, what will be different at the end of it?"

O – Observable definition of the objectives, "what will you notice?", "what others will be noticing?", "how will you react to what their reactions?".

L – listing all relevant elements around the situation about which you are reflective.

U – understanding more about what went well.

T – taking time and thanking, which implies that the reflective practice process should not be something that is condensed into a certain amount of time, but rather an emergent process, and that you can park it and come back to it at different parts of the process or at any time that fits you best.

I –   innovate – as with any "innovation" process, this implies that several ideas will emerge, and that collecting those ideas will create the foundation of the next steps.

O –   optimising the ideas generated by considering what you want to bring more of to your clients.

N –   next step: "What is the smallest thing that you could do in the next 24 hours?"

The same process of reflection can be used as the facilitation technique for a team coaching workshop.

Other reflecting practice models

One model frequently referred to was defined by Borton (1970). It takes a very simplified perspective of inviting you to work through three steps:

1   What? (describing what happened).
2   So what? (analysing the situation).
3   Now what? (extracting learnings and take-aways).

Schön (1983) pictures it as two dimensions: the first dimension is reflection *on* action, which is probably the most traditional way we reflect. We look back at the coaching session that we concluded and gather our thoughts, observations and impressions. We encourage you to observe how you reflect immediately after the session and at some additional time interval. We encourage you to apply this approach to individual sessions and the longer coaching engagement. Both reflections offer you significant opportunities to grow, and we encourage you to do it while also recognizing how things such as memory, accuracy and your own bias may impact your reflection.

The second dimension is reflection *in* action. This type of reflection happens, as Schön (1983) describes it, in the "midst of the activity" – most likely during your coaching session. This type of reflection offers you the ability to adapt while in the coaching session, to the people who are with you and who you are serving. It is especially powerful because it offers you chance to make a difference in a situation that is still happening.

We encourage you to create your own structure of reflective practice. Here, we are sharing a few ideas that we apply, and they help us and our mentees and colleagues to develop and grow.

1   *Coaching meetups.* These are non-formal group meetings where we invite any coach to come and bring the topic they would like to discuss. They involve non-judgemental, inclusive group discussion, which helps all of us to reflect and learn from our experience and that of others.
2   *Self-reflection.* Ideally structured, potentially written and/or voice-recorded reflection on your coaching practice and cases, looking at areas of your work that

you found particularly well developed and those you believe could be strengthened. If you are more into technology, there are a couple of coaching chatbots already available that walk you through a reflective practice model. You can offer the same type of chatbot to the team members so they can embrace reflections after the team coaching sessions.

3 *One-on-one reflection.* This involves finding a reflection partner – for example, your mentor, supervisor or peer coach, to create a safe space for you to reflect on action.

4 *Peer group.* This means reflecting in your peer group, with coaches who ideally know you and can offer diverse and inclusive approaches to coaching in general.

Reflection practice is a key element of the EMCC accreditation process, and is also reflected in the EMCC team coaching core standards. At each level, you will need to provide five reflections: three on team coaching practice, one on a team coaching supervision session and one related to continuous professional development on team coaching (book, workshop, webinar, course, etc).

As an accredited EMCC team coach, you will be encouraged to maintain the habit of reflecting and engaging in continuous supervision. We believe it is best to start early and experiment with different tools to capture different perspectives.

Deliberate practice

Deliberate practice (Rousmaniere et al., 2017) is a way to improve in fields where objective performance measurement is very hard. Since we don't have two universes, we cannot really compare the skills of one team coach with those of another: no team situations are the same, no team is the same, so we can never know who was better and who was worse. The idea of deliberate practice for a team coach is to identify what they need to get better at by establishing a baseline. They can do this by asking their clients what they appreciated about the process and how happy they were with the outcome (knowing that there are many factors that play into the outcome, not just the team coaching). If there is consistent feedback around managing discussions, for example, and the team coach has decided to work on this, they might ask for even more detailed feedback around that skill:

- "I am working on my ability [insert description] — on a scale of 1 to 10, where 10 is that I demonstrated this in a way that is exactly right for you today. Where would you put this session?" You could even prepare a little form with a line from 1 to 10 that the client marks.
- "What were the instances where this was just right for you?"
- "Where would you have wanted me to do this more?"
- "Where would you have wanted me to do this less?"
- "Do you have any other recommendations for further collaboration?"

The main idea is to get client feedback, determine what you would like to work on, get more client feedback and then work on it in preparation for the next session. Don't work on it during the next session – you want your coaching to be focused on the client and not your performance!

Supervision

Team coaching requires the proficient use of several modalities by the team coach. The team coach needs coaching skills, facilitation skills, conflict management skills, training skills and more. It is not possible to learn all these skills by reading a book or in any kind of theoretical way. You can only develop them in practice, and you can get better by deliberate and reflective practice. There is no one way to coach or one way to facilitate – every coach and team coach develops their own style. Everyone struggles with different situations: one team coach might have trouble helping a team reaching a clear goal, the other might shy away from mentioning potential conflicts. Therefore, after your initial training, the best way to develop your skills is by regularly working with a team coaching supervisor.

A good team coaching supervisor can help you to develop your skills. Supervision is not only a method for quality assurance, but can also help a team coach process any negative experiences or stressors that may have occurred during team coaching. It also has a restorative function. Both learning and receiving support are best done with someone you respect, who you believe holds you in unconditional positive regard.

When you are in the process of selecting a good supervisor to develop your team coaching skills, it seems natural to look for someone who embodies what you want to develop. While it might be very useful to learn from someone who has the competency that you are willing to develop, bear in mind that this might be a trap. We don't expect from coaches that they know more about the subject matter than their client – what is more important in a supervisor than their ability to demonstrate the skill that you are looking to develop is their ability to help you in this process.

Questions for the selection of a good supervisor could be:

- Do I trust that my supervisor has my best interests at heart?
- Do I feel comfortable to be open and vulnerable with my supervisor?
- Does my supervisor understand what I want to develop?
- Do I feel positively challenged and acknowledged?
- Is there enough breadth of experience for me to profit from?

The most important factor is that you feel well, challenged and supported after a supervision session. If you have any doubts about the relationship with your supervisor, let them know and then work on it – a good relationship with your supervisor is key. If you see that the relationship is not developing in the direction you would like, end it sooner rather than later.

Team coaching supervision can be reflection on past engagements, figuring out what went well and what could have gone better. You might explore your intentions and interactions in any given team coaching engagements. Team coaching supervision can also be a preparation for a team coaching engagement: you can share your plans with your supervisor, ask for advice, brainstorm together and help you go into the next engagement prepared mentally, emotionally and organizationally.

In order to make best use of team coaching supervision, prepare! Sorry to give you work – but if you want to make the best use of your session, reflect on what you want from the session. Ask yourself, "Suppose this was the most helpful session possible, what difference would that make for my team coaching practice?" Think about yourself, who you want to be as a team coach and how your supervisor can help you develop into that. Be clear on what kind of supervisor you want: a mentor, a coach, an adviser, a quality assurance person, someone who will give you confidence. Don't hesitate to share this with your supervisor.

Both ICF and EMCC require team coaches to take regular coaching supervision to attain certification. Since both certifications are rather new and the field of team coaching supervision is also just beginning, we thought it might be useful to reflect on what happens in team coaching supervision, how you can make use of it and why it is a good idea in the first place.

Accreditation and certification

Accreditation is an important element in the continuous development of a coach. It is a powerful development tool for a coach who strives to grow and become better. In our view, it is really important that when you consider the accreditation or certification, you take into consideration your needs as a coach, development areas, focus areas and potentially business needs. We encourage you to think through those and invest your effort, time and often money into not only well recognized accreditation or certification, but also the accreditation or certification that will further enhance your practice. In other words, choose the accreditation or certification that is truly aligned with who you are and want to be as a coach and who you serve as clients.

This book is focused on team coaching. It has emerged as one of the more exciting and popular developments within coaching space. This has been recognized by the organizations representing coaching community, such as the ICF, EMCC and AC, and is reflected in the provision of the team coaching certifications and accreditations that you may want to pursue.

We believe the accreditation process helps you to grow as a coach by providing clear structure of requirements, which is a great framework for your development. It requires you to complete certain number of hours of accredited team coaching education, which we believe is very important. Selecting quality training in preparation for accreditation, together with experience of working with teams, and reflecting and engaging in supervision, offers the most comprehensive and impactful development.

Practise, practise, practise

And the most important point comes at the end: practise, practise, practise! Do reach out to potential clients, acquaintances, local NGOs and so on, and offer your time and skills to build that muscle of team coaching. With each process you will grow tremendously. And if you need some confidence, team up with a colleague who also wants to grow as a team coach and approach organizations together.

All cases mentioned in this book would not have been possible without the desire of each team coach to grow and sharpen their skills by engaging with real clients, in real business contexts, working on real objectives.

References

Borton, T. (1970). *Reach, touch and teach*. London: Hutchinson.
Rousmaniere, T., Goodyear, R. K., Miller, S. D., & Wampold, B. E. (Eds.). (2017). *The cycle of excellence: Using deliberate practice to improve supervision and training*. Chichester: Wiley-Blackwell.
Schön, D. (1983). *The reflective practitioner: How professionals think in action*. London: Temple Smith.

Chapter 8

Team coaching cheat sheet

We are aware that each team coaching process and each team is individual and needs to be seen as an emergent process, and at the same time we recognize the mix of feelings that appear once you step out there as a team coaching professional and start working on your first team coaching case. Hence we have decided to include a "cheat sheet", a structure of questions for each step along the process. Please use it as an example of what you could do, rather than as a rigid and formal process. You will know best what the team needs and wants, and how that should shape the process.

Ticket office

Initial explorative conversation with the sponsor/team leader

Opening: Problem-free talk (optional)

- What do you do? How are you? What has been going well?
- If the client is going through a tough time: How are you holding up? How are you coping?
- Pre-session change: What has happened in the time between making the appointment for our conversation and today that is going in the right direction?

Exploring the scope of work

- What are your best hopes from this conversation?
- What difference will it make for you/the team if we reach that?
- What is your boldest hope for what can be a result of our work together?
- Have you worked with a team coach before?
- If so, what did they do that helped you to develop as a team and work towards your goals?
- Details around the team: how many members, what is the structure, etc.?

DOI: 10.4324/9781003370314-8

- Are there any relevant stakeholders that should be taken into account for this process?
- Will this be an online or onsite process?
- (If any suggestions come to your mind, do offer them to the sponsor/team leader, and co-create the best course of action.)

Further contracting conversations – similar structure for additional conversations with HR, stakeholders, etc.

Interviews

The minimum structure for the individual team member interviews can be addressed in about 20 minutes of conversation:

- Is there any information that you might need before we start?
- What are your best hopes for the team coaching process?
- Suppose we reach that at the end of our interactions, what difference would that make to the team?
- How will you notice that difference?
- Who else would notice that and what will they be noticing?

Mind map

Cluster the input collected around strategy, operational, interactional and so on.

Workshop 1

Potential structure

- Welcoming the team.
- Introduction of the team coach.
- Introduction of the team members with an ice breaker (make it light and specific to the team) – who you are, what is your role in the team and what happened in the last week that makes you proud of the team (pass the ball in the room).
- What do you need from all of us to make this a useful conversation today and in general? All team members collect sticky notes on a flipchart or a virtual board.
- Introduction of the mind map. The coach shares it with the team and reminds everyone that it is anonymized and that the purpose is to support shaping the team coaching process on something that is of value to the team.
- Invite the team to reflect on the mind map. What do you notice from the summary? What surprises you about it? What seems to be of importance to everyone? (short conversations in groups of two to four members).
- Debrief in the main group.

- Team coach facilitates the debrief and note-taking of the objectives that are emerging.
- If additional elements are raised, partner with the team to understand whether they can be added to the parking lot.
- Based on the elements collected, try to a make a summary and ultimately a prioritization of the objectives.
- If needed, cluster some objectives, reformulate them or simply, based on their decisional process, vote or determine the priorities.
- Once you have those sorted, invite the team to a round of reflection on what went well in the session.

Workshop 2 to … (depending on how many you have contracted)

- Welcome.
- Ice breaker.
- Introduction of the session objective in line with the ones identified in Workshop 1.
- Preferred future on that specific objective.
- Scaling, with 10 being the future described and 1 you have only started, where are you right now?
- What does this tell you as a team that you are there?
- What would be the next step that you might want to take towards your objective?
- Who and until when?

Follow-up (four to six months after the last team coaching workshop)

- Welcome.
- Ice-breaker.
- Conversation in the main group or in small groups on what has been working better since the last meeting.
- What do you want to do more of?
- What are others observing?

Index

follow-up 43, 64, 105, 116, 117–118;
  questions 33, 34, 99
Furman, Ben 6, 17, 116, 176

Galveston Declaration 7, 21, 46, 48, 55, 56,
  58, 59, 60, 140
gift shop metaphor *23*, 24, 39–40, 60,
  108–118, *109*, **128**
"glues clues" 87
goals: conflicting 26, 44, 50, 95–96;
  congruent 158; eliciting of 132; team
  72, 73, 75, 103, 121, 195; team coaching
  9, 26, 27, 28, 31, 43, 69, 71, 174; team
  member 47, 139; and team supervision
  127; visualizing discussion of 95–96
going for a walk 102
good working relationships 24, 45, 131,
  173

Haley, Jay 2
hierarchies, and team coaching 10
highlights from the past 106
hospitals 136, 141–142
Human Resources (HR) 49, 59, 67, 77,
  132; team coaching request from 68–72
humming 106

ICF (International Coaching Federation) 8,
  12, 24, 48, 52, 74, 103, 186, 193
"If it isn't broken, don't fix it" 9
implementation interviews 112–113
improved communication 32
inclusion 11, 16, 57, 59, 118, 155, 186–187
individual coaching 5, 25, 28, 40, 41,
  44–46, 57, 58, 83, 88, 132
initial training, as a team coach 188–191,
  192
inner picture, of the client organization 66
interdependence 51
International Coaching Federation (ICF) 8,
  12, 24, 48, 52, 74, 103, 186, 193
interventions 60, 93, 131, 132, 150, 156;
  change 7, 15–16
interviews 47, 106, 127, 169, 196;
  appreciative 21; and definitional
  ceremonies 182–183; executive team
  138; implementation 112–113; and
  negative groups 158; Solution Focused
  64, 66–67, 77–83, *81*, 93–94; team of
  teams 140
introduction round, in a workshop 84
invitations, to a workshop 84

isomorphism 4
*It's Never Too Late to Have a Happy
  Childhood* 17

job-sharing conflict 13–14

Kanban board 112
kickoff meeting 122
kitchen table 149–151
Kline, Nancy 177, 178

language of the client 25, 45, 65, 139
large groups 101, 106, 143–151
laws 54
leadership 10, 11, 51, 60, 69, 70, 71, 76, 77,
  78, 84, 150
leadership team 124, 136, 151, 167
legal compliance 54
letter from the future 97–98
liberating structures 118
listening 24–25, 45, 60, 79, 89, 116,
  148, 149; in difficult situations 180,
  181–182, 183, 187; *see also* curious
  "not-knowing"
long-term success 109

mandated teams 155, 158–160
Manifesto for Agile Software Development
  6, 20
Māori method 173
mentoring: in initial training 188; team
  49–50
merger of two teams 42
microstructures 118
mind map, results as a 79
mindset: Agile 121; of Solution Focused
  coach 54–55, 83, 93
miracle award 103
miracle board 100
Miracle Question 11, 15, 32–35, 98–103,
  100, 132
More than Miracles 9
motivation 14, 19, 30, 65, 127, 131, 181,
  185
moves *see* team coaching moves
multi-directional partiality 46–48, 53, 90,
  186
multipartiality 46–48, 53, 90, 186
multiple social realities 7, 9–11
multiple "truths" 7, 8, 140
mutual influence 7, 12, 147
Myers-Briggs Type Indicator 132